THE KATRINA PAPERS

Cover Art:
"All mothers are boats" by Herbert Kearney
67 x 106 inches
Paint, driftwood, lumber, dirt, masonry, glass, etc.
See colophon (page 235) for further information.

Cover Design:
Bill Lavender

Book Design:
Erin Gendron and Bill Lavender

Editorial Assistants:
Kelcy Wilburn and Nathan Ware

Printed in the USA

Library of Congress Control Number: 2008937285

ISBN: 0-9728143-3-7
ISBN 13: 978-0-9728143-3-1

The Engaged Writers Series

University of New Orleans Publishing
UNO Metro College
New Orleans, LA 70148
http://unopress.uno.edu

ACKNOWLEDGEMENTS

Portions of *The Katrina Papers* were published in *African American Review, The Grinnell Magazine, Drumvoices Revue, Konch Magazine* [ishmaelreedpub.com], *ChickenBones: A Journal* [nathanielturner.com], and the Project on the History of Black Writing website [www2.ku.edu/~phbw], and I am grateful to the editors. I am especially indebted to Kim Lacy Rogers (Dickinson College), Bradley Bateman (Grinnell College), Andree Nicola McLaughlin (Medgar Evers College), Tara Green (Northern Arizona University), Wilfred D. Samuels (University of Utah), Violet H. Bryan (Xavier University), President Marvalene Hughes, Provost Bettye Parker Smith, and Thomas King (Dillard University), President Beverly Hogan, Larry Johnson, and Candice Love Jackson (Tougaloo College), Dave Brinks (17 Poets Series), and colleagues affliated with Educational Testing Service and the College Board for their extraordinary support. And without blessings from my friends Edgar Smith, Maryemma Graham, Lolis Edward Elie, Julius E. Thompson, Kalamu ya Salaam, Raymond and Quo Vadis Gex Breaux, John S. Page, Jr., Chakula cha Jua, Ernest Jones, and Reginald Martin, I would have terminated the project. I am especially grateful to Herbert Kearney for allowing me to use his gnomic art and poetry for this book, to Hank Lazer for seeing what I did not know was there, and to Bill Lavender and Erin Gendron at UNO Press for their perspicuous editing.

THE KATRINA PAPERS
A Journal of Trauma and Recovery

Jerry W. Ward, Jr.

DEDICATION

For Valerie Matthews Crawford, Stefan M. Wheelock, Rian E. Bowie, Howard Rambsy II, and Candice Love Jackson.

And for my relatives and friends who always provide the safety nets.

KATRINA: A MATRIX OF STORIES

In those brief, rare moments since August 29, 2005 when I am my old self and not taking daily walks on a tightrope of despair, I think about the importance of stories. In the unsettling aftermath of Hurricane Katrina, my focus is on narratives and natural disasters. Mark Twain delivered a mouthful of truth when he proclaimed that nothing in our country is as interesting as the human mind. Despite the unprecedented damage that Hurricane Katrina and her sister, Hurricane Rita, accomplished, the minds and bottomless imaginations of survivors prevailed. The survivors refused to release their grips on their dreams of life, refused to cast faith in God and themselves to the winds. Women, men, and children told and are telling stories of bodies and psyches in pain. And in the future those stories will become more polished and more suspect. That is unavoidable. What is most valuable is the fact that elements of genuine literature are preserved in raw, passionate, uncensored stories of survival rather than in media-constructed stories about survival.

The first type, in addition to the narratives of local victims and evacuees, must include the immediate stories of newspersons who defied the most basic human instinct and became intimate witnesses. The latter type is marked by the reporter's sense of what is a "good" story, the newsworthy replete with inventions, ideological and political baggage, unverifiable rumors, threadbare stereotypes, angles and staging, cosmetic departures from "truth." The former is marked by the sense that story and survival into a future are symbiotic. The types are not discrete; formal and emotive features overlap. Uncertainty is all.

We are still in the whirlwind of production. We are enslaved by professional habit and tempted to theorize and interpret immediately. There is virtue still in the caution that one must have distance in order to render judgment. It is difficult, however, for literary and cultural scholars to resist automatic metanarratives. We want to be on the cutting edge.

For some of us displaced scholars, the cutting edge is elsewhere. It is to be found in listening even as we speak or write. Perhaps we would do well to resist our acquired, self-conscious tendencies and test our abilities to do some preternatural listening to the rich multitude of stories issuing from the matrix of hurricanes. A renewed appreciation for the power of story comes as the sympathetic ear listens to the tale of spending twenty-six or more hours in a fetid attic with roaches and no water and no ax to break through the roof and being saved by the providence of a neighbor who returned in a boat, heard your cries, chopped a hole in the roof and transported you to an evacuation station; listens to the eloquent outrage of a woman who trudged through a water-logged New Orleans with family and friends— a band of criminals in the eyes of some who had the authority and means to rescue them— endured many indignities because she was female and non-white, suffered the crowdedness, stench, hunger, heat,

9

and frustrated displays of self-centeredness and ill-temper among strangers, and reluctantly accepted deportation to where she did not wish to go; listens to parallels between the New Orleans Superdome, the slaveship, and Dante's Inferno; hears the pain-stitched final cries as water enshrouds the elderly and infirm abandoned in a nursing home. Let the ear smell the stench political and racial. Our ears will reach into our hearts and bless us with an humble wisdom we have never known.

These ur-stories, I admit, may not be breathtakingly "literary." They are merely real. They give evidence of how human beings always use languages to depict situatedness and resilience. From sympathetic treatment of such materials we should forge our literary and cultural histories. Privileged gazing upon the matrix without entering it may only lead to curious rewritings of Sister Gertrude Morgan's stunning statement: "I was so busy with the Lord, I didn't notice the house across the street had burned."

Early September Preludes

Entry: September 2, 2005

Being in the First Baptist Church shelter means... damn, the words don't want to come out of the pencil... that thousands of us have been abused by Nature and revenge is impossible.

Entry: September 4, 2005

I went to Mass this morning at St. Paul's, but prayer and anxiety are muddled. The priest welcomes all of the visitors from New Orleans. I am conscious of my looking like a tourist.

Entry: September 7, 2005

I have to register online with FEMA. FEMA is very intrusive. What is my social security number? List the types of insurance I have on my home. What was the gross total of my income at the time of disaster? Provide contact information. Provide bank information for electronic funds transfer. List my current address and telephone number. Prove my identity by checking addresses at which I formerly resided. I had to write out all this information. Fortunately, I did put the crucial documents in the car. This is a slow process. There are glitches in the information system. I got kicked out a couple of times and had to start over. Kicked out. Yes, the weather has kicked us out.

FEMA gives me an identification number. I also have to have a user ID number and password for the computer and a PIN. I guess I am now a legitimate item in the national database of the needy. The volunteer workers at the shelter are very attentive to our needs. I try very hard not to have too many needs. I need to know when I can go home.

Entry: September 13, 2005

I have got in touch with a few people. Or they have managed to get in touch with me. I have managed to send some emails out. The happiness that comes from knowing people are still alive is brief like the flame of a match. Be happy, then be miserable.

I have to watch all this gut-twisting stuff on TV— water, angry people, lies, familiar street signs in water, pregnant women wading in the water. *Wade in the Water* is part of the title of my poetry anthology. Irony.

A boat is anything that floats.

I do not have a cell phone. I use the pay phone at a gas station to call some of my relatives. They are all alive, at least the ones I call. I can not go to my relatives in Moss Point, Mississippi. Their homes got flooded by the surge from the Gulf.

My relatives in Convent, Louisiana want me to stay with them until I can return to New Orleans. I politely refuse the offer. I don't want to be a burden for them to bear. I will try to carry my own cross. I am very like people in my father's family: we appreciate help when it is offered, but we try our damndest not to need help. We are independent to a fault. Given that I have accepted help from the good people in Vicksburg, I see no reason to make accepting help a habit. I am critical of people at the shelter who make up lies to get more help than they really need.

They are not showing my neighborhood on TV. It may be I have no neighborhood, no house, no nothing. How to start... to start over.

Faces and hands, waving from rooftops and overpasses and bridges and out of the water. They need water. The heat is killing them. They don't have toilet facilities on an overpass. Suppose someone has diarrhea....

All the faces and hands are African American. The news informs us all the people are black. I feel miserable, sick. I guess I have trauma. Unlike the common cold, trauma affects the mind, the soul, the body. I am restless. All the African Americans are....

My friend Chakula Cha Jua stayed in New Orleans with his siblings. Are they dead? Did any of my dozens of friends in New Orleans drown? I don't know. I worry. I want to cry, but crying would make me more depressed. Be strong. Save tears for funerals.

Guns, gunfire. Who is shooting? Some people in the shelter make ugly comments about the stupid people who are still in New Orleans. It does no good to respond. They are convinced anyone who stayed was stupid. They are convinced thugs are shooting at helicopters. Anger makes my body hot.

Sick people getting sicker in the nursing home, the hospital. The old woman died on the bus. What is killing? Oil is killing St. Bernard Parish. People at the shelter who are from St. Bernard say over and over "We can't go home ever again. We have no home." Do I have one?

That is a dead man in the water? Who is killing? Time. Football lives.Writing something other than the information people give me for their FEMA applications helps. Dead. And no drinking water. And wading in poisoned water with the snakes and the dead bodies of animals and people floating by.

Writing. Help! I have not been writing the way I want to write. I have been thinking about writing, the fragility of writing, how personal it is. Water can wash it away. Baseball games— the national pastime lives. Boats and helicopters and the military... the people who could help are over there— Iraq— killing terrorism. Sand. They must be killing shadows in the sand. The terrorism is here— hurricanes in the South, on the Gulf Coast, in and around the Crescent City. Yes, I have to write.

I. You Don't Know What It Means

Until Sunday, August 28, 2005

You defied Hurricane Ivan, but Hurricane Katrina makes you enter the I-10 contraflow traffic and flee New Orleans for Mississippi. Katrina is a 5, a force to retreat from. You hurriedly pack– vital documents, granola bars and water, sports clothing and toiletries for a week, put on your Army dog tags for good luck [You did survive Vietnam], lock up the house and leave at 12:06 with a backward glance at John Scott's "Spirit House" on the corner of St. Bernard and Gentilly. Is Katrina a post-modern war goddess or God's agent come to punish New Orleans or Satan's gumbo, poisoning for Lake Pontchartrain? You don't clock the miles or the hours: New Orleans to I-55 North to MS 98 and Natchez (no available rooms), Vicksburg (no rooms), Monroe, LA (not room), and back to a rest stop and fretful sleep after 15 hours of driving. Monday afternoon you find shelter, a much-needed hot shower, and food at the First Baptist Church Vicksburg. You had planned to teach Rousseau's *The Social Contract* this semester? You shall live it now as a "houseless" person among other displaced strangers. It is not easy to accept your fate– no comforting words from the friendly, caring Baptists erase the horror of losing house, forty plus years of manuscripts, first editions (esp. Richard Wright 1st editions), correspondence with fellow writers– the horror smolders. For many days you can not write. You can send brief answers to emails, you can read a popular novel, you can pull your share at the shelter by cleaning the men's restroom– why do adult males drop towels and soap everywhere?– hauling the trash the "community" creates, and helping your fellow-inmates complete FEMA applications (when the overworked computer terminals decide to cooperate). You can not or will not write. Despair shrouds you; the Mississippi River looks like an attractive place to drown it all. Suicide becomes a preoccupation. Only the crying of babies and the yelling of the football and basketball crowds on TV remind you death is not "the" answer, not yet at least. You do have unfinished work at Dillard University, and suicide, damning your Roman Catholic soul, would hurt the relatives who love you. Wear the mask. Smile. Pretend you do not hurt.

II. To Miss New Orleans

Monday, September 12.

The other world remembered 9/11 yesterday. I don't know how to measure tragedies. This confinement to being one of the wretched is child's play by comparison with the American institution of slavery and the AIDS /famine/ ethnic laundering crises in Africa and the triumph of evil elsewhere. A shelter is a microcosm of universal ills and potentials. I visited people in a nursing home last week. I must respect being more blessed than they are. Rereading the Book of

14

Job inspires belief that cosmic justice is beyond man's grasp. Remember, Lord, I am not John Donne. Please. Do not batter my heart. I am a mere singer of sorrow songs.

Tuesday, September 13.

I am waiting for a call from Magnolia Commons, the gated apartment complex I am to move into this week. I recall the necessity of gates from reading Octavia Butler. I recall also that not having taught any undergraduates for more than two weeks is like sitting on death row. I must get out of this cage. All one speaks at a shelter are simple sentences, even with those who have college educations. Complex sentences and witty turns of phrase would reveal too much, leave you disarmed, would insult the majority of the displaced. Theirs is vicious honesty. A thirteen year-old humorously reminded me yesterday, "Professor, I am not in college, so leave my language alone." Reality is all. There will be time to talk politics, to raise one's voice against creeping fascism in America. There will be time to resume the *Richard Wright Encyclopedia* and *Cambridge History of African American Literature* projects and time to rebuild my home and life with old friends in New Orleans. I make the existential choice to believe in renewal.

September 15, 2005: Entry

Note from a psychiatrist to Katrina, September 3, 2005

Dear Madam,
Yours is the most pristine case of Oedipal menopause I have yet had the pleasure of examining.
You must no longer deny that you are of a certain age,
the age at which females reclaim their adolescent appetites.
If the sex was bad, the reason is not far to seek. Your reason was quite beyond satisfaction.
That explains why your too much love went mad.
Very sincerely yours,
Dr. F_____

Katrina replies to her psychiatrist, September 5, 2005

Beloved doctor,
Do not fall out of love with self-pity. [period] It may warm your bed in winter. [period]
As always, with love,
Katrina

The psychiatrist responds, September 10, 2005

Dear Madam,

You are past due to have a session with me. Check your periods.

Sincerely,

Dr. F____

Katrina pleads her case, September 30, 2005

Dear Dr. F____:

You are most cruel. I did check my periods. Give me some credit. I know something of grammar, good usage, and gender. And I have put my colon in the right position. A salutation only deserves a comma when you are in a coma or in love. At this moment, permit me to assure you, I am in neither.

If you want my opinion (and at the prices I have paid you, you do want my opinion), I am convinced you are a refugee, evacuee, mental migrant, ego-exiled, displaced, and displeased person.

You are the Other inspecting and sprinkling judgments without sufficient reason upon the Self, on my motives. Do not transport or beam Your Self into My Self. I do no take kindly to such invasion of my privacy or my territory. Nor do I take kindly to your arrogance, the arrogance of a St. Charles Avenue heir of new money who had to take his degrees from LSU. You could not earn them in a true gentlemanly fashion from Vienna or in the mirror image of Lacan's seminar. The only reason that I submit to you is your being an amusing distraction, which you have proved no longer to be.

Of a certain age? My dear boy, you have utterly no appreciation of what age can bring you, and you are enormously ignorant about Oedipus and his menopause. But then, you are not Greek. So I will not assume you understand mystery or history.

Dr. F____, I am no longer receptive. Henceforth I shall please myself as women of a certain age have learned to pleasure themselves.

Respectfully yours,

Mrs. Katrina Stigmata Krism-Claus

THOUGHTS

Do not fall out of love with self-pity; it may warm your bed in winter.

Where did you meet plain, semi-civilized, trash-making America? In the shelter of a convention center.

Katrina deported me to another country. Rita insisted that I dwell there much longer than I wished.

If you are the wretched of the earth, riding in the Ark of Bones at the bottom of the Mississippi is a seductive option. Then along comes Job, meddling with your business, whispering to your guardian angel that you best be patient and put your hand in your mouth.

Only the brain-dead should be blessed by despair.

Hurricanes are Satan's gumbo, environmental gumbo, gumbo with toxic flavors— Swamp New Orleans is a filthy bathtub.

September 16, 2005

I was able to rent an apartment in Vicksburg on Wednesday, September 14. I had been a "homeless" person in the First Baptist Church Vicksburg shelter with approximately 149 other homeless people. Some of them are pleasant, decent, affable people. Some of them are enigmas. Some of them make a habit of inviting your dislike.

The level to which you will descend in exile is proof that neither education nor breeding nor class nor skin privilege makes you immune to human error and foibles. In the absence of good literature, you will read Wilber Smith's *Wild Justice* and Michael Prescott's *Stealing Faces* and enjoy the occasional interesting description or turn of phrase in them. You can discriminate nothing in these popular novels from the undemanding stories you have watched in movie houses and on television. For the moment, these books constitute good literature, literature that is good for what it enables you to grasp about the people around you whom you have mistakenly judged to be lacking in complication. It is you who are lacking in your powers of observation, you who have been blinded by all the fragile filters an academic life has allowed you to take for granted. Once inside that sociological construction called "the masses," you bemoan your previous ignorance.

I have become weary of the small talk, the mumbling and grunting that passes for conversation. I am saddened by the loss of rich conversations with my friends in New Orleans. I am going deeper into a Grand Canyon of dissatisfaction. I begin to feel listless. I mumble and grunt. I watch television only because it is in the shelter and unavoidable. My ears perk up when something called "news" is shown. Otherwise I am watching colors and shapes as they shift this way and that, and I hear recognizable words without paying attention. I am becoming a chair potato. My bottom is glued to the seat. I should be doing meaningful work, but I do not move. There is relief and contentment in being dull. I am no longer who I was on August 28, and I do not applaud what I am becoming. I hope the scars are not permanent.

The Katrina Papers

September 20, 2005: Tuesday.

After a pleasant drive from Vicksburg to Jackson, my first stop is Exxon for gas, then Office Max to have a house contents worksheet for the insurance company downloaded and printed; onward to Circuit City to pick up a wireless mouse. When I purchased the laptop last night, I forgot or the salesperson forgot or we both forgot the mouse I had purchased. Forgetting is much in evidence now. Remind me what is the pluperfect tense of a verb. Did I use it correctly? Surely I know what it is. And I will have to fight my way back to recalling what it is before I set myself up as a master tutor in the Writing Center at Tougaloo College for however long I volunteer my services. I shall want to tell the undergraduates who seek help with the writing process that control of tense is crucial as one creates verbal tension and texture. After years of writing, use of tenses, embedding, sentence variety and the quest for nuance become matters of reflex rather than thought. Undergraduates have their own reflexes. They come to us for assistance with doing, performing, earning, or getting the grade by whatever means. I digress, for now is a time of regression and digression.

September 21, 2005

Crisis begets crisis. It is difficult to triage priorities as each new reason to hope has its fingers amputated by a new reason to lament. Katrina and her sisters insist on revenge, and it seems these wild women are the blood kin of Shylock and Titus Andronicus. In the matrix of Shakespeare, in the turn and counterturn of languages incapable of naming the tissues of emotion absolutely, one discovers the pedigree of the heifers. Katrina, Ophelia, Rita, Ursula– KORU– bastard kinship. It is no accident that all the hurricanes this season have women's names and are identified with the worst properties and capabilities of the female. It was mainly males who named the hurricanes, and under the guise of being non-sexist in the naming process, they imply that woman is a wind and water weapon of mass destruction. Worry wants and gets several pounds of your flesh, and mercy becomes just what Bob Kaufman named it: the ancient rain. Literature, frantic use of imagination, can lead to such a dreaded conclusion. The conclusion is real but not actual, attractively misleading.

September 28, 2005

A Modest Proposal to the Roman Catholic Church

Xavier University in New Orleans is unique. It is the only black Catholic university in the United States, and it has done an exemplary job of providing spiritual and practical education to God's children in America. In recognition of that legacy, the Roman Catholic Church should provide rebuilding funds for Xavier that exceed the recent donation from the Mellon Foundation. I propose that Pope Benedict XVI sell a few old relics from the Vatican vaults and donate the profits to Xavier. Surely God would bless the Church for doing such a good deed in the wake of Hurricane Katrina.

Advice to Self about Writing: This is not about me. ME is US.

T. Monk Quartet with Coltrane at Carnegie Hall, November 29, 1957– Blue Note 2005

September 29, 2005

Dave Brinks, a fellow poet from New Orleans, called with good news. My house at 1928 Gentilly Boulevard seems to have suffered less damage than I feared. I am not off the hook yet. I am still not in possession of ocular proof, as bereft of ocular proof as Othello when he made a rash decision. I now savor the anxiety of not knowing completely. I still have freedom to fear the unknown.

September 30, 2005

Life is a wave. You move up. You move sideways and down. It is about motion. You rush and ebb, flow and flood and ebb again and repeat the variations. Accounting for your lifetime persuades you to descend into the mathematics of nonsense. How many seconds have you been alive without counting the aliveness in your mother's womb? There are 3600 seconds in one hour. And 86,400 seconds in one day. Ignore leap years and time adjustments, and you find a year is made up of 31,536,000 seconds. One decade is 315,360,000 seconds. At age 60, you had endured and prevailed for 18,921,600,000 seconds. The cells in your body are keenly aware of this magnitude. They complain of pain and shriveling. The cells in the skin family have it worst of all. They are constantly losing neighbors and relatives at a faster rate than their sisters and brothers below the surface. Perhaps something similar happens to the sea, to the portions that have to deal with sunlight and wind and the portions that commune only with themselves in the cold that light never visits or violates. And here's the killer. It took Hurricane Katrina and Hurricane Rita and 18,984,672,000 seconds for you to discover a fact that is at once fantastic and quintessentially untrue. Such games does the mind in misery play.

Saturday, October 1, 2005

Finished reading Budd Schulberg's *What Makes Sammy Run?* today.

Had this 1941 novel been published by a Gentile writer, it would have been condemned for its excellent stereotype of the greedy and crafty Jew in the early twentieth century. Only in America can a Jew write a bitter satire about a Jew and not be stoned to death by zealots in the Anti-Defamation League. It seems that Schulberg learned some wonderful lessons from F. Scott Fitzgerald about letting an unreliable narrator tell the story, borrowing as he did a few choice bones from *The Great Gatsby* in characterizing Sammy Glick and the narrator Al Manheim. It is noteworthy that Schulberg borrowed next to nothing from Shakespeare (*The Merchant of Venice*) or from Marlowe (*The Jew of Malta*) and that he was politic in his fleeting references to the Italian and the Irish. Perhaps because the novel is artfully melodramatic and cliché-tainted, white Americans in particular have saluted Sammy Glick(stein) as an icon to emulate. In the afterword he wrote for the 1978 Penguin edition, Schulberg mildly regretted such misuse of his novel, but his collaborating in the republication tells us something about what made Schulberg himself run. It would not be a waste of time to explore how he embedded a complex and even contradictory ideology in his factoidal fiction.

Return to New Orleans: Executive Summary 10/06/05

By way of prelude

You can go home again. It would be my first trip into New Orleans since I evacuated myself on August 28. I did know what to expect. A colleague from Dillard University, then in Houston, was almost certain that my house had water damage. Television had supplied a surplus of dreadful pictures of the Big Easy as the American Venice and of those citizens who did not leave as well-to-do and defiant or as poor and stress-stricken. Newspapers, magazines, and online journals force-fed me what I should believe. Chakula cha Jua was thoughtful: he sent an interactive site that allowed me to see aerial views of my house and neighborhood. Dave Brinks, a brave, purposeful poet, made a site visit to my house, confirming that I had little damage that he could see. "Come home," he said, "as soon as you can. It is crucial that we begin rebuilding immediately." Raymond Breaux, in a deadpan voice, stirred all my anxieties when he said, "New Orleans as we knew it does not exist." He echoed what Tyrone and Tina Albert said after their visit a week earlier. I was well prepared to be unprepared.

The Findings for 1928 Gentilly Blvd., New Orleans, LA 70119

1) The roof suffered little damage and the ceilings have no water stain.s
2) 3-5 inches of water flooded the house. The carpets were soaked. The wooded flooring buckled. These must be removed and replaced. The marble tile must be cleaned and treated. The detached garage and workshop was flooded; any books in those areas were destroyed.
3) The 24 windows suffered no damage.

4) All rooms in the house must be treated to eradicate as much mold as possible. Removing mold must take place immediately to prevent further damage, especially to books.

5) The refrigerator, hot water heater, washer and dryer must be replaced.

6) Paneling in the kitchen and den areas, the interior and exterior doors and some furnishings (dressers, beds in the master bedroom and guest room) must be replaced.

7) To ensure that there are no electrical accidents when the house is inhabited again, it should be completely rewired; the attic, where most of the wiring is located was not inspected.

8) The room used as an office sustained losses that will cause Mr. Ward to be in agony for months. He will grieve over the loss of his two-volume *Oxford English Dictionary*. Many reference books, autographed books, papers pertaining to the *Richard Wright Encyclopedia* and the *Cambridge History of African American Literature*, Ward's manuscripts for *Reading Race Reading America, Hollis Watkins: An Oral Autobiography*, and *To Shatter the Iris of Innocence* (poetry) are beyond recovery.

The same is true for some videotapes. The PC and hard drive, 35mm camera, tape recorder, vacuum cleaner, some photographs and the rare *Black Box* tapes are ruined. Manuscript materials from Tom Dent and Lance Jeffers and Chakula cha Jua were not damaged.

9) Most of Ward's clothing and shoes have to be replaced; the mold damage is severe.

10) Ward is luckier by far than 89% of the residents whose homes suffered wind and water damage.

Tentative conclusion: Yes, Margaret, "A race of men shall rise and take control."

I am far luckier, thank God, than 89% of my fellow New Orleanians. I have been blessed by the prayers of my relatives and friends. My fortunate circumstances strengthen my resolve to return permanently, to restore my house, to help to restore Dillard University and other educational institutions, to join Dave Brinks and others in grassroots efforts to prevent the NEW New Orleans from becoming a "corporate colony" with a minimal non-white population that is controlled by wealthy and extreme neo-conservatives. I must encourage more people to return. The natural disasters that are now elements of a national tragedy persuade me to fight a repetition of the Reconstruction era and the nadir of African American experiences, to speak loudly against a replay of the Great Migration. Commitments must gradually erase the depression and periods of near-insanity that have afflicted me since August 29, 2005. I must devote myself to the practice of civic virtue in New Orleans.

Saturday, October 8, 2005

Can this brief essay I delivered at Mississippi College in Spring 2005 be relevant during the Fall, the post-Katrina season?

THE BEST ADVICE

When you are asked to identify the best of anything, you may be stricken with mental paralysis.

That was the case when I was asked "What is the best piece of writing advice you have ever received?"

Piece? Only one piece? And it has to be the best? I guess I best grab the Jack Daniels.

The best advice I ever received was an umbrella to cover all cases, coming as it did at some moment of crisis involving my report card very long ago, and the advice did not pertain to writing but to behavior. "Always do your best," my mother said. She did not smile, but the soft tone of her voice was an invitation for me to fill in what she had left unfinished: "and I'll be proud of you for having exhausted your potential." I like that kind of advice. It is pleasant, straightforward, inviting. It is not the kind of advice I fell into the habit of giving my students.

I would write sidewise advice on student papers in a future I never imagined. "Take the weeds out of your paragraphs. I lost the trail." If that appeared on the margin of a paper, it meant the student should avoid an excess of adjectives and repetitions that choked any sense of where she was going. "Your writing is like light on water; it dances everywhere. In short, young man, focus your ideas. They must not dance according to some obscure laws derived from chaos theory." The question I am trying to avoid had nothing to do with my mother or my students. It has everything to do with my self.

To make a proper answer regarding the best piece of writing advice, I would have to dig through several decades of listening to other people's comments on my writing. It is honest labor but dirty work. The good stuff is always buried in the crud. Even when I got to the good stuff, I'd have to sort it out and make judgments about what deserved to be called the best. On what grounds do I decide what the best is? The best compared to what?

What I found down there at the bottom concerns my memory about writing at the age of four. At that age it was not called writing. It was called playing with letters. My father had the daily habit of putting letters in strangely arranged little squares that appeared on a certain page in the *Washington Post.* I figured there was something important going on when you did the crosswords. I was anxious to play this game with letters. Here was magic. You put letters on a page, you make visual sound. One day after drawing a picture with letters under it, I proudly presented the piece of paper to my father. He said nothing about the drawing. He told me I had not spelled the simple word "the" correctly. But I had, I had. I knew I had, and through my tears I babbled that T-E-H did indeed spell "the." Couldn't he see that I had all the letters right? My father was not the most sympathetic man in the world. He informed me I was to show him nothing until I got it into my head that T-E-H was nonsense and T-H-E was what I was trying to write. I was crushed. My ego was flattened like the body of a cartoon character run over by a dumptruck. When I was finally able to reinflate myself, I got his point about how necessary it was to observe what one put on paper.

By trial, error, and observation I eventually got the spelling under some control, but grade school and high school had more challenges in store. Spelling correctly was not enough. The teachers wanted you to arrange words in the proper order according to parts of speech and then you had to diagram them so that relationships could be etched on your brain. That didn't satisfy them. They demanded that you use certain marks called punctuation. When you got to paragraphs, you should have neither too many nor too few sentences. That, please remember, was in the old days before some English teacher with vision sold the idea that a paragraph should have eleven sentences. You had to learn vocabulary, but when your vocabulary got too fancy, the teachers complained that your writing was pretentious. You had to learn the fine art of outlining, because you needed to predict the development of your thesis or topic sentence. And if I followed the outline too carefully, I was told the writing was awkward and stiff. It did not flow. Well, hell, the outline wasn't flowing.

Writing was an uphill struggle. The mountain got steeper and more treacherous the higher up you went in education. But I did have enough mother wit not to fall off the mountain. The memory of my early schooling turns up not one fragment of best advice about writing.

The advice I got in my two semesters of freshman composition with Miss Helen Kelly often reminded me of what my father had said about observation. She worried me about the development of ideas. It was not that I did not have good ideas. I just did not articulate them in a compelling fashion. Miss Kelly said I lacked style. She urged me to study the prose of one Norman Mailer. Now, I had decided back in high school that James Baldwin was a better writer than Mailer. The advice to imitate Mailer just did not make sense. What would I be imitating? I did not ask that question. I didn't want to be called stupid. She wanted me to study the structure of his sentences, his use of vocabulary, his arrangement of paragraphs. But I could do the same thing with the writing of Rachel Carson or James Michner and come up with the same result: zero! Besides, I was not an English major; I was doing math.

At some point during my college career, the best piece of advice about writing did arrive. I was taking a creative writing course with Dr. Elizabeth Sewell, a wonderful poet/scholar who knew everything about the Orphic voice and the human metaphor and how to get us excited about words. I took on the very ambitious task of writing a sequence of twenty-four sonnets as my final project. The sonnets were not very good, but something that has remained invaluable was my reward. I discovered the first sonnet in Sir Philip Sidney's sequence *Astrophel and Stella*. The final line of that sonnet hit me like the sound of a trumpet announcing the Last Judgment.

"Fool, said my Muse to me, looke in thy heart, and write."

Yes. Precisely. That's it. None of my writing instructors had advised me to do that. So, I really took to heart what Sidney's muse advised, and stopped worrying about grand ideas and inventions and models coming from other people's writing and tried to find the location of genuine expression. Robert Frost lied when he said, "nothing gold can stay." Sidney's advice stayed. Everything I have written since my undergraduate days has in greater and lesser degrees been a matter of trying to do my best, observing carefully, and looking into my heart.

As far as my post-Katrina heart is concerned, the pre-Katrina presentation is still relevant.

October 8: When Music is a Poet's Tool

"Rising from the ashes," my friend Alice Lewis said, "is a hard job when everything is wet." Creating the poem is hard too when your spirits are soaked by tragedy. Turmoil, if you don't fight the feeling, will assassinate imagination. "What do you do to relax," Alice asks, "until the inner turmoil settles enough to function?" Go to war. Kick ass. Fight the evil stimuli. Listen to music, to jazz, to blues. If there is no electricity, sit in the dark and play your memory of "Backwater Blues," "So What?," "Meet Me with Your Black Drawers On," "I'd Rather be Blind," "Take the A Train," or "A Love Supreme." If all that is brewing in your head is Sarah Vaughn's "Black Coffee," use it.

Tame turmoil. Transform all that bile-flavored anger and anxiety into words. Vent. Review the outburst to discover the pattern the turmoil never told you it had. Reshape the pattern into stanzas or lyrics, dramatic monologues, and narratives. Polish. Repolish. Publish.

There are times when poems must respond to natural disasters and subsequent pandemics, to the reflux acid of war, racism, genocide. At those times, it is only normal for poets to let the turmoil roll. If you want a poem rather than the droppings of a vatic pigeon, you must dance in a music that takes you to the other side of natural disaster and national tragedy.

New Fears in October

This week I have begun to notice that my mind is asserting a certain unhealthy independence of rationality. I forget the names of new people I meet about 30 seconds after they have introduced themselves to me. Sometimes I lash out at people in a way I never did before, especially at clerks in stores. I do not hate the clerks because they are clerks. I turn nasty because the clerks are symbolic of American enterprise at its worst. Companies are dishonest about their products, selling ever cheaper products at ever ascending prices. A loaf of decent bread costs as much as a gallon of gasoline.

My sense of direction is failing. I make stupid exits from highways, and sometimes I am on the wrong highway going in the wrong direction. I misplace things each hour and have to waste time relocating them. I am developing a new fear of opening mail or email, even from my friends. I do not know why I am afraid of mail. I am not comfortable with my new cell phone, because it is so alien. Its buttons perform many functions that I do not understand. There are too many codes and procedures to remember. Portals on the Internet will not let me enter without passwords and PINs. Human beings rarely talk to human beings when they call companies; they talk to recorded sounds made by artificial intelligence. I resent the worship of numbers and being talked at by machines. I resent being exiled from my home. I have a log on my shoulder when it comes to natural disasters. I fear that I am being seduced to walk on a path that leads to the end of life.

Sunday, October 9, 2005

*Epiphany #1: The name Webster has no authority to guarantee anything!

Dear Mr. Robert Davis,

When the police beat you at Bourbon and Conti, when Officer S. M. Smith spit profanity as he jabbed the AP cameraman on the scene and screamed, "I've been here six weeks trying to keep alive; go home," did you reconsider that you might have been mistaken for Rodney King?

Monday, October 10, 2005

Epiphany #2: In order to be absurd, one must have remarkable talent.

I had never heard of Black America's Political Action Committee (BAMPAC) until this afternoon. Surfing for useful information about New Orleans, I happened upon a posting entitled "BAMPAC Expresses Opposition to Bennett Comments." Earlier today I read Jabari Asim's article on "The Black Bogeyman" in the *Washington Post*; William Raspberry's parable about South African elephants and black people also caught my interest.

I made a connection between the efforts of BAMPAC and Asim to deal with the import of what Bennett said about aborting black babies and reducing crime. For my money, Asim used the far more effective strategy: he put Bennett's remarks squarely in the continuing tradition of racist discourse in the United States. The BAMPAC article was just another of those polite, reactionary gestures that the William Bennetts of American read and laugh at. The schmuck and his ilk have no intention of alienating their entitlement to be morally reprehensible. The U. S. Constitution, at least up to the passage of the USA Patriot Act, protects that entitlement. BAMPAC seems not to understand the tyranny of the majority.

Since the organization theoretically speaks on my behalf, I thought it only right that I speak to it by emailing one Mr. Curtis Midkiff. I informed Mr. Midkiff that I appreciated BAMPAC's demand that Bennett retract his statement about the efficacy of genocide. It seems to me, however, that Bennett has already succeeded in adding gasoline to the embers of racism in America; it is impossible for him to retract the damage. His making an apology would be an act of bad faith. I reminded Mr. Midkiff that Bennett's comments were related to the mass media's demonizing of black New Orleanians in the aftermath of Hurricane Katrina and not devoting so much as thirty seconds of air time to the fate of Latino/Latina and Asian American evacuees. American mass media is as clever as the serpent in the Garden of Eden. It plays the game of divide and contain the "ethnics" well. And it should be noted that law and order communities are expressing grave fears about the black New Orleanians who fell among them like manna from the skies. It is not Bennett that we should target exclusively. The real issue is permanent racism in the United States. BAMPAC would serve us best by putting that issue on the floor of the United Nations and in other international forums. Katrina pulled the covers off a social order that is a monstrosity. The world should gaze upon it and wonder.

Thursday, October 13, 2006: Poetic Rebirth

Thanks to Dave Brinks, we had "a critical gathering of New Orleans artists, poets, and friends" at the Gold Mine Saloon (701 Dauphine). We joined hands and minds dedicated to continuing the production of various arts in the city. The event was titled "STILL STANDING." Whether the writings were old works or ones newly forged in the tense climate left by Hurricane Katrina, the works by more than thirty poets proved to be effective. Some were healing. Others were brutal. They kept the wounds open and throbbing. Fortified with red beans, rice and French bread, we sought solidarity. Diverse ideologies and voices can coexist without bloodshed. Did it matter that reunions in the back of the saloon ignored performances in the front? No one cared. No one complained. What mattered was that Dave managed to pull off the affair, to persuade us to return. Revitalizing the 17 Poets Series and helping artists to help one another loosened the stranglehold of trauma. That was crucial. We are still standing rather than merely standing.

Saturday, October 15, 2005

Epiphany #3: Q: Why did New Orleans flood?

A: The engineers, being in possession of godlike power, conspired with pseudocrats to punish those who could not evacuate before the Storm. Anyone who pays careful attention to fables will understand. Fortunately, floods are not racist.

Hurricane Katrina brewed a large batch of "jes grew." Remote sectors of the United States have been infected. The actual flooding in the Northeast has caused a few people to behave as if they were citizens of New Orleans. They are disturbed by flooding in their homes.

October 15: A Birthday Gift

The lawyers Lolis Edward Elie and Ernest Jones became a part of my extended 62nd birthday celebration in July 2005.

We were having breakfast at Hotel Richelieu on Chartres Street, spending a leisurely Saturday morning to discuss the fate of the world and the forthcoming New Orleans Word Festival (September 25-October 2). I had noticed a copy of *Guns, Germs, and Steel* in the back seat of Ernest's SUV. I asked him what was the subject of the book. He launched into an extended explanation, telling me about animals, climates, domestication, and the formation of cultures. I began to think the book might be worth reading. When we returned to Lolis's house in Treme, I announced that Sunday would be my birthday. Ernest immediately said I must have Jared Diamond's book. He signed it "Happy B'day/From Ernest/7/05." Lolis gave me two bottles of white wine. The book and the wine were compatible. I spent the late hours of Sunday getting acquainted with the extraordinary work of Jared Diamond in evolutionary biology.

October 16, 2006

Lenard D. Moore's poems remind me that fingers make piano keys sing.

Tuesday, October 18:

On not awakening at 6:00 a.m.

I wanted to get up at 6:00 a.m., get an early start on the day. My body would not cooperate. It was tired from its trip to New Orleans yesterday to talk to the insurance assessor. "No way, buddy," it said to me. "I'm sleeping." So, my body stayed in bed until 8:15 a.m. and only slid out of bed because I had a phone call from a *Wall Street Journal* reporter. Then my body decided it wanted a cup of coffee before it got showered. So I was tolerant. My body said, "We really should complete the contents worksheet and fax it to the insurance adjuster this morning, write a thank-you letter to Harryette Mullen, and write a check for the rent." Just when I had persuaded my body that a shower would make both of us feel better, the doorbell rang. Body and I, looking quite unkempt in our pj's, cracked the door. A smiling lady handed us a UPS package. My body said, "I wonder if she thought we looked sexy?" I refused to honor his ill-bred question. I promptly opened the package. It contained Keith Byerman's new book *Remembering the Past in Contemporary African American Fiction*. My blurb for the book is handsomely printed on the back cover. Now it was my turn. "You see, old buddy, using the brain has some rewards." My body was not listening. He was humming, "Water, Lord, water. Flood us with the water of Thy grace." I suppose I will have to sit my body down and give him an hour's lecture on the difference between grace and water.

Wednesday, October 19:

After the Hurricanes
(for the radical writers in New Orleans)

Poverty is not devoid of its dignity,
Nor is the Ninth Ward a fractured mirror
For minor gods to behold factitious laughter.
Beware of aliens, of inside agitators, of vultures
Who would batten on grief and broken hearts,
Kidnap our cultures and dreams, wondrously aged,
Transport and auction them for abuse.
Against such tragedy within tragedy we stand
In solidarity for life, for liberty, for return to happiness.
Hope is not devoid of its deceit,
Nor immune to misleading into swamps.
Careful. Don't move left. Quicksand be there.
Don't move right. Gators will kiss you.
Learn from the fugitive enslaved.
Befriend moccasins.
Capture and coffle the cruel,
The arrogant, the mammon cold.
Send them on middle passages into the blues.

October 20, 2005: 1:56 a.m.

Remembering has no mercy. "The outside has begun to look abnormal, so I have settled down to discover the jewels in my soul." I have perhaps misquoted my friend John Milton Wesley, a poet and superb prose writer. Nevertheless, I have retained the gist of his meaning. A wonderful phrase— "jewels of my soul." This is no commonplace metaphor. "Jewels of my heart" is commonplace. What strikes me is the location of material— jewels, raw rocks and minerals transformed and transvalued— in a spiritual place. But one expects no less of John, a man in quest for the rare and provocative. He often finds treasure, or makes it. At present, the quest is of more importance to me than the discovery. Are we writers from the Gulf Coast region endowed with the credibility of trauma, the authority of disbelief? Do we see these scars on writers from other parts of the world?

Are survivors of tsunamis, the death of loved ones, cancer, AIDS, earthquakes, genocide, hurricanes, rape, famine, and nuclear explosions endowed with authority without any effort on their part? I think not. I think that we, like John whose fiancée was killed in one of the 9/11 planes, are driven to track the contours of sad memory in places we deem sacred. Like John, we grind and polish our grief into something precious.

At Grinnell

Entry: Sunday, October 23, 2005

If there had been no sunshine in Des Moines when my plane arrived on Saturday afternoon, I would swear that Iowa is permanently cold and gray. I would swear to an untruth. Iowa does have sunshine and bright, healthy smiles. The sun warms the soil here in due season, and farmers grow more resigned to what shall be as harvest nears. And despite having been in Grinnell when rain, ice, snow, and temperatures of seven below zero taught me how to ballet on slick sidewalks, I will praise this piece of the Midwest for being a fine site for reviewing the sense of depression. A cold, gray Sunday in Iowa increases the weight, the baggage of emotions one has carried from New Orleans to Vicksburg to Jackson to New Orleans to Vicksburg and from Jackson/Evers International Airport to Grinnell College. One can coffin oneself in depression here.

And that is very much what I do not wish to do, however inviting death of awareness might be. Doing nothing would only bring the paralysis of will from which I might opt not to recover.

Yesterday, Brad Bateman picked me up at the airport. After visiting his favorite coffee shop (one of the earliest in Des Moines), we go to his house for dinner and delightful conversation with his wife Sheryl and two (Thomas and Lydia) of the three Bateman children. Henry, the middle child, is off DJing at a birthday party for his new love interest. The leg of lamb, fresh green beans, potatoes, and an American pinot noir in a screw top bottle constitute a fine first meal for my two-week visit to Grinnell College as a Minority Scholar-in-Residence. Brad drives me to the College from Des Moines, a trip of approximately 60 miles, gets the keys and directions I'll need from his office, and drops me off at Ricker House, a huge bungalow in the style popularized by Frank Lloyd Wright. Some features in the house have been modified, but much of it remains in an "original" state. It will be nice to inhabit, even for a brief time, an architectural space that announces something as opposed to the carelessly planned structure that insults: the typical house of 2004-2005. Ask people who once lived in costly homes in East New Orleans about the quality of materials and workmanship. As I try in various ways to negotiate the return to New Orleans, the path back is littered with death things that shall never return and money and the evil smiles of dishonest contractors as they loot the wallets of the recovering.

My being at Grinnell College is a part of the recovery. I can reenact the role I played early in 2001, in a less troubled time. Only the surface of the act can be repeated. Whatever satisfaction I dream was attached to the role will be altered by time past. I can't recover the illusion of happiness through the same portal.

Replication of the past is impossible. It is also undesirable. Such fantasy is rice paper tossed into a roaring fireplace. Automatic consumption.

Yesterday, Brad asked if writing *The Katrina Papers* was a kind of travel. I hesitated before I answered. Writing = discovery = exploration = journey somewhere = destination requires travel = discovery of a vast geography of imagination = travel in the mind. I hesitated until I could work out several analogies. Do not confuse the motions of remembering and forgetting with the travel motions involved in going from New Orleans to Convent, LA for Christmas; from the threat of inevitable destruction to safety. Yes, Brad, I suppose it is.

Additional entry for October 23, 2005:

Carnegie 111, the office I have been assigned is larger than those I have had at Tougaloo and Dillard. It does not have a telephone. I don't have the password that will allow me to access the Internet. After purchasing a loaf of wheat bread, Folgers instant coffee, Blue Bonnet margarine, Lipton chicken noodle soup mix, and crackers at McNally's, I return to Ricker House, plug in my laptop, and prepare for Monday's meeting with my students. Tomorrow, I'll get the password, an office phone, and the ID card (Pioneer Card) that allows me to eat in the student dining halls. At the library I read Zeleza, Paul Tiyambe. "Rewriting in the African Diaspora: Beyond the Black Atlantic." *African Affairs* 104.411 (January 2005): 35-69. Zeleza complicates the issue well.

Monday, October 24, 2005:

The day begins with a shave and a shower. I pretend to have breakfast— two slices of toast heavily buttered and strong instant coffee. The coffee is a sad substitute for the coffee that used to make my day in New Orleans. Nevertheless, it enables me to deal with life.

Life was quite obviously prepared to deal with me. The first person I greet in Carnegie is George Barlow. I am in Office 111; George is down the hall and around the corner in Office 104. George helps me secure the code for the copier, the computer password, etc. I hurry through the accumulated email messages, make short answers, delete the unwanted. Angie Story takes me to get my Pioneer Card. Brad takes me to get my "official" photograph taken by Steve O'Connor, and then we have lunch at the Forum Grill. After lunch it is back to the office and fixing my mind on central ideas about Wright's travel writing. The 18 students in the seminar were lively and forthcoming about their reasons for taking the course. I enjoyed the first day with them.

I have dinner with English Department colleagues at the Phoenix after giving George a whirlwind tour of Ricker House. I remember to call Bettye Parker Smith, Dillard's Provost. It is a joyful reunion of our voices; we had not talked since the end of August. And there is pain: the extreme weariness in Bettye's voice, weariness from planning for January 2006 when too many unknown variables preclude the making of good decisions. The future conceals itself in weariness. Then it is off to the library for books to quicken my thinking about *Black Power, Part One.*

Public Lecture at Grinnell College: On Richard Wright and Our Contemporary Situation

I.

"Are you still," someone asked my young colleague Howard Rambsy II, "interested in Richard Wright?" Imagine substituting another writer's name in the question. "Are you still interested in William Shakespeare?" Anyone who asked that question might be considered odd. So too do I regard the unnamed person who posed the question to Rambsy. I have discovered no justifiable reason for not being still interested in Wright's challenging works of fiction or in his provocative non-fiction. Indeed, our contemporary situation, which is constituted by a welter of immediate and long-term anxieties and denials, invites me to have a more profound investment in Wright and in how the body of his published and unpublished works might assist us in dealing with the chaos of the twenty-first century. Our contemporary situation invites our dwelling with writers ancient and modern, especially those who raised disturbing questions about the designs human beings have upon other human beings. Focusing on Wright is both a professional and personal choice; it is, for me, an existential choice, a choice to confront rather than be lobotomized by the absurd.

II. Wright orients us to points of reference

It is not a single work by Richard Wright that assists us to deal with the lack of metaphysical absolutes to secure our sense that life has meaning; it is the whole body of his work that serves as a question-generating machine. The short fiction in *Uncle Tom's Children* forces me to deal with the idea of regional differences in the United States, with social and labor relations, with the permanence of race, racialism, and racism in America, and with the fact that terrorism threatened certain Americans at least a century prior to 9/11. *Native Son* forces me to ponder possession or absence of free will among my fellow citizens, to think about the nature of our vernacular political economy, and to view the drama enacted in the spider web of the urban. Consider that Bigger Thomas has been rescued from the electric chair, displaced from Chicago to New Orleans, and refashioned as a dedicated looter rather than as an environmentally determined adolescent. *12 Million Black Voices,* which Wright proclaimed in 1941was a folk history, exposes the unstable grounds upon which human histories are constructed and revised. Moreover, given that some photographs used in the book came from the Farm Security Administration, my interest in the uses of visual evidence to broadcast state propaganda is quickened. *Black Boy,* Wright's autobiography, forces me to consider that life writing is an inscription of the self within a tradition and a quest for understanding, that book titles are often gendered. Wright's 1953 novel, *The Outsider,* obligates me to consider that philosophical meditations and common sense thinking about life can result in abject alienation. *Eight Men* bids me to examine stereotypes and *Savage Holiday* provides a glimpse of non-black pathologies. *The Long Dream* begets questions about fathers and sons, economics and amoral corruption, and death. The posthumously published *Lawd Today* takes me into the realm of folklore and generic imitation of James Joyce's *Ulysses*; Wright's 817 haiku (*Haiku: This Other World*) lead to questions about American uses of Oriental aesthetics.

Wright's travel writing– *Pagan Spain, Black Power, The Color Curtain,* and *White Man, Listen!*– provides yet another frame wherein I can pose my unanswerable questions about world order and disorder; about human responses to natural disasters and recovery; about imperialism and its relationship with terrorism.

III. Wright promotes deeper inquiry about the aftermath of recent disasters

Richard Wright's works did not suddenly cease on August 28, 2005 to be the objects of my research, but they did become, in a rather new sense, instruments or catalysts for thinking about the aftermath of September 11, 2001 and the aftermath of Hurricanes Katrina, Rita, and Wilma. Wright hinted in his writing at the end of his life that the history of Western imperialism might be usefully examined as surreal, irrational, and effective immoral acts in the service of power. One of the key phrases in our current situation is "homeland security," a phrase that served as a warrant for the passage of the USA Patriot Act, a legal entity that authorizes suspension of constitutional guarantees. This Act has done much to create a climate for "legitimate" transgression of human rights. To the extent that American citizens can be persuaded to be patriotic without question and to survive on a diet of misinformation, the immense power unleashed by the Act can oil that path that leads from American democracy as we knew it to American fascism that we imagined would never come into existence on our soil. What has slouched into our lives is a horror that not even Wright's most prophetic vision could prepare us to deal with.

Wright's fictive treatment of the Mississippi River flood of 1927 in the short stories "Silt" (later retitled "The Man Who Saw the Flood") and "Down by the Riverside" does prepare us partially for the national tragedy that is unfolding as the national gaze on the plight of New Orleans segues into macrodiscourses about government preparedness for responding to natural disasters, about poverty (which is being treated as an amazing new discovery), about the long-term effects of various toxins on ecosystems and on public health in the southeastern United States, about race as an inevitable American dilemma, about probable government appropriation of private property in New Orleans by using a fairly obscure concept– USUFRUCT – as one recovery strategy.

Wright's story "Down by the Riverside" makes us aware that natural disaster and its subsequent traumas do not necessarily lead to any transcending of racial differentiation and skin privilege, as can be seen in the way our mass media used various kinds of print and visual narratives to report on New Orleans, a regressive process of demonizing one portion of the city's population and of erasing the existence of other portions. The classic binary of black and white was showcased with a vengeance. It is now very easy to believe that no Latinas/Latinos, no Haitians, no Vietnamese, no Japanese, no Chinese, no people of Asian descent inhabited the city. They are a significant absence in the ongoing discourse.

So, what is the fallout that might be anticipated? Listen to this small excerpt from the screenplay of *Hotel Rwanda*.

Paul [Rusesabagina]: I am glad that you have shot this footage– and that the world will see it. It is the only way we have a chance that people might intervene.

Jack glances down. Jack: Yeah, and if no one intervenes, is it still a good thing to show?

Paul: How can they not intervene– when they witness such atrocities?

Jack: (sighs) I think if people see this footage they'll say "Oh my God, that's horrible," and then go on eating their dinners.

Hotel Rwanda (New York: Newmarket Press, 2005), p. 170

A more scholarly forecast comes from Slavoj Zizek, a senior researcher at the Institute for Advanced Study in the Humanites in Essen, Germany: He concluded his article "The Subject Supposed to Loot and Rape: Reality and Fantasy in New Orleans" with a chilling paragraph:

...New Orleans is one of those cities within the United State most heavily marked by the internal wall that separates the affluent from ghettoized blacks. And it is about those on the other side of the wall that we fantasize: More and more, they live in another world, in a blank zone that offers itself as a screen for the projection of our fears, anxieties and secret desires. The "subject supposed to loot and rape" is on the other side of the Wall– this is the subject about whom [William] Bennett can afford to make his slips of the tongue and confess in a censored mode his murderous dreams. More than anything else, the rumors and fake reports from the aftermath of Katrina bear witness to the deep class division of American society. [http://www.inthesetimes.com/site/main/article/2361]

The best that Richard Wright's works can do to alleviate our pessimism and near despair is to remind us that human beings survive enormous tragedies. I grant that may be very true, but I still ask if, in the absence of ruthless conversations about what it means to be an American it is possible for Americans to survive one another. It is quite conceivable that benign, highly selective genocide can occur here under the guise of homeland security or whatever the buzzword of choice might be. Wright's example of engaging dangerous issues by way of his actively reading contemporary situations and writing about them is one we might wish to follow.

34

When I sum up my investment in Richard Wright and our contemporary situation, my attitudes are expressed concisely in the third stanza of my poem "After the Hurricanes".

> Hope is not devoid of its deceit,
> Nor immune to misleading into swamps.
> Careful. Don't move left. Quicksand be there.
> Don't move right. Gators will kiss you.
> Learn from the fugitive enslaved.
> Befriend moccasins.
> Capture and coffle the cruel,
> The arrogant, the mammon cold.
> Send them on middle passages into the blues.

Permit me to leave you with an unarticulated but certainly intended warning in the final line: "Send them on middle passages into the blues." Remember, of course, that you will be on the same awe-filled journey. Richard Wright and I are very unlike Ralph Ellison's invisible narrator who spoke for you perhaps at the lower frequencies. Our current situation demands that we speak to you of anguished efforts to uncover a truth.

Friday, October 28

Epiphany #4: The night is scarlet / the moon is blind / mudbugs have invaded the sun.

A film directed by Nagisa Oshima is a rare treat. Tonight I watched *Gohatto* [against the law] which was distributed as *Taboo* (1999). It was visually of great interest to me, but I remain baffled by the content. And I am more baffled after reading Andrew Grossman's critique of the film's reactionary treatment of homosexuality. I am content to complain that the swordplay in the film was mediocre and that I am in the dark about the historical accuracy in representing the samurai.

Saturday, October 29, 2005

Epiphany #5: Katrina obviously did not consult Thomas S. Kuhn or Jared Diamond about the nature of revolution. She confused a paradigm with a puddle.

October 30, 2005: Covering and Recovering at Grinnell College: Exile and Writing

Writing has no mercy. Like the nails used to accomplish a proper crucifixion, writing can inflict pain or deeply wound with impunity. And quite unlike those nails, it can heal. It can practice medicine without benefit of license. Writing surprises the hand. Sometimes it assumes a remarkable balance of content and form, function and shape; it manifests an equilibrium the mind thought was impossible. Yet, when the mind most desires that writing should organize dissimilar parts and reveal their interrelatedness, it can refuse to expose connection. It behaves like a spoiled child who performs outrageously in public to defy, embarrass, and manipulate the frustrated parent. There is no peace until the poor parent relents and gives in to the child's desires. A few parents reach into memory, ignore the strictures of the correctness police, and apply ancient methods of behavior modification. These methods work. The child remembers well into adulthood and old age why thou shalt not abuse thy parents. For better or worse, writing has no mercy until violence becomes palpable and the taste of bitter medicine induces restoration.

As an evacuee, a survivor of Hurricane Katrina, an exile from the city that care forgot, I have begun to give abnormal attention to how the violence of one natural disaster followed by a second, a third, a remote fourth can severely change one's perspectives on life. In Vicksburg, Mississippi, the Union dead and the Confederate dead who populate the national battlefield are of minimal interest. I prefer to inspect the beauty of a single flower blooming on the grounds of the First Baptist Church. The wind and rain of Katrina did touch Vicksburg, leaving the shelter where I was given refuge without electricity for three days. The flower, this token of beauty, survived. I will not question how a seed reached it telos or its ordained end. I admire. With astonishment I ponder the survival. Is this how early man came to inscribe himself in the vocabulary of nature, how early woman adjusted and improved the language?

Human creations also endow me with a renewed sense of pleasure and mystery.

In Grinnell, Iowa, Ricker House– Frank Lloyd Wright's angles rearranged in the alembic of Walter Burley Griffin's architectural imagination– this Ricker House impresses upon me a simple fact I had for too long taken for granted: people live within geometries. Straight angles versus curves. The defining power of the line. Passage through boxes not cylinders. My mind wonders and wanders in spaceshapes until a view through a rectangular pane brings daydreaming to a halt: multicolored autumn foliage against an ominous gray sky is a sufficient invitation to return to nature, to reality, to what must be dealt with after natural disaster. Illusion and magic vanish.

The taste of bitter tonic is heavy on my tongue. I must face the violence as certainly as the criminal must face the music here or hereafter. Violence you are the cause of death, the cause of rot and stench and sickness. You are a primal agent in the creation of debris. You murder dreams. You kick hope in its ribs. You sponsor enormous projects of emotional wreckage. You engender tears, trauma, curses, the dreadful thought that the Almighty was taking a nap when the violence of a natural disaster occurred.

You welcome me to the trashheap. Everything has become surreal. You have made me the trashman's helper. You have made me wear a heavy surgical mask and cover my hands with heavy duty rubber gloves. I look like an out-of-work actor ready to audition for a minor role in a science fiction film. The work is too much for me alone. My friend Dave Brinks lends his strength to cut stinking, soggy carpet and haul it to the curb. He is giving me assistance and courage. I cannot let Dave see me cry. No tears will stream down my face. They will just have to drip into my stomach.

He warns me not to open the refrigerator. We do not want to see what might be inside. We do not want to inhale the stink. We bind the refrigerator with yards of duct tape and angle it out to the sidewalk. Books that dampness and mold have rendered beyond salvation are tossed into large trash bags along with shoes and other items of clothing. Although my more than two hundred LP albums are ruined, I can not bear to expel them. Not yet. Eventually the lost and damaged contents of 1928 Gentilly Boulevard must go. I don't have a digital camera. Flooding has made my 35mm as useless as my PC. Much of the lost and the damaged— can I sell that phrase as the title for a new soap opera series?— will sit and wait for the flood insurance adjustor to come. Dave has gone, and I have the freedom to cry. I opt not to. Let the tears remain in my guts. Use the energy it takes to cry to strengthen your effort to write.

Yes, Hurricane Katrina violated my house. But that violation was minimal when I recall that many people who lived in various sectors of the greater New Orleans area no longer have homes. I have been blessed. Because you are in exile, at a distance from your relatives and friends and from what remains of the unique cultural gumbos of New Orleans, those social and spiritual foods that nourished you, you must write. Should you fail to write your own story of survival and amplify it with the physical labor of recovery, writing will truly have no mercy. It will be a stern judge. It will consign you to the prisonhouse of guilt.

November 1, 2005: Words

"CONSTRUCTION"— Cutting-edge people in the academic world repeat this word over and over. They begin to sound like one-dimensional gnats. These people are not carpenters, architects, brick masons, or civil engineers. What do they think they are constructing?

"LOSS"— *The Wall Street Journal* finally prints a story about people who are more to me than names I recognize, people with whom I have broken bread and laughed.

Daniel Golden, who called me at least six times as he was writing the story, published "Words Can't Describe What Some Writers in New Orleans Lost" on pages A1 and A10 today. I grieve as I read what my friends Mona Lisa Saloy and

Niyi Osundare lost. And I don't know what to say to them when I see them. I'll embrace them, be overjoyed that their hearts are beating.

"CURTAINS"– Pieces of cloth that filter our vision. Are they really necessary?

"RECORDS"– Only a few people learn from them 100 years after they are created.

November 2, 2005: Of Writers and Sociology

Professor Kesho Y. Scott has invited me to attend her Sociology 275: Race and Ethnicity class at 11:00 a.m. I spend much of this morning trying to anticipate what the students might want to know. I have no grand ideas to share with them. I do not habitually follow the procedures sociologists and psychologists use in raising questions about people and environments. My questions spring up unannounced. The answers I want often play cat and mouse games. I will not pretend to know what I do not know. I will use reductive clarity and pray that my simple ideas can be verified.

Hurricane Katrina has made me willing to be humble, to expose degrees of stupidity if it comes to that. The students had prepared some good questions for me. One student asked: "After we listen to all these feelings from survivors, then what are we suppose [sic] to 'do' with them?" I guess the student surrounded the word DO with quotation marks to signal that I ought to interpret "to do" as something other than action as usual. I ponder the question for several moments, blending thoughts about the feelings those who have survived atomic bombing, holocausts, genocide and natural disasters probably have. People who fortunately have never occupied the subject position of survivors tend to acknowledge misfortune is a fact of life and get on with their business. They do not have time for empathy. Conventional sympathy must suffice. I gave the student a blunt answer: "Become human."

I was more generous in responding to the student who asked: "Has there been a lot of writing and response to people's Katrina experience yet or are people still drownng in the recovery process? How has the process of being displaced affected you? Is the process of writing about it theraputic in a way?" People in the southeastern United States may indeed believe that they are drowning or being overwhelmed. Yet, they are able to articulate the drowning. The disaster did not render them speechless. They talk. They may not write but they are receptive, I believe, to recording oral histories. Some may be reluctant to submit themselves to elaborate interviews, but the majority of the victims will find words to describe their loss and their faith or despair. For me, the act of writing is a form of therapy. Were I to refuse to write, my pent-up feelings would make me very ill.

Professor Scott had shared a few pieces of my writing with her students. I was momentarily puzzled by two straightforward questions: "How did you go about

receiving these stories? Are these people you knew before the disaster?" From
the relatively safe distance of Vicksburg, I had received stories by way of talking
with people from New Orleans, from telephone conversations with my cousins in
Moss Point, Mississippi and Convent, Louisiana, from the stories about stories on
radio and television and in newspapers and magazines. I assumed I was hearing or
listening to stories, not receiving them in the sense of fencing stolen goods. The
student was teaching me something about nuanced communication. Given that
I did not know many of the people I listened to before the hurricane, I probably
was "receiving" their stories. She followed up the simple questions with ones
that asked about the sociology of knowledge: "At one point, you mention how
literary scholars, like yourself, have felt the need to start 'theorizing' about these
events immediately after they occur. Do you think that you may be too close to the
situation (as you lived in New Orleans, I think??) to give an accurate portrayal of
what occurred and what people are feeling? Would someone from the 'outside'
(outside the areas, the state, the country, etc.) be more objective? How have
you worked to be 'objective?' When have you recognized that you are not being
objective? Is objectivity important at all in the case of a sociological study?"

When one is hit by such a tidal wave, one sinks or swims or surfs. I chose to
surf. I do not feel compelled to theorize a hurricane (an impossible undertaking)
or to theorize the responses to natural disaster. I do not especially want to
speculate about the mixed genres people use in responding– vicious jokes about
FEMA, prayers, bitter ancedotes about mistreatment after they have risked
their lives to reach higher ground, conspiracy theories, poems that thunder with
memories of past and present and unseen future, memoirs, comic signs and
symbols, photographs, paintings and videotapes. Indeed, I referred to theory to
caution against haste or inaccurate portrayal. I evacuated before the hurricane
struck, so I am a virtual outsider from the perspective of those who remained in
the city and experienced horror firsthand. As a person who chose temporary exile
along with the politically incorrect status of "refugee," I am an insider. I have
no desire to be objective, to be a social scientist. I elect to be creative, to exploit
language and my own emotions. I have not made any effort to be objective. The
art of what I am doing depends on being deliberately non-objective or of not
striving for a certain kind of realistic representation. In the case of a rigorous
sociological study, one would have to seek objectivity in accounting for minute
factors. The early sociological papers I've heard were less than objective. The
speakers were mesmerized by precooked theory rather than theory created from
empirical specificity, probably as a result of wishing to avoid the messiness of
"insignificant" factors. The questions provoked a mini-lecture, more theory than
I was interested in releasing.

I could not answer all of the questions within the time limits of the class, but
I felt obligated to answer the one that dealt with literature: "For English majors

and other students interested in literature, which works of Richard Wright would you recommend we read to gain insight into the situation in New Orleans? What questions should we ask ourselves as we read these works, and what themes should we keep in mind that are still relevant today?" You should read "Down by the Riverside" in *Uncle Tom's Children*. You keep in mind the pains of man's limits in the face of natural disaster, fear and race, and the difficulty of reaching a moral terminal point.

Writers create sociological possibilities with broad paint strokes and sociologists must become art historians who inspect textures with magnifying glasses.

As a guest professor at Grinnell, I do feel obligated to answer all the questions somewhere in this journal. They are integral parts of its making, sociological elements that affect writing.

November 2, 2005: The Cutting

Having spent a considerable portion of your life in dealing with disappointments, fears caused by events and circumstances you did not invent, and the statistics of bad luck, you are not surprised that Dillard University terminated about 59% of its faculty and staff as of November 1. The institution was more severely devastated by Hurricane Katrina than you had estimated. $400 million in devastation is not chump change. As life-threatening as would be the misfortune of having your jugular vein sliced by a razor, the damage alarms you. It does not surprise. It just alarms like an impolite clock.

The fact that you are a tenured faculty member at Dillard does not shield you from the foreclosure of a future, a future in which whale-sized uncertainties swim. The future contains a surplus of unknowns. Yes, you too can be terminated by the iron rule of financial exigency. You too can join the parade of jobless Americans. Your pale security can be erased.

In a split-second the ground can disappear, and you can find yourself swirling in the storm of Kunstwollen and gazing at self-portraiture by Käthe Kollwitz and Oskar Kokoschar. Cliometrics, climate control, climax and closure. The letter/sound "K" is the key.

You are done and undone. Welcome at last to the working class. The rains and winds of change have issued you into history, handed you the tribulations of your ancestors. What is this? A stick of dynamite? Will you dare to light the fuse? Potentials. You can design an exit from the turmoil and trust God to be your witness. In a split-second, your life could imitate your art.

The little voice that squeaks in the outhouse of consciousness says, "No. No. No." Remembering the students you love, you cut these threads. You decide in a split-second to let your art imitate your life.

November 3, 2005:

It has been another long day. The hours unwind with their usual rapidity, but I am sensing time's movement being retarded by tar or chewing gum or glue. Speed is not measurement but impression. I had a smaller breakfast than usual at Cowles. I scanned portions of *Native Son* and did not make any notes. Notes would only muck up my talking with students at Grinnell Community High School. Brad drives me to the school. We discover I am to talk with two sections of composition and literature classes, a two-hour job (11: 00 a.m. to 1:00 pm.) Scratch having a leisurely lunch with Brad. I feel just a little put upon, being used like the beet from which blood plasma is drained. What the hell? Something good will come out of talking with the students.

I launch into my talk by reminding the students that the novel begins with sound and ends with sound. The clang of the alarm clock. The clang of steel on steel. Awakening. Closure. A complete cycle. This is a simple observation, but it seems to get the attention of these adolescents. Brief comments on Fear, Flight, Fate and why Bigger Thomas is a most unlikable character. I get a mixture of very good and fairly stupid questions. So much for the first set of students. The second set are different. Some are taking the AP English class, and they have not read Wright. They have read *Lord of the Flies* and *Fahrenheit 451*. No problem. I flip the script and escape the noose. They have to ask questions before I make any comments. The session is being videotaped. I ignore the camera. I do pull up from somewhere appropriate allusions– T. S. Eliot's "there will be time to murder and create" is compressed into "murder to create." That is what Bigger does. One timid youngster asked if Bigger was a combination of bigot and the N word. He seemed incapable of uttering the N word. I asked, "You can't say NIGGER, can you?" He gave an affirmative nod. "Well, just say it." And the word "nigger" escaped from his mouth as the color red spread into his already pink face. "You see," I said, "you did not die, and I did not jump across the chairs to kill you." End of lesson on niggers. The students were mildly shocked but only mildly. How many of the tight lips looking in my direction had uttered the word many, many times? I don't know. I don't want to know. I do know this: young white students have to be tricked into uttering in public what they have absolutely no difficulty saying within the circle of whiteness, the gated and guarded community where prejudice has never ceased to breed.

At 1:03 p.m., I leave. Brad is waiting for me outside. We drive off to have a quick lunch on campus, a fine chat over sandwiches. Brad has to teach an afternoon class. I go to my office, read the email, grade a few English 195.01 papers, and review what I want to share with the elderly people at the Mayflower residence. After dinner, I walk the six blocks down to 600 Park Street. As I near the Carmen Center where I will speak, an odd thought flies through my mind:

writers-in-exile should talk to those who are in exile from good health.

Note to self: Read Paul Gilroy. *Small Acts*. London: Serpent's Tail, 1993.

View www.quilombofilm.com = maroon societies in Brazil

5 November 2005: Leaving Iowa, Re-entering Mississippi

Epiphany #6: The greatest gift of the post-postmodern is the restoration of the state of nature.

During the flight from DesMoines to Memphis, I prepare a rough draft– very rough– of a letter of recommendation for Candice Love-Jackson. Tone is so important because I am writing as her former teacher/mentor (undergraduate). The letter can not be streaked with unqualified praise. It should incorporate an observation about one of the small shortcomings that encourage people to grow. There is more than an hour's layover before my flight (NW 5792 @ 2:35 p.m.). I call Reginald Martin for a brief chat. Might as well itemize the things that must be done once I reach Vicksburg.

1. Write checks for bills
2. Get a haircut
3. Write notes for Tuesday's presentation at Mississippi Valley State
4. Buy gas on Sunday and food for the week
5. Write thank-you letter to Brad
6. Write additional notes for Friday's presentation at Tougaloo
7. Press shirts
8. Outline schedule and papers for Dickinson, esp. new poems
9. Call flood insurance company on Monday

November 8, 2005: THREE OF MY FRIENDS NEED LETTERS OF RECOMMENDATION.

My three friends have conveniently forgot that I am not at home. They have failed to remember that my previous writings about their achievements are either in my office at Dillard University or in my house, water-soaked and moldy, quite beyond use. I shall write honest letters, of course. These letters on plain paper rather than Dillard letterhead will not be as splendid as my friends might deserve.

I surprised myself at Mississippi Valley State University by not sticking to the script. Dr. Zheng wanted me to talk about "Reading *Black Boy* in the 21st Century." I have written about the autobiography, and our current circumstances demand, I think, something more expansive by way of putting one's finger on Wright's contemporary importance. I announced to the audience of students and faculty members, approximately 75 people, that I would say very little about the autobiography and talk instead about Wright and our contemporary situation. The talk was a success, sending small shocks of recognition through the audience.

I was prepared in the afternoon to talk with the honors students, but again

Dr. Zheng was insistent that I talk with them about Wright's late poetry, his haiku. Zheng is Chinese, and he knows the oriental forms much, much better than I. Moreover, I have not made my study of what Wright was up to in the poems. So, I led the students in some general discussion about Wright's last years, his paranoia and tense feelings, and suggested that haiku was a form of therapy, which ignored all the nice considerations of aesthetics in the production of the form. We read the haiku randomly and tried to figure out together what Wright was doing. I insisted that we focus on words, on how his words transgressed the implicit emotions and sentiments that obtain in classical haiku. Zheng was sitting behind me. The eyes in the back of my head did not detect that he was annoyed by my treatment of the material. And I really did not give a damn if he was annoyed. I have my own Richard Wright agenda and I will follow it to the letter.

I could not leave MVSU until nearly 4:00 p.m. That meant arriving in Vicksburg at dusk dark. I called Chakula after I ate a quick supper and then went off to have good luck at the Ameristar casino. God must have answered my wishes. I left the casino with real money in my wallet. And I want to write a poem about those who sing with mouths of diamonds and gold.

Peace, spell me for a while.

Wednesday, November 9: Trying to organize papers in the apartment. Now I miss my filing cabinets.

Poem notes: "Tears in a Bullfrog's Eyes"

Wind. The wind. Just the wind
And a grain of sound, sound wailing
In dust, in sand like a music, sound
Swirling where diamonds stand for teeth,
Where he who likes it like that and has it like that
Plates his tongue with a foolish gold.
Just a stench of wind croaking in the distance,
The wind that makes your nostrils vomit,
The wind that bloats a bullfrog as his eyes fill with tears.

Entry notes:

Today is a jigsaw puzzle. Some pieces are chilling in the refrigerator. Some are hyperactive, jumping out of and into the laptop screen. Others are playing hide and seek in telephone messages. A few have made a pilgrimage to Mount Anticipation. Dumb reverence is a sucker for miracles. I guess they will show up at some point bearing sacred tablets of cardboard. The fat and lazy ones have potatoed themselves on a sofa to watch imaginary sit-coms on a non-existent television. As a child, I delighted in solving jigsaw puzzles.

Now, late in 2005, I can't even call up nostalgia. Puzzles infuriate me.

November 9, 2005

KATRINA, YOU ARE NOT A KNIFE

A cutter of cardboard and carpet;
A sharp point deveining
The delicate curve of a shrimp's back;
An edge slashing wing, breast,
And leg of gospel bird;
A blade thrown archly in a sideshow;
A dangerous toy
In the dangerous fingers
Of deranged aristocrats;
A surface paring a surface;
A weighted line mincing onions;
A crude, passionate
Chivving of an inmate's heart;
A complicit witness in samurai ritual;
Slitting tendons and tender loins, severing muscles and bone;
Tempered steel gleaming sterile and disinterested,
Exploring a cadaver's cavities;
A tool forged to section grapefruit,
To divorce Creole tomatoes from their vines.
Katrina, you are not a knife.
You are a morbid corkscrew in motion.

Thursday, November 10

Made some progress with the organizing. Had a good conversation with Michael Reddix at Barnes & Noble as I ate a bagel with cream cheese and coffee. Visited Candice's class and talked with two of the students about how to write their essays. Wrote introductory material for my talk at Tougaloo tomorrow.

Friday, November 11

Epiphany #7: Never play the dozens in bed.

Dear Rudy,
I do not want to hook into this conversation, but I just can not resist saying that you are not exotic. As a child in Mississippi, I used an outhouse until we got indoor plumbing. When one's family had a very limited income, one did the best one could until times got better. Given that the "white" ethnic popped up, I should say that I do find some "white" ethnics of various classes to be quite exotic. People who insert

metal rings and other objects in their genitals and other body parts are
exotic; so too was the woman I saw at Yale who was wearing a snake
for a scarf. Southern women and men who lacked certain advantages
and privileges in the 1940s, unless one buys into William Faulkner's
descriptions of them, were rarely exotic. They may have been eccentric.
Their exposure to certain aspects of American "civilization" may
have been delayed. It puzzles me that an intellectual who ought to
understand the nuances of the "different" would want to keep it at a
remote distance from his consciousness.
Jerry

November 13, 2005: Going to Dickinson College

At Delta, it is business as usual. A delayed flight from Jackson to Atlanta
and a rocky ride. Lucky I'm wearing jeans today. Coffee spilled on my pant leg.
The *NY Review of Books* (November 3, 2005) piece on higher education sparks
an idea about the exclusion of HBCUs from the conversation. One might argue
that social stratification and economics and privilege constitute the barrier; that
race is rather a tertiary factor, given that Asians have a slight edge on whites in
mathematics and science programs at the most prestigious universities. Blacks,
of course, are as invisibly folded into the statistics as any other ethnic grouping.
Nevertheless, I had expected to see the names Hampton, Howard, Spelman, and
Clark-Atlanta appear at least once in the article. They did not. I would have to
inspect the books under review to determine whether any of them mentioned one
HBCU. It is a bitter consolation to recall that Native American colleges like the
one in Lawrence, Kansas, are habitually ignored in national discussions of how
well or how poorly young Americans are being prepared for life.

November 16, 2005

Epiphany #10: Beware. Life has begun to frit the elements.

The Agony of Recovery: Abandon Romance. Embrace Reality.

When the dentist sliced through my gums to the underlying bone structure,
I signaled him to stop. "Spray on anesthetic," I demanded. "I am less tolerant
of pain as I grow older." Since hurricanes swept through and dumped disaster
on the Gulf Coast, aging occurs with surprising rapidity. Productive anger alone
prevents one's collapsing into dead-end resignation. Like that shiny scalpel in
the board-certified hands of the dentist, the agony of recovery invades sensibility
with its own brand of pain. The excruciating jolts leap like jumping beans along
the network of nerves. Now you know a little how the innocent convict feels as the
first nanosecond of electrocution sets her body twitching.

Unlike the compassionate William K. Jenkins, D. D. S. of Carlisle,
Pennsylvania, the recovery process ignores any individual pleas for relief. It is a

juggernaut of one-dimensional dedication. It rolls over and onward, smashing, crushing, and flattening things and people and the emotion to have emotion. We have to move from romance to post-post-modern logic. Sentiment must be repressed or obliterated. It does not belong to the order of things, and it would compromise the validity of analysis. You have to wear a mask. As you navigate the sprawling discourse of natural disaster and national tragedy [and you will accept those as the correct narratological categories in line for imminent deconstruction], your face must be the face of an American president destroying a Middle Eastern cockroach or of a cult leader mixing batches of Kool-Aid with cyanide. The face/ mask must be grim and comic. It is a serviceable device. Add feathers and ribbons of green, purple, and gold, and you might gain admission to any number of Mardi Gras orgies or reasonable caricatures thereof.

Accept Lady McBeth's advice, and unsex yourself of the personal. Become "objective" social observer number N, the one who after a few weeks of "helping" New Orleans recover can return to his hamlet, town, or mansion where all is normal. Wherever "home" is for that person, the subway runs on a fairly reliable schedule; the supermarket is usually stocked with staples as well as gourmet foods, organic oranges and hydroponic lettuce; there are usually three or four hospitals in the town with doctors and nurses and candy-stripe girls; the postperson arrives at least once a day; school children romp and squeal away the recess; cell phones spend large amounts of time planning assignations or checking stock quotes; only 4.13% of the residents are unemployed; beauty parlors and barbershops are anxious to help you keep up appearances; churches are anxious to help you shore up your soul against floodtides of evil; holiday prices have begun to season the air. Virginia, there is no Santa Claus. Your parents are liars.

Begin with a trivial fact and move to facts of greater consequence. Electricity has been restored at Xavier University. As of November 16, 2005, electricity had not been restored at Dillard University. Request full disclosure from Entergy about the cause of discrimination.

If you are a property owner in parts of New Orleans where working class people once lived, give attention to how on June 23, 2005, the U.S. Supreme Court made a 5 to 4 decision that allows the term "eminent domain" to migrate beyond its traditional habitation. In *Kelo v. City of New London, Conn.*, the Court decided it is "constitutionally permissible for the city government to take a group of working-class homes from their owners and turn the parcel of land over to private parties for the purpose of economic development" (3). [See Carla T. Main. "How Eminent Domain Ran Amok." *Policy Review*, No. 133 (October and November 2005): 3-24] The imposition of eminent domain might apply to parts of New Orleans other than the racially demonized Ninth Ward, but oddly it might not apply to blighted homes in the French Quarter or the much touted Garden District. Such homes might be quickly accorded benefit of history in legal proceedings; the unblighted home in Mid-City in certain Louisiana courts might be accorded the distinction of being a sacrificial lamb for the "public good," geological and biocultural factors notwithstanding. If you do not have a Ph.D. and have some difficulty reading the Court's decision on eminent domain, you obviously do not understand the rare legal term "ususfruct." You are a person who needs to ask a law student from Tulane or a senior from Dillard or Xavier University for help with interpretation immediately. You are in danger, as any streetwise kid can tell you, of being legally bamboozled. Of course, for the sake of objectivity, I must add that there is a very high probability that the randomly-chosen at-risk juvenile would use the past tense of a word deemed vulgar by most conservative dictionaries, a word whose initial letter is "F."

Labor will play a crucial role in the recovery of New Orleans and of all areas of the Southeastern United States affected by hurricanes. But how will labor be constituted? What percentage of the workforce in New Orleans by March 2006 will consist of residents who returned; what percent of migrant workers from Central and South America? How will questions regarding fair wages be adjudicated? What will be the daily quality of life for workers regardless of race or origin? How extensively have legal procedures been ignored up to November 1, 2005, in the U.S. government's awarding of contracts? Is it a matter of morality, of justice, or of plain common sense for black workers to argue that selective confirmation (the obverse of affirmative action) was used in blocking minority-owned contractors? Labor statistics and labor histories in the context of political contests for power must be studied to sharpen vision of how recovery in New Orleans evolves. **[[As a footnote that is not one, I submit that musicians, especially jazz musicians, are artists who are also laborers. Some excellent New Orleans jazz musicians did play venues in the French Quarter, but it was an open secret that they were not overjoyed with the conditions created by club owners. They were often happier playing on the edges of the Quarter. Part of the total recovery process must involve measures to improve working conditions for jazz musicians.]]**

The footnote was an instance of slippage of the kind not to be brooked in tough-minded social science, especially political science. Can we say that a New Orleans voter living temporarily in Flagstaff, Arizona, is being disenfranchised if she or he is not notified about forthcoming elections in 2006? This question must be debated from many angles in hope of arriving at an answer that will stand up under judicial scrutiny.

As I engage in preliminary designs for a story of survival, I am feeling a throbbing pain from the invasion of reality. I was beginning to enjoy the magic, the creative joy of writing inside the vast and changing zone where imagination can shake hands with facts. Once the necessary mask separates me from such romantic ventures in narration, I have to make a separate peace with raunchy reality.

Dickinson College

November 17-18: When It Is Genuine

"When it is genuine, when it is born of the need to speak, no one can stop the human voice."

Eduardo Galeano. *The Book of Embraces* (NY: W. W. Norton, 1991). 25.

It becomes more genuine, the need to speak becomes more genuine. The voice becomes engaged to another need, the need to record. To record is perhaps some attempt to sew the odd patches back into the heart. Re/cord. Recordar: to remember, from the Latin.

Re-cordis: to pass back through the heart. Cor ad cor. Heart to heart speaking. The passing back of words can be genuine and fragile. So too is sitting in front of television watching your dreams die in living color.

Galeano speaks of two kinds of colonialism under the title "The Culture of Terror." See page 159 in *The Book of Embraces.* Blatant colonialism forbids you to talk, to act, to exist. Invisible colonialism convinces you it is not possible to speak, to act, to exist. Either type is deadly.

Ideas parachute into your mind each morning. Cameras pan to St. Bernard Parish. There, at least 99% of the homes were destroyed. Fatigued by a glut of post-hurricane representations, a cook in Wyoming flips another pancake. A truck driver from Toledo, Ohio, lights a cigarette. He ponders how to create happiness for his wife and children on Christmas Day. In China, a mother weeps. Her daughter died of avian flu. All of her chickens are also dead. At Dickinson College, the cold wind complains against your face. Life is an intelligent design.

November 28, 2005: Arizona

When you are giving a speech, the audience usually expects you to greet them with a joke or anecdote. I tell jokes poorly. I do not like to spill my stories or anecdotes freely. I know I am supposed to establish a sense of automatic community with my audience, but the "tried and true" formulas do not work for me. I have tried them. They are not true for me. This is what is true: dispense with introductory ritual and get to the point. Yes, there is an undeniable charm in the linguistic acrobatics Nigerian speakers perform before they get to the point. I am neither Nigerian nor in Nigeria.

My audience in Flagstaff needs to hear two sides of my story, to listen to both sides of the record. Side A is public information, the words and data used to shape ideas about social tragedies. I have no control there. Side B is personal, dependent on autobiographical authority. Side B is *The Katrina Papers*.

I have written a ten-page presentation for Northern Arizona University. It is too long. It is too short on anger. It needs spice.

I want to share sting and heat with people 7,000 feet above sea level. I should do so by abandoning words as written. I must embrace the WORD as primal sound not as signified signs that emit sense. To depart from the prepared script is to depart from the domination of print. Go. Depart. Freedom is not totally independent. Freedom is dependent on my inventiveness, my subjective agency. There must be an adequate sounding of pessimism, of the mood swings between resignation/defeat in the faces of the Hurricanes Katrina and Rita and defiance. Terrorism. Show me a piece of terrorism. Put it on the floor so I can step on it.

November 29, 2005: Northern Arizona University

The practice of recovery may be marked by the exercise of power. For example, there is an assumed use of power in finding a connection between miner Allen Martin's fortitude as he is about "to lose his career after almost 30 years of dedicated service" to the Peabody Western Coal Company: "Peabody is weeding out the old, the sick and the uneducated." [Curtis Cartier, "A miner's life forced to change." *The Lumberjack*. Nov. 23-30, 2005. pp. 1,5] New Orleans is weeding out the old, the sick and the uneducated. Substitution enables a truth to emerge. Note: *The Lumberjack* is a student publication at NAU.

December 1, 2005: Two Epiphanies

1) Let us learn from Katrina. When we must deal with such government agencies as the Army Corps of Engineers and FEMA, we should review the mental health records of people who work for them prior to negotiating.

2) After her psychiatrist informed her that she was inviable, incapable of frisson, Katrina retorted, "My dear, dear Doctor, you are an asexual monstrosity."

KATRINA PAPERS, 4 Dec 05: Woman Points to Pearls

The Newark Airport is one of the least appealing places in the United States, but it is a good place to lose oneself in a book or in the pages of the Sunday *New York Times*. I am on standby, waiting to learn whether I will be able to take an earlier flight to Atlanta. The Atlanta Airport is more urbane than the one in Newark, and I would prefer to spend four hours there waiting for the late flight to Jackson, Mississippi, rather than two hours in this Northern hub of rudeness. The article on Barney Rosset's efforts to realize a triptych of films by Pinter, Ionesco, and Beckett intrigues me for reasons I will not explain.

The gate attendant calls my name: *Jerry Ward.* I walk to the counter, and he greets me with good news. I have a confirmed space on the flight. As I return to my seat, the woman who has been sitting next to me with her significant other or husband or whatever, asks "Jerry, did you lose your earring?," her arm pointing to two paste seed pearls on the filthy floor. Earring? A blind woman could see that these specks of white never adorned an earlobe, that they had fallen from someone's outlandish sweater. "No. I don't wear earrings. Some woman dropped them." End of dialogue. Return to the *New York Times*.

I always have a delayed reaction to such American breach of true civility. Had I been in a mood for equal vulgarity, I would have replied, "When did I last sleep with you that you should address me with such familiarity?" But I fear the humor would have been lost on such a post-modernly ill-breed woman. She was nondescript, a typical victim of her skin privilege. Perhaps she was a reincarnation of Mary Dalton. Her rude question was predicated on the assumption that black men wear earrings, on her failure to notice that more white men than black men wear earrings. She was an annoying reminder that careless white women in the twenty-first century still carry a gene that forces them to desire the lynching of black men. They are, like Hurricane Katrina, alien females who wish to transform the black men upon whom they gaze and prey into death-bound subjects. Her question was not an act of kindness. It was an invasion of my privacy. Such women deserve to be treated as RAID treats bugs.

December 6, 2005: Reckoning with Displacement

People are possessed by hope, sensing at once its promise and its futility. One hopes to resolve economic difficulties by winning several million dollars. The probability that one can warp from poverty to wealth overnight is farfetched, a transparent fantasy. One might hope that tribesmen, dusted by Islam, would honor the Words of Allah and not murder, in the name of honor, women they believe have been violated. It is unlikely such virtue can unsettle the male-defined tribal mind. One does not discard root and branch, an idea that has been growing since the invention of antiquity. In the fervent mind of the tribesmen, the hymen must be either intact or totipotent.

When such brave Muslim women as Serap Cileli (*We're Your Daughters, Not Your Honor*) and Necla Kelek (*The Foreign Bride*) expose mortal sins, we may hope the lesson is not lost on Euroamerican wife-abusers. Hope on. The words of those who dissent, who transgress the pseudo-sacred, receive scant attention. Their words are hangnails to be clipped and discarded. Nevertheless, in our brave new world of electronic possibilities, hope refuses to die. It is brash and determined and survival-oriented. It lives.

One might hope that ordinary civilians would not become the collateral damage of warfare, knowing even in the moment of hoping that the God of War is blind and thirsty, incapable of discriminating the blood of the innocent from the wine of the guilty. Hope is absurd.

Strangely, it is within the hopeless confines of the absurd that one hopes to find meaning in exile, in the diaspora occasioned by Hurricane Katrina.

From the vantage of a writer, the lack of a good library, or the pain of not having one's dearly loved books at hand, is a bittersweet blessing. The writer in exile recalls that other writers have sometimes volunteered to exile themselves in artist and writer colonies. This places exile in arguable perspective. The disadvantages of forced exile, you can freely lie to yourself, are sweeter and yield higher dividends. Matthew Arnold thought sweetness and light were primal ingredients of the civilized mind. He was dead wrong. The truly civilized mind is a product of recurring darkness. It can not flourish where the dirt is not saturated with bitter toxins like the soil of post-Katrina New Orleans. Examine the fabulous textures of writers exiled from the Crescent City for evidence. Or explore the weavings of writers who have returned to the Big Easy to create in the moldy stench, in an "exile" from the normal.

The writer in exile becomes a rabbit. She or he navigates the briar patch of memory. The rabbit does not forget convoluted paths, the tracks of reading and witnessing that have become matters of instinct. The rabbit remembers the lettuce of the King James Bible and munches on the carrots of expanding canons. Emersonian self-reliance increases tenfold and enables the rabbit to explore geographies of imagination. There, critical foxes do not run you down and snap your neck. There you are immune to the intimidation of the book, to its power to batter you with exactness. You hop blissfully over alien terrain. The rabbit remembers what is most worth remembering.

Exile forces the writer to live outside the box, to be remote from textual or referential certitude. The writer has hope that odd combinations in a new context do work.

TKP 12/9/05: On a book by Tillie Olsen

Although it was written between 1932 and 1936, Tillie Olsen's *Yonnondio* was not published until 1974. I bought the book thirty years later in Princeton, but I did not get around to reading it until Hurricane Katrina whipped up the need for alternative anchoring. The title, borrowed from one of Walt Whitman's yawps about the aboriginal, hints that Olsen's fiction is very much in the Old Left American grain, in the tradition of laying bare and critiquing morphological stages in the shift from cultural democracy to capitalist tyranny. Critique in Whitman is often so buried in celebration that it is overlooked. Such invisibility is the price one pays for embracing optimistic romanticism. Olsen's work is proletarian, modernist, and suspicious of romantic sentiments; critical ideology and feminist ideas inform its pages and highlight its perspective on capitalist dynamics of change. It is unlikely that a reader would overlook how *Yonnondio* resonates thirty-one years after its initial publication.

In narrating the story of the Holbrook family's progress from a coal-mining town in Wyoming to a tenant farm in South Dakota to a Midwestern city of slaughterhouses, Olsen employs hard-boiled romanticism (an aesthetic that is almost anti-Whitman) to illustrate how the sweet dreams of sacrifice and a Puritan work ethic can be eroded by American realities. Her strategy of using the consciousness of a young female protagonist to lead readers from airy innocence to afflicting knowledge is a prototype for what Harper Lee did most effectively years later in *To Kill a Mockingbird*. Lee's novel addresses more directly our continuing uncertainties about human rights and justice, but Olsen's unfinished novel throws us into a snake pit of concerns that are ultimately broader and more universally historical than a facile discourse on civil rights in the American South— despite the useful service the South has rendered the nation as a bellwether. *Yonnondio* has a better purchase on the dialogic imagination. It is a novel that Herman Melville and Richard Wright might have applauded.

What did I seek to have anchored by my reading of Olsen's novel, which it might be claimed is a less than extraordinary example of tradition and individual talent? I was unsure how I ought to answer such a question for several weeks. Would Sherley Anne Williams's *Dessa Rose* or Chinua Achebe's *Things Fall Apart* or Ernest Hemingway's *The Old Man and the Sea* have been a better vehicle for my purposes, for locating chthonic elements of narrative? No. These novels are too devoid of the primitive, too "good" on the subjective scale of goodness in literature. *Yonnondio*, on the other hand, was rough, one-dimensional in its focus on unrewarded labors and the recurrent dashing of hope, curious about how the Greeks reinvented constellations, just the right degree of "bad." Because it is a book that, in Olsen's words, "bespeaks the consciousness and roots of [the 1930s]," it anchored me in the realm of what is primal, mediocre, ordinary, and problematic. It provided a vantage for seeing how the environmental problems, class and racial issues, and social dislocation that led to the creation of the New Deal is an analog by back-formation for those same issues in the aftermath of Hurricane Katrina. Should my reading to be so anchored need a supplement, the most probable candidate would be John Steinbeck's *Grapes of Wrath*. But I do not need more. Olsen's novel is a sufficient new beginning for exploring what is contingent and continual in American time, natural disaster, and national tragedy. What it brought to consciousness will serve me well as I investigate the slow motion of democracy as it descends into tyranny and fascism, as I seek to complete Tillie Olsen's reversing of Whitman's lines:

> Race of the woods, the landscapes free and the falls.
>
> No picture poem, statement, passing them to the future:
>
> Yonnondio! Yonnondio!— unlimn'd they disappear;
>
>   *From* "Yonnondio"

Dec. 12, 2005

I do not leave the apartment today. Derrick sent the rough, rough draft of his Wright/Katrina paper for review.

New entry ideas for TKP

1. Xmas story
2. Mr. DuBois on Asia
3. Public education in New Orleans and Everywhere Else
4. The Invasion of Philosophy
5. Silent Word Poetry
6. Redemption, Race, and Capital Justice
7. Missing Libraries
8. Having an argument with St. Paul
9. Why I do not address the topic of rap/hip hop
10. Cornel West and the Laundry Room
11. On Lines from Shakespeare
12. On Lines from David Brinks
13. Harold Pinter's Moment of a Truth

It does not matter if I don't write these ideas up as paragraphs or essays. TKP is not about essays. It is about necessity.

December 13, 2005: A Post-Katrina Motive

When I wrote my 2005 end-of-the-year letter, the distinction between what **is not** literature and what **is** marched to the front of the combat zone. Misquoting Shakespeare can illuminate something that is happening in the writing of *The Katrina Papers*. One of his famous characters said, "Bring me my shroud; I have immortal longings." Writing those lines without acknowledging Antony and Cleopatra as the source would be an act of glorious plagiarism, an imitation of Shakespeare's creative penchant. Not acknowledging my deliberate substitution of words would border on the unethical, the criminal. Without any fear of being caught in the act by masses of people, I might easily pass on the misquoted words as my own and be rewarded by literature for my theft and deception. Such is the state of general intelligence in our nation.

Choosing not to plagiarize is remote from any longings for moral perfection. The choice involves delight of walking on the transgressive margin established by literary pundits to define what they believe literature is at any given time.

Arguments among the pundits about what is and what is not literature, about what is worthy of sainthood and worship, entail wondrous confusions of the secular and the sacred. Arrested by the spider web of language and imaginary power, the pundits construct elaborate theoretical and philosophical treatises in styles appreciated mainly by the priests of the inner temple. They stake all their bets on Western philosophical traditions, ignoring any alternative systems of explanation that have legitimate claims on the activities of mind. Decorum demands that one be tolerant of such people, even honor their First Amendment right to be arrogant. It does not demand mute and blind membership in their speech communities. One does not have to be a parasite. One can practice interdependent subversion.

Despite their illegitimate, and sometimes illogical, claims to be universal, the literary pundits are innocent enough. They do little harm in matters of public and foreign policy; in fact, they rarely admit that a public which uses L/literature does exist or that the managing of relations with other countries can have the most devastating impact on the quality of our lives. Their names are unknown among people who do medical research, deal with environmental issues, health care, and social justice, or seek to analyze the causes of poverty and human exploitation. People who need help with providing shelter, food, clothing, and jobs for the dispossessed, with reconstructing a thoroughly devastated urban area, or with funding levees that can withstand category 5 hurricanes, do not consult them. From those vantages, the literary pundits are mere shadows in the landscape. The best of them do have a social consciousness and will occasionally step outside the academic castle to fight in solidarity with the victimized serfs. More frequently, however, they remain on the other side of the moat and entertain themselves at the masque of the white death.

We must recognize, however, that the pundits who promote literature as an ethnocentric imperative do excellent work as factotums of the State. They are not politicized. They are political and irreversibly ideological, the mirror image of their opponents. They might urge us to deconstruct the deconstructive language of Harold Pinter's *The Homecoming*; they would not encourage us to listen to and revoice the tintinnabulation of a "truth" in Pinter's Nobel Prize acceptance speech. They effectively castrate significant numbers of people who might otherwise become a menace, dangerous and thoughtful citizens and candidates for seizure under the USA Patriot Act. Their opponents manufacture and distribute social and cultural Viagra.

I may be a literary critic by choice or by default, but I opt not to live in the castle. I much prefer, as Walter Rodney put it, to be in the grounding. In that sense, *The Katrina Papers* is an example of creating what is not literature. I refuse to steal and then wash my hands in the blood of guilt. I subvert interdependently with my friends.

TKP: December 14, 2006

Hurricane Haiku

Aqua vitae heard
Mad death massing in their throats:
Blues, disaster hymns.

Tkp 17 December 2005:

I had scheduled myself to drive to New Orleans this morning. I did not drive to New Orleans this morning. I awoke late, my nose feeling much like a clogged drainpipe. Did I undergo metamorphosis in my sleep? Do I have the first stages of bird flu? Is my process of dying accelerating? *What's up, doc?* Why is a Disney cartoon character mocking my misery? If I can unclog the drainpipe, I shall drive to New Orleans tomorrow morning. If I can't unclog the drainpipe, I shall drive to New Orleans. I shall be in New Orleans tomorrow morning.

Ten new erotic cocktails will be available for tourists during the Mardi Gras season in New Orleans:

1. The Katrina

2. Aftermath Looter

3. U B Nagin

4. Blame Who?

5. The Red Cross Cherry – you must show proof of virginity to be served this drink

6. FEMA– New Orleans version of Long Island's infamous "Skip and Go Naked"

7. Shelter– New Orleans flavored tap water and secret ingredients served at room temperature in a freshly smoked glass

8. The Rapist

9. Levee Break

10. The Funky Bourbon

Gulf Coast Towns Revisited

Before Katrina came

Before Colonel Sanders
Reinvented fried chicken
Only to be undone by the Cajun craftiness of Popeye

Before the wrong side
Of the tracks began
Driving on the right
Side of the road

Before the flush toilets and oil rigs
Made the wasteland of wetlands

Before Katrina Came

Southern towns were
Eternal units of talk,
Vernacular musics,
Vibrant histories

All that's gone
As if yesteryear's wind
Turned towns into vacuums,
God's little acres of blight,
Weathered backboards
For the sport of hit and run
Language among people
Too wet to pay attention.

On Being Silent in New Orleans

This year the jaws of the Howling
Wolf are tight as a stingy clam;
Butterbeans and Susie will not sing
"Papa aint no Santa Claus, and your mama
Aint no Christmas tree" at the Roofgarden.

Big Al Carson is not belting out miracles
In the Funky Pirate, instructing anxious ears
To take their drunk asses home

The ladies of Storyville
Lie like nuns in St. James Infirmary,
Afloat on holy water

The River is not flowing into spring,
And Creole tunes cannot perfume the air.

Listen. The streets are as loud as termites
Dancing the second line on a live oak tree.

Katrina Fatigue: Words on the Way to Elsewhere

And you expect yet another "Katrina" poem,
So you have excuses to say "how sad, how terrible, how unimaginable,
How tragic" as you sink into forgetting
Any speakable motive for sympathy?

What you saw in your mirror this morning
Is not sufficient to excavate those words for you?

Representing Anxiety

Imagine driving from Durham to Raleigh when suddenly a billboard blocks your view of the trees that have begun to bud in the spring. In the best art that an ad agency can offer, there stares at you a man wrapped in Arab headgear who holds in his right hand a North Carolina driver's license and a grenade. The garish lettering on the billboard sends a plain message: Don't License Terrorists, North Carolina. We have reached a stage in national history where it is impossible to distinguish an immigrant who comes to eat a piece of America's pie from one who comes to blow up the kitchen. Thus, we are anxious to represent our anxiety about the power of license.

The Coalition for a Secure Driver's License (www.secure license.org) had planned to sponsor such billboards in several states. Lamar Advertising decided at the tenth hour not to mount them. Christine Saah Nazer of the Arab American Institute (www. aaiusa.org) claimed the message is racist. Why did she make that choice rather than another? Whom did she fear she might offend? It is obvious that the portrayal plays an ethnic card from a deck stacked by the U.S. Bureau of the Census. Nazer chose to pull out a race card. The point worth debating, however, is whether the message is racist or anti-Semitic.

The Jewish Virtual Library (www.jewishvirtuallibrary.org/jsource/gloss. html) explains, in succinct terms, that Anti-Semitism "literally means opposed to Semites (which would include Arabic and other semitic peoples as well), but usually applied specifically to opposition to Jews (anti-Judaism)." Blind fidelity to the traditional usage of the term "anti-Semitic" would make us hesitate to say the message on the billboard was "anti-Semitic." The radical thinkers among us, however, are bold enough to say that the message does stereotype Semites, admitting that the visual evidence does shift attention from those who might worship in synagogues to those who might worship in mosques. This leaves still unanswered the question of why Ms. Nazer would call the message racist and not anti-Semitic.

If Ms. Nazer is Arab American, her fluctuating ethnic and racial identities may, for reasons of rhetorical strategy, have precluded her using the ethnic card when the race card is obviously the trump in discursive card games. The Census Bureau classifies Arabs as whites, using the tacit understanding that in the United States there are only two races: black and white. One race invents and re-invents the rules of the game; the other race is expected to concede that the rules are just. Whether we agree or not, Ms. Nazer, if she is of Arab descent, is a government-certified white woman who proclaims that an anti-Semitic representation is racist, thereby preventing (in *language* only one must note) the possibility of her voice being cast into the shadows with the voices of women who transcend racial description. If Ms. Nazer were *seen* on the streets of our nation's capital, the anxiety of stereotype might cause one to mistakenly identify her as the non-white Other. Had she called the message what it really is, she would have invited the dreaded possibility of critical thinking about the term "anti-Semitic" and the concept of a Semitic race. She would have evoked a terrifying post-Holocaust racialism.

This is but one of several plausible, speculative explanations of what Ms. Nazer might have intended beyond naming the offense conceptualized by the Coalition for a Secure Driver's License. Nevertheless, it exposes a seemingly permanent danger in representing anxiety that plagues us: the burden of white anti-white sentiments that white people are doomed to carry. It is counterproductive to deny that the burden exists by tossing it into the convenient dumpcart of race. Such a gesture intensifies our anxiety, our complicity in the machinery of terrorism, our failure to ponder the license of language.

Hurricane Haiku

Aqua vitae heard
Mad death massing in their throats:
Blues, disaster hymns.

Written on December 14, 2005

TKP: December 17, 2005.

The project of understanding can begin with a tall tale or a short story. Which does not matter. Beginning is all. Beginning is hard. Either you plunge or you stand like a gawking statue on sands of ignorance. Plunging, however, has its own terror. Hurricane Katrina taught us that water can rip you asunder.

Hope in New Orleans

December 18.

Hope is a very fragile emotion, but I dare to savor it after a visit to New Orleans. Entergy has restored electricity at my house. When I plugged in the radio, I heard music from WWOZ. This radio station has survived underfunding and the disaster of Hurricane Katrina through the efforts of volunteers who steadfastly refuse to be daunted. By anything. Even after a nuclear strike, WWOZ volunteers would broadcast records from the crypt and CDs from the contaminated debris. We must do more than salute and support WWOZ volunteers. We should imitate them as we fight to reclaim New Orleans from natural disaster and to prevent the greed that has no heart from consuming the city.

December 20: When one poet dedicates a poem to another, the gift resounds endlessly.

December 20: The Idea is the Gift

Today, my friend Dave Brinks sent me "the caveat onus:::twenty-six," which he has dedicated to me. The gesture is a lovely gift, and I am not finding the right words to say what I mean with precision. "Thank you, Dave" is too weak to bear the weight of my gratitude, or the gratitude experienced by readers sensitive to how a poem might astonish. Let me try again. Gift-giving is a gesture of caring, of regard, of acknowledging another person's importance to oneself. A gift, especially the gift of a poem, pleases and further secures the bonding of intellects and imaginations, those of the receiver and the giver. The pleasure is in the surprise. The intangible counts. Especially among poets and artists.

Healing observation about words and memory is brought time and again to our attention in the work of certain Renaissance poets who chose to remark on mutability and how the power of language (Nommo, the Word, the naming) defeats the strong claims mutability would make upon us. We have a fine modern instance in Robert Hayden's "A Ballad of Remembrance." In our post-post-modern condition, particularly in the moment that Hurricane Katrina dumped upon us the damnation of negativity, Dave's gift is a relief-valve. The uncanny wit of recognition in its final lines mocks post-Katrina depression, transforming gloom into bright laughter. The dross we must discard in recovering is made lighter by Dave's corrective:

O Felicity you can't have it both ways
I don't care what street it is

December 21, 2005

Notes on Book Reviewing
Mozart and Leadbelly by Ernest J. Gaines.

Book reviewing long ago lost its purpose of shaping tastes and educating readers. The review is little used these days to socialize readers, to make them receptive to the idealized status quo that the reviewer champions. Reviewing is an exercise in rendering as little communal criticism as possible about the book or books in the instance of the review essay. The reviewer uses the occasion of talking about the book to spew the fetid, festering contents of his or her psychology; class identity is worn like armor, and the lance of random desire pierces the reader. Book reviews tell us much about reviewers and their cultures. The reviews are not necessarily things that ought to be condemned. They are just not overwhelmingly commendable as a genre.

Under the pressure of globalization, the sense that readers have a shared community of values has shrunk. Why measure a book against a set of assumed and wholly imaginary communal standards of goodness, excellence, or utility? Why should the critic be a saint, holding fast to antiquated dreams of a unified culture that people no longer believe ever existed?

I have written elsewhere with reference to the Black Arts Movement that the illusion of community was valuable. I have not, despite the raving of postmodern thinkers, changed my opinion. I simply recognize the opinion as opinion with gusto. It is my opinion that Gaines's recent collection of essays and stories is a useful book for writers to read.

TKP: December 22, 2005

It is 11:04 a.m. The air is cold. The sun is bright in Vicksburg. It is less than 72 hours before Christmas Day 2005, the day when the bright eyes of children who are still capable of being surprised are surprised. I shall be glad when December 26 arrives, bringing with it the colors and purposeful celebration of Kwanzaa and the eyes of children and adults, the eyes so utterly conflicted as they search for meaning. The eyes that interest me are those of people displaced by Hurricanes Katrina and Rita, the eyes of children orphaned in the Sudan, in Calcutta and Jerusalem, in Iraq, in stranger places where they are subject to be auctioned off for adoption or something worse, or terminated if they annoy the tourists too much. Eyes that speak loudly of hunger and wrecked spirits. The eyes of people who are out of work, out of homes, out of love, and damn near out of hope. As I look at the world through those eyes, the signs of Christmas seem to be grotesque, obscene, on the brink of being Satanic. St. Nicholas the obese and Santa Claus the drunk and the excessive costs of commercial bread and wine. The truly wretched of the earth can not afford the price of such communion.

The cold air and the bright sunshine and the decorations on the apartments of neighbors do not remind me of a yam festival. In fact, overcoat, scarf, gloves, and a grinning reindeer look slightly out-of-place at a yam festival. Nor do miles of gift-wrapping paper, bows and ribbons, and Hallmark messages belong to the same space as the fruits of the harvest. For once, be for real. Strings of lights and costly trinkets made in China or Japan are not life-saving; yams are. I render unto Christmas what belongs to Christmas: worship at Mass and prayers that the Prince of Peace will one day deliver what has been promised. The silence of night in New

Orleans is an echo of pain. Kwanzaa offers the possibility of finding a healing balm.

TKP, 22 December 2005: The ideas above should be entitled "Prelude to Kwanzaa."

I want to remember that Gaines does not use the word "sculpture" in the essay "Bloodline in Ink." He makes the idea dominant. This is one of the strong points of his art: to let what is absent or not said manifest itself and manifest more than an entire dissertation. I want to remember also that he ends the essay by advising teachers to pass on the tools to those worthy of receiving them. Of course, Gaines does not use the word "worthy."

"Worth" diverts my attention from Gaines's words to my own thoughts as a teacher. Not every student will accept the tools you offer. Be content with the few who do. Be proud of them. Be pleased that they use the tools to do something noteworthy, or that they fashion new tools from old ones. Continuity is a reward. Be content with it. It may be the only confirmation that you did not waste your life before dying.

Sidebar: In telling stories about the South, Faulkner worked like Jackson Pollack. He dripped ink all over his pages to achieve the sense of plenitude. In contrast, Gaines does not fear a vacuum. He tells stories of the South with the economy of a gifted Chinese painter. A few words suffice.

TKP: Christmas, December 25

I drove from Vicksburg to Moss Point, Mississippi. I should not have been surprised, but I am. The evidence of severe damage is still visible on Highway 49 between Hattiesburg and Gulfport. I enjoy being with my cousins. We laugh and tell lies about the old days. My cousins laugh with genuine pleasure. I laugh to disguise the horrible sound of the time-bomb in my brain. I drive past the property where I used to live, where my father died on Christmas Day in 1957, and where I spent the last Christmas of my mother's life. I begin to cry.

TKP, December 26: Umoja (Unity)

Kwanzaa– straw mat, candles (3 red, 3 green, 1 black), candleholder, corn (the children), vegetables, fruit, and unity cup (chalice)

"We all should see ourselves as citizens of the world."

Danny Glover

If you lack a sense of personal sacrifice, you see nothing people gained by dint of fear and blood.

Check information on Claudette Colvin.

Christmas night, 11:22 p.m.

The image of a toy found in my Easter basket in the 1940s is inside my head. It is a round box with a clear plastic inset top. The side of the box has a design of stripes. At the bottom of the box is a chicken. The chicken stands on green grass against a yellow sky. Just where the chicken's legs begin is a small indentation. There is a tiny white egg in the box. I get the picture fairly quickly with help from my parents.

I am supposed to turn the box this way and that. I am supposed to make the uncooperative egg fit in the indentation. I often succeeded in making the egg fit vertically. Making it fit horizontally was an achievement.

After we moved from Washington, D. C. to Moss Point, Mississippi, I saw a real chicken lay a real egg. What a surprise. The membrane that surrounds yolk and albumen is tough and soft. It becomes a shell after it is exposed to the air. Being a city kid, I discovered late what my country cousins had known for a long time.

Foolish is the egg who would teach a bird to fly.

If you read William Faulkner with some care, you discover that, among his characters, only niggers and old virgins are capable of telling the truth. Faulkner was not a virgin. He was a nigger.

December 27: Kujichagulia (Self-determination)

Book Tip:
Gaines, Ernest J. *Mozart and Leadbelly*. Compiled and edited by Marcia Gaudet and Reggie Young.
New York: Alfred A. Knopf, 2005. 159 pp. Hardcover. ISBN: 1-400-4472-3.

Several times in this collection of essays and stories, Gaines mentions leaving Louisiana in 1948 with "a block of oak wood in a sack." In California, he earned "the hammer, the chisel, a grinding stone, and a few sharp knives to do the work." The work to which Gaines refers is an embracing of one's cultures and a witnessing of human dignity in robust, graceful language. Gaines has many useful lessons for writers who would be at once in the tradition and innovative. His downhome theory and skillful demonstrations in this collection are more valuable than a dozen books on how to write. *Mozart and Leadbelly* is itself a lesson to be learned.

Jerry W. Ward, Jr.

Portrait of a Suicide/Death in Yellow Flooding

It was disconcerting
    The music of madness
        Demanding its moment

        Demanding its fragipanic
    Its raw eternity
In photo-painting

        Primal colors flooding
    The Garden District
Shame-shaping Stonehenge Ballet

Primal man knifing air
    Killing spirits killing him,
        His face an Easter Island rock

        Fourteen cop-columns circle
    This mute trauma
        Fourteen cop-columns contain
A violent self-destructing, a yellow rose bleeding at noon

Jerry W. Ward, Jr.
December 27, 2005

December 28, 2005: Ujima (Collective Work and Responsibility)

If you write "Thinking of New Orleans conjures remembrance of things past. It puts your grief in a loud light," one reader will note your allusion to Proust. Proust is too afraid of sweat to carry your baggage.

In this water, my grave, I scream when necessary. Many centuries from now, my voice shall worry the critters of the Earth.

Howard Rambsy's email "The Miles Question; or, a preface to my responses to your KP entries" 12/28/2005 6:23:45 p.m. CST is an example of ujima. I wish I had taught at least a dozen other students who are as brilliant as Howard. Alas, there is but one Howard Rambsy in this world.

TKP Note for Reading Race Reading America

I recall only two noteworthy instances of American poets reading at the inauguration of a President. Robert Frost read "The Gift Outright" in 1961 for Kennedy. Maya Angelou read "On the Pulse of Morning" for Clinton in 1993. In both instances, the poetry dealt with nature, race, and culture. From the perspective of 2005, the choice of poet and poem for these national occasions seems judicious.

Frost– New England Yankee, American exceptionalist, imperial affirmation that might is right

Angelou– Arkansas, African American woman, democratic affirmation of hope

Neither poet could speak for the First People upon whose backs they trod.

The contrasts of persona and person, the clash of ideologies at work in each poem, and history, as an ecosystem over a period of thirty-two years, invite notice. Examine the form, the language, and the rhetorical stances of the poems.

Other writing can provide basic touchstones and parameters for thinking about the significance of the two poems. Machiavelli's *The Prince* and Shakespeare's *The Tempest* are convenient choices. Myth and oral tradition are also useful for beginning analysis. Kennedy is mythologized as King Arthur in the Americanized Camelot. We can parade a new myth: Clinton repossessed and inscribed his Negritude. We can examine the poetry of Frost and Angelou for clues about their exploitation of oral traditions. Given what significance as defined by E. D. Hirsch might be, it is just to account briefly for the impact of natural disaster (Hurricanes Katrina and Rita) on how one thinks about poetry that evokes nature.

The primary theme in the two poems is possession through appropriation. The theme ensures that neither poet could speak for the First People upon whose backs they trod. Contexts are vital in dealing with these poems, for they reveal the invisibles of creative psychology. They are acts of autobiography. Each poem pushes forward a persona to mask the undeniable presence of the poet in the words. Or the presence of the words in formal moments in the history of the American republic. The poems resist dislocation. Even if deconstruction succeeds in murdering the poems and disemboweling their assumptions, the poems defy death. Like the phoenix, they rise and raze us. They throw us down to the ground of racialized politics.

Need a copy of:

Annette D. Sahar, Sebastian M. Brenninkmeyer, Daniel C. O'Connell, "Maya Angelou's Inaugural Poem," *Journal of Psycholinguistic Research*, Volume 26, Issue 4, Jul 1997, Pages 449–463.

December 29, 2005: Ujamaa (Cooperative Economics)

NOLA SPEAKS

In this water
My grave
I scream

When necessary

Many centuries from now
My voice shall worry
The critters of the Earth

Essay sent to leespeak@cox.net for "49 Days" project
New Orleans is my "Spirit House."

I yearned to live in New Orleans long before I took up permanent residence on Gentilly Boulevard in 2003.

As a young boy in the 1940s and 1950s, I made many trips by train from Washington, DC, or Mississippi to the Crescent City. There my parents had met and married. I think they fell in love over bowls of gumbo. My mother had spent the most glorious days of her life in New Orleans, enjoying Mardi Gras, her exceptionally large family of uncles, aunts, and cousins, and dancing to the best jazz on earth. I vowed I would one day have the magic of her city. My New Orleans relatives, whose musical speech put clipped accents and drawls to shame, treated me to breakfasts of warm French bread, café-au-lait, and creole cream cheese, 3-D movies, rides on streetcars, sneaked sips of Dixie 45, and intriguing tales about my rainbow Catholic family. Mr. Dunwood's lunch room on Delachaise Street made the best beef stew that a kitchen could produce; the highlight of a summer's night was getting Brown's Velvet ice cream on Louisiana Avenue, and I much preferred my godmother's exotic seasoning to my mother's subtle St. James Parish Creole flavoring. How well they cooked was one way of discriminating between the relatives I liked most from those I visited only as a matter of obligation. Krauss, Kress, Maison Blanche— shopping on Canal Street was special. I knew I belonged in this city. The people, the food, and the life-pulse of the city were ideal.

As I gaze each morning at John Scott's remarkable "Spirit House" sculpture at Gentilly and St. Bernard and listen to the bells from St. Leo the Great, I know that my soul has found home.

Bio: Jerry W. Ward, Jr. is a Professor of English at Dillard University.

Image to use: "Spirit House" sculpture

December 30, 2005: Nia (Purpose) Friday

Essay for WWOZ project accepted and is to be recorded on Monday, January 2, 2006.

Contact person is Lee Barclay at leespeak@cox.net

Gave permission to Jeannette Drake, a visual artist, to use "NOLA Speaks" Kswpoet@yahoo.com

The politician encouraged us "to be weary of all things that appear too good to be true." We are weary of such things, but we must also be wary of them.

65

Prospects for 2006

Death monopolized 2005. Let us hope it has fewer claims on our attention during 2006. The Spring semester at Dillard will find me involved in some events that may help with returning to "normal" or with entering a new state of normal:

January	Zora Neale Hurston Festival
February	Ishmael Reed program at Howard
	Natchez Literary and Cinema Celebration
March	Shabazz Conversations, the Schomburg

A new year begins tomorrow night, but I am more interested in the progress of *The Katrina Papers* than in the change of date. TKP is taking me in a new and powerful direction as far as writing is concerned.

I am definitely experimenting with the shapes ideas can assume and how those shapes affect human actions.

The reading and thinking that informs what I write now has led me to believe that our country is in the first stage of preparing for a class/race civil war. It shall be interesting to see what the Asians stand up for, if they stand up at all. And the Jews, the problematic Jews, who have long insisted that they were natural allies in our struggle as they sleep with the enemy (mindless capitalism). And who shall make common cause with the First People (the Indians of the Americas). Latinos play a major and quite divisive role in the coming struggle. All of this will get explored to some degree in TKP, not that I am consciously setting an argument or prophecy about war as the subject. It is just appearing and reappearing as I explore the life problems in their pre-and post- Katrinaness. TKP is truly an organic enterprise.

December 31, 2005: Kuumba (Creativity)

Warning from La Papessa to the tourists

If you are
In New Orleans
Before, during, after
Mardi Gras

And see people
In the streets weeping
Oily green tears

Do not touch them
Or speak to them
They are Katrina's children

They are the virgins
Of the city
Repossessed by stigmata

Stigmata are contagious

This Garden You Will Not Explain
Good intentions backfired.

Flowers bloom in my brain.

Their magenta petals wave
As neurons go to work.
12/31/05

A Lady from New Orleans
"No, Mr. St. Peter, I beg your pardon to differ.

And anyhow, when did God authorize you
To fix your mouth to tell folks
They can't come in
Because they did not have time
To put on their dying clothes?"
12/31/05

January 1, 2006: Imani (Faith)

What is faith? Why should people acquire it or nurture it or lose it? Possible answers are dramatized in the lives of those who survive natural disasters. The play of faith certainly lacks intelligible design. Seeking answers in its acts and scenes, in its dialogues, monologues, and performances, is an insatiable exercise of the human will. In the long run, you no longer know if you are the author or the authored. You just whirl endlessly in the vortex of theater, scripting as best you can once and future deeds. You write like a blind mouse drawn into a trap by the scent of cheese. Unfortunately, the trap does not kill you and bring answer-seeking to an end. The special trap that faith is keeps you in perpetual motion. Such is the gift of 2006. Such is the sentence that humankind must serve.

TKP: January 2, 2006: THE BURDEN OF POSSESSIONS

You hate packing for your trip from Vicksburg to New Orleans. When you came to Vicksburg on August 29, 2005, everything could fit neatly in the trunk of your car. When you leave now, the trunk is packed to the hood; the backseat groans under the weight of boxes and bags. How did it happen? Why did you accumulate more possessions, more bloodsuckers to feed on mind and body? Habit. Simple habit. You acquired a few books in Vicksburg, and you brought a few books back there from your return trips to your house. You rescued clothing from your closets and had them cleaned; you rescued washable items, laundered and ironed them, packed them as neatly as you could in the single closet in your Vicksburg apartment. You have recording equipment for the oral history project. You have a laptop. You have papers from Grinnell and Dickinson, papers from Tougaloo, and essential files. It all adds up, this pile of stuff to be transported. You are reminded of moving things and furnishings from Moss Point, Mississippi, to Ridgeland in 1993 and ten years later those same things plus newer acquisitions got moved to New Orleans. The lessons Hurricane Katrina should have taught you about the necessity of reducing possessions to a bare minimum seem to have dissolved. Just as the turtle is condemned to carry her or his shell for a lifetime, you are damned endlessly to deal with the burden of possessions.

January 3, 2006

Yesterday, the full emptiness of death in New Orleans stretched across the horizon. Your late afternoon arrival ensured that you'd see the city in a softer light, in what Kalamu used to call the golden time of day: darkening hues and diminishing intensity put streets, buildings, and plant life into softer focus. Home, despite its most unaesthetic appearance and the lingering smell of mold, seemed right and comforting and final. Home is gravely golden. Lively music from WWOZ (90.7) helped as did the prospect of recording "New Orleans is my 'Spirit House'" for a WWOZ program. The lamplights on Gentilly Boulevard gave your dead neighborhood an aspect of artificial urban aliveness. Only as you drove through deserted streets to get to St. Charles Avenue did you begin to feel uneasy, to feel that you were trafficking with the dead. The very few people you see in the streets remind you of monks following an open coffin. Both BRAVO, an upscale Italian restaurant, and The Trolley Stop, a dive of an eatery that was the favorite of locals, are dark, dusty. Igor's is happening, but that only reminds you of Gothic associations with Mary Shelley's novel. As you pass the corner of Jackson and St. Charles, you remember having had breakfast exactly a year ago in the Garden District Hotel with Irvin Mayfield to plan a musical tribute to Ernest Gaines. As you strain your eyes to see the dimly lit street signs and to prepare to turn right on Washington, life in death hits your shoulder like a 25 pound block of ice. You are to tape the reading at 1634 Washington, Apt. C. You can't see the house number, so you park as close to Washington and Carondolet as possible and walk back to the house that might be the right one. It is. Despite your conflicted emotions about your semi-permanent return to New Orleans, your recording voice must not sound like that of a miserable gravedigger; you must sound like a prosperous funeral director.

This morning you arose, congratulating yourself for having slept in your moldy house. You do not especially enjoy having to heat water in the coffeepot so that your wash-up will not be a cold one. Nor do you enjoy discovering which books you have to discard. In a fit of false creativity, you begin to record authors and titles:

Eudora Welty, *Collected Stories*
William Faulkner, *Collected Stories*
Olympia Vernon, *Eden.*

And you stop. The obituary for books is nonsense. Do not memorialize. Let the ache of loss settle in gradually. You abort the project and turn to removing more evidence of mold from the walls. You try to feel good about the light coming through the open blinds. The effort is wasted. Trepidation about leaving the house again and moving into a room at the Hilton Riverside Hotel, where many of your Dillard colleagues will be and where all the returning students are to be housed is just too strong. You are moving from the discomfort of your damaged home into the restrictions of living in a hotel. You had begun to grow comfortable in your Vicksburg apartment, but that is now 234 miles northwest of New Orleans. You had registered for your room at the hotel shortly before 1:00 p.m. You ball your fist and give discomfort a solid punch. You pack enough clothing for a week, the unfinished drafts of entries for *The Katrina Papers*, and your notes for your Dillard courses. You are in your car and headed back to the hotel and unknowable adventure by 4:00 p.m. The spirit of a New Orleans that will never return haunts you. You must not let the past be an albatross. You have to move into complaint-filled futures. At midnight, you still have not written the entry you wanted to complete about your reentry. You can go back. You can write about returning later, a week or so later when distance again brings you to your senses. The necessity of talking with your colleagues will replace for a time the solitude and raw creativity you have lived with for the past four months. As you read portions of *The Katrina Papers* to Thomas King, who is amused by the humor of which you are only vaguely aware, you become more self-conscious about writing. You would have it be otherwise, but you are no match for destiny.

January 4, 2006: THE TRUTH IS NOT

Distance, you realize after several hours of suffering, will not bring you to your senses. Nor will distance produce a consensus among the citizens of New Orleans at home *chez moi* or those abroad in the wilderness of America that is not. You realize that the truth is not...Like you, the truth is in constant motion, changing, always changing. Statements that try to represent the truth only represent what is not existing; they are excellent representations of illusion.

January 5, 2006: TASTING THE PAST AND THE FUTURE: A TRIBUTE TO DAVE BRINKS

It is a typical Thursday night at the Gold Mine Saloon, home of the 17 Poets Series. You find the usual crowd of artists and the friends of artists, appropriately costumed, communing and conspiring over their drinks and their smokes and the languages they squeeze from living. The range of talent is remarkable, and your ear helps you to distinguish what is genuine from what is only a sad need to emote. Thanks to Dave Brinks, the Gold Mine Saloon is one of the best venues for cultural experimentation in New Orleans. It is decidedly democratic. Truth be told, it is hyper-democratic. No attempt to be expressive is excluded. Anyone can sign up for open-mike and have five minutes of the audience's attention. It should be noted, however, that hearing a conservative voice in the Gold Mine Saloon is unlikely. Perhaps the conservative artists who have the answer for everything fear uttering their version of "the truth" and exposing it to the withering inspection of the radicals. Perhaps the conservative artists, like the conservative political brotherhood, think it would be beneath them to engage in any true dialogue with leftists and those who are neither left nor right nor central. Perhaps those who think they are most radical are ironically conservative. They conserve cultural variety. The spirit of artistic democracy that Dave Brinks fosters does force one to reckon with how conflict makes its presence known by absence. Demons are exorcised in the Gold Mine Saloon.

The panel discussion about saving creativity in New Orleans planned by Loyola University for January 19 is anti-climactic before it occurs. The academy, unfortunately, places the highest value on clean hands. Clean hands do have a place in this world, but they are so easily co-opted by the sinister forces of the status quo. They will talk about saving creativity in the city as though creativity was an endangered species of human activity. If Hurricane Katrina could not murder creativity in the Crescent City, we must wonder what is in our midst that could. It may be the case that members of the panel have some privileged insights about New Orleans creativity that we lack. We should listen to them. It would be folly to turn a deaf ear. Nevertheless, the talk will be anti-climactic in the context of what has been occurring at the Gold Mine since October 13, 2005. Thanks to Dave, there has been weekly continuation of creativity. The 17 Poets Series is a model of how to save creativity. It is action rather than learned discourse that saves anything. Dave, like my late friends Virgia Brocks-Shedd and Tom Dent, has a knack for keeping creative people connected with one another and for suggesting, often by indirection, what directions must be taken to be on the cutting edge. In this sense, Dave is a professional mentor, and he has taught us how noble it is to have dirty hands. His genius resides and resonates in his Caveat Onus poems. Those poems give evidence that a thousand butterflies bless Dave's work inside and outside of poetry. Little would be accomplished by inflicting praise upon him. The most meaningful tribute to Dave Brinks is our dwelling for a time in the space for life that his words, both poetic and practical, create, and then using our minds and bodies to create space for the lives of others.

January 6, 2006: Twelfth Night

The Mardi Gras season has begun in New Orleans. The official chant for 2006 should be: I ain't calling New Orleans no gold-digger, but you know it ain't giving time to no broke...ugh-ugh. Let the chant signify how the wheel of misfortunes broke the bones of this city and forced it to cry for corporate sponsorship.

Today, I feel tired. Alone. Somewhat abandoned by the shadow of happiness. Exhaustion possesses my body. My language does not lie. It plops on the page like bird crap. When I glance to the side as I walk on Poydras Street, I see a shadow behind my shadow. My ideas are Jello. Losing it? Yes, I fear losing it. What I recall from last night's reading by the poet Michael Tod Edgerton could hasten my losing it. He quoted a line— from some other poet— "I want to be in my life." I want to be in my life, but how does one be in a sieve? Whatever I pour in lately comes dribbling out. Poets resow themselves into home. Poets resew themselves into home. The metaphors of planting and stitching sound trite, mundane, anti-poetic. The poets resent themselves into home. By way of a creative misreading, the word "resew" became "resent." There is strength in error. Am I feeling a loss of nerve, the result of ingesting fear of error? Is that why I want to hang on to the lifeline that having an apartment in Vicksburg has come to represent? Confess. Otherwise, the talons of the Holy Ghost will tear out your liver. O.K. Yes, fear has become or is becoming more real. I can touch it, just as I can touch the surface of the desk. I do not want to pass my hand over the textures of fear. I don't want to have those blues. None of us who survived the hurricanes want those blues. We will not want to be roaches in a red light seeking darkness. We will not want to be lunatics by Lundi Gras. Witnesses of nightmare. Like thunder the feeling is frightening. Whom can I beg to rescue me?

TKP, Friday, January 13, 2006

Since I returned to New Orleans on January 2, I have acquired a new friend, Mr. Lawrence Seagull. Mr. Lawrence is one of the most intelligent members of his tribe, and his English is far better than my efforts to communicate in avian sound structures. He has declared that I have the accent of a grackle. It would be best for both of us, he continued, if we agreed to communicate in ESP. The silent sharing of ideas is economical and more rapid than the jerky stops and starts of talk. Mr. Lawrence is intelligent and wise.

During our conversations on the outside deck of the Riverwalk, Mr. Lawrence perches on the railing like a member of a royal family. Head erect, feathers perfectly groomed, he scans my face with one eye and scans the swirls of the Mississippi River with the other for his next meal. He noticed traces of powdered sugar on my sweatshirt and chided me for not sharing my beignet with him. "Seagulls do not live by fish alone," he quipped. I promised to bring him a whole beignet when I visit Café du Monde at the French Market again. I explained to him that beignets at Riverwalk lack the excellence of those prepared under the sanctified gaze of St. Louis Cathedral.

An expert on wind and water, Mr. Lawrence has advised me to get my evacuation kit together, to keep the gas tank in my car filled, and to watch the Weather Channel faithfully. "You people don't have the instinct to know what's coming. There will be hurricanes of great magnitude in 2006, and one of them will visit the Gulf Coast." I think Mr. Lawrence assumes a few words to the wise are sufficient.

I hope my colleagues at Dillard University never discover that I converse with a bird. As Mr. Dunbar said, it is good to wear the mask and to let the world think that I am admiring Mr. Lawrence just as I might admire a Siberian tiger or a penguin. I hope that people will assume Mr. Lawrence is taking a rest break. If people discover I have given in to post-Katrina temptations and have violated the code of separation which Intelligent Design ordains should exist between the human and the non-human, they will condemn my childlike innocence as an act of moral turpitude. Even before Hurricane Katrina changed everything, people were like that.

TKP, Saturday, January 14, 2006

The fine art of survival:

Water must
enter you
before you
enter water.

TKP, Sunday, January 15, 2006

A Tribute for Dr. Stephen Caldwell Wright

Excess of delight in the arbitrary and unpredictable troubles us. We sense in such contemporary behavior a forecast of a day when the sun shall neither rise nor set; indeed, we sense that random barbarity has smashed the gates of the New Jerusalem. Are the inhabitants of the city are irreversibly doomed? Time is not merely out of joint. It is dismembered. We quest for some evidence that wholeness, truth, beauty and goodness have not fled the world like people who know a hurricane is coming.

The human condition in the twenty-first century is unsettling, and it is quite rare to find people who deserve encomia. Unlike the majority of mankind, such people are unwavering in their principles. They champion civility, compassion, and moderation. They are steadfast in believing that standards of excellence in craftsmanship and everyday life are real, not dim shadows of Platonic ideals. They hold that virtue, reason, service, ethics and judgment, intellectual honesty, and character are matters of sustained practice rather than free-floating abstractions. They are true to themselves and do not chase after things that are ephemeral or merely common. One member of this distinguished community is Dr. Stephen Caldwell Wright.

As an accomplished poet, teacher, editor and Gwendolyn Brooks scholar, he has devoted many years of his life to exploration of how languages function in human affairs and of how literature, especially poetry, often serves as an instrument of critical insights, as a window through which we gaze upon human aspirations and foibles. Through our shared interests in language and higher education, tradition, Zora Neale Hurston, and cultural preservation, I have developed great respect for his fortitude, his forthrightness, and his genius. How could one fail to admire a person who is so genuinely responsible?

Whether he was teaching and mentoring students in the classrooms of Seminole Community College or serving as one of that institution's administrators, creating poems or editing the poems of others for magazines and anthologies, fulfilling his political and social duties as a citizen, conducting research and writing on substantive issues of cultures, or using his considerable imagination in resolving ambiguities, Dr. Wright has been a consistent role model. Like the best of his fellow poets, he has found his voice; he speaks with authority. He refuses to compromise the values he has acquired through experience and reflection. His essential dignity is inspiring. His integrity merits praise.

It has been a privilege for those of us who serve as National Planners for the annual Zora Neale Hurston Festival of the Arts and Humanities to have enjoyed many hours of Dr. Wright's delightful, witty presence and to have benefited, often in ways that are quite beyond language, from his extensive knowledge of Florida's history and cultures and from his ineluctable wisdom regarding the necessity for balance between celebration and cerebral obligations. Truly a man of character, Dr. Stephen Caldwell Wright deserves gratitude for all he has done to improve the quality of human life.

Jerry W. Ward, Jr.
Dillard University
January 15, 2006

TKP, Monday, January 16, 2006

Dreamers Die Young; Dreams Die Eventually

One of the more compelling editorials to appear on Martin Luther King, Jr. Day is Cynthia Tucker's "Did King die so thug culture could live?" [The Times-Picayune, January 16, 2006, p. B-5] My automatic answer to the questioning title is YES. When King was assassinated in 1968, there was no thug culture as we now know it. Thugs have existed for eons. A few outlaws have achieved international fame. Brotherhoods and sisterhoods of the criminal have flourished for centuries in hamlets, villages, towns, and cities. They were a part of human cultures, but they were not generally discussed as a discrete culture. Prior to the late twentieth century, none of the thugs lived in "hoods," although some of them wore hoods. They were not commercial objects to be sold back to themselves in the forms of expensive but trashy fashions and overpriced CDs that preserve and broadcast dubious talent. Martin Luther King, Jr. died because he, and thousands of other unnamed people, confronted the hypocrisy of the United States and demanded Freedom. Freedom embraces thug culture. Ms. Tucker's calculated framing of the question by way of contextual displacement invites ironic affirmation.

Ms. Tucker's indirect answer to her question is NO. She does not wish to consider that in time ultimate sacrifices may slip into the category of things done in vain. She wishes to protect the glory of the sacrifice against erosion. To be sure, King did not die so the clever and greedy might more easily exploit the oppressed. She castigates affluent blacks for pimping and earning handsome profits from the lawlessness and the outlaw choices of some young black women and men. She fails, however, to criticize the source: white, corporate America, the major sponsor of benign genocide. Pimps, we should recall, are themselves pimped by systems. "The popularity of thug culture," Tucker claims, "is among the most serious of modern-day threats to black America, far more dangerous than any lingering institutional racism." In this sentence, the weakness of Tucker's informal analysis erupts like a boil. Institutional racism is the very backbone of the industry that champions and valorizes thug culture. That some presumably intelligent African Americans should be gears in the machinery of institutional racism is not astonishing. They have embraced the current version of the American Dream. After all, they have no obligations under the laws of brute economy to be more noble than Africans who sold other Africans to Europeans. If Reginald Hudlin and Tracey Edmonds and the non-black black-oriented BET celebrate Kimberly Jones (aka Lil' Kim) for her crimes, they are acting in ways that historical narratives allow us to predict. Although King did not include either thug culture or racial treason or sinister commodification in his dream-script, these things are undeniable components of our post-1968 America.

Ms. Tucker's juxtaposing the memory of King's death with the success of trafficking in lawlessness is sobering. It is regrettable, on the other hand, that she failed to place the abuse of King's sacrifice in the context of the pervasive lawlessness that is honored at the highest level of American government and business. Her critique only urges us to recall that some dreamers die young and that their dreams eventually become material for nostalgia. Ms. Tucker teaches us a lesson that is probably quite remote from her intentions. History is a hurricane. It has no respect for the integrity of dreams or dreamers.

TKP, Saturday, January 21, 2006

Epistle to Dr. Rambsy

Dear Howard,

Being Roman Catholic, I find it necessary to abandon the confessional of the Church and its suspect orthodoxy and to enter the estranging emptiness. No, I am not disowning belief in a Supreme Being. Quite the contrary. Indeed, the mystery of a Trinity that lacks a female component— I have always conceptualized God the Father and God the Son as male and the Holy Ghost as presence devoid of gender— continues to inspire belief. I am moved to believe we pray to a strange god who has as little respect for yin and yang as Hurricane Katrina had for the sanctity of human life. The belief, however, shifts and slips like a house in a hurricane. And there is no adequate theory to account for where either house or belief shall come to rest. From the vantage of New Orleans in this post-Katrina moment, it is possible and reasonable to entertain the idea that anything is everything. Ashe.

You have asked for my opinion by way of the question "What's with Mayor Nagin?" a question raised by his Martin Luther King, Jr. Day address at City Hall. I do have strong opinions about Mayor Nagin. To avoid the accusation that I am a threat to national security, I shall write my opinions slantwise.

It is doubtful that his speech will rank in memory on a par with famous speeches by Abraham Lincoln, Frederick Douglass, Booker T. Washington, Winston Churchill, Mrs. Mary McLeod Bethune, John F. Kennedy, and Martin Luther King, Jr. Nevertheless, it should not be forgot that in the performance of the speech, the jeremiad, Mayor Ray Nagin was in direct contact with God through Dr. King's serving as God's linguist. Please note, Howard, that such communication is not governed by American rhetorical conventions but by elaborate Akan protocols. **The Word is replaced by Nommo**. When **Nommo** trumps **Word** print representation fails us.

Did not some ancient authority once propose that those whom the gods would bless, they first make mad? Was the ancient authority uttering a lie from the foundation stones of Western Civilization? I will not claim that our mayor is mad in the clinical sense. I do suggest that the pressure of being in a questionable position of leadership in the dark, empty horrors of post-Katrina New Orleans has driven Nagin to speak in the churchy cadences of an Old Testament prophet. Who am I, marked in my baptism by Jeremiah and St. Jerome, to cast stones at a prophet? Should I cast any stones, it shall be at the words, the language, wherein the prophet fabricated a message. Let us go to the source, a transcript of Nagin's speech as printed in **The Times-Picayune** of Tuesday, January 17, 2006, on page A-7. The newspaper's source was WWL Radio. The punctuation of the transcript betrays the discrepancy between what Mayor Nagin vocalized and what the transcriber heard.

Transcript of Nagin's Speech

I greet you all in the spirit of peace this morning. I greet you all in the spirit of love this morning, and more importantly, I greet you all in the spirit of unity. Because if we're unified, there's nothing we cannot do.

Now, I'm supposed to give some remarks this morning and talk about the great Dr. Martin Luther King, Jr. You know when I woke up early this morning, and I was reflecting upon what I could say that could be meaningful for this grand occasion. And then I decided to talk directly to Dr. King.

Now you might think that's one post-Katrina stress disorder. But I was talking to him and I just wanted to know what would he think if he looked down today at this celebration. What would he think about Katrina? What would he think about all the people who were stuck in the Superdome and Convention Center and we couldn't get the state and the federal government to come do something about it? And he said, "I wouldn't like that."

And then I went on to ask him, I said, "Mr. King, when they were marching across the Mississippi River bridge, some of the folks that were stuck in the Convention Center, who were tired of waiting for food and tired of waiting on buses to come rescue them, what would you say as they marched across that bridge? And they were met at the parish line with attack dogs and machine guns firing shots over their heads?" He said, "I wouldn't like that either."

Then I asked him to analyze the state of black America and black New Orleans today and to give me a critique of black leadership today. And I asked him what does he think about black leaders always or most of the time tearing each other down publicly for the delight of many? And he said, "I really don't like that either."

And then finally, I said, "Dr. King, everybody in New Orleans is dispersed. Over 44 different states. We're debating whether we should open this or close that. We're debating whether property rights should trump everything or not. We're debating how we should rebuild one of the greatest cultural cities the world has ever seen. And yet still yesterday we have a second-line and everybody comes together from around this and that and they have a good time for the most part, and then knuckleheads pull out some guns and start firing into the crowd and they injure three people." He said, "I definitely wouldn't like that."

And then I asked him, I said, "What is it going to take for us to move and live your dream and make it a reality?" He said, " I don't think we need to pay attention anymore as much about the other folk and racists on the other side." He said the thing we need to focus on as a community, black folks I'm talking to, is ourselves.

What are we doing? Why is black-on-black crime such an issue? Why do our young men hate each other so much that they look their brother in the face and they will take a gun and kill him in cold blood? He said we as a people need to fix ourselves first. He said the lack of love is killing us. And it's time, ladies and gentlemen.

Dr. King, if he was here today, he would be talking to us about this problem, about the problem we have among ourselves. And as we think about rebuilding New Orleans, surely God is mad at America, he's sending hurricane after hurricane after hurricane and it's destroying and putting stress on this country. Surely he's not approving of us being in Iraq under false pretense. But surely he's upset at black America, also. We're not taking care of ourselves. We're not taking care of our women. And we're not taking care of our children when you have a community where 70 percent of its children are being born to one parent.

We ask black people: it's time. It's time for us to come together. It's time for us to rebuild a New Orleans, the one that should be a chocolate New Orleans. And I don't care what people are saying Uptown or wherever they are. This city will be chocolate at the end of the day.

This city will be a majority African-American city. It's the way God wants it to be. You can't have New Orleans no other way; it wouldn't be New Orleans. So before I get into too much more trouble, I'm just going to tell you in my closing conversation with Dr. King, he said, "I never worried about the good people– or the bad people I should say– who were doing all the violence during civil rights time." He said, " I worried about the good folks that didn't say anything or didn't do anything when they knew what they had to do."

It's time for all of us good folk to stand up and say, "We're tired of the violence. We're tired of black folks killing each other. And when we come together for a second-line, we're not going to tolerate any violence." Martin Luther King would've wanted it that way, and we should. God bless all.

Comments on the transcript and other opinions

Howard, given the expertise you have developed in dealing with visuals, print, and sound in your "cool black consciousness" project, you will no doubt see and hear what the transcript leaves as a faint trace. The rhetorical structures of the speech eventually fall apart. They implode from the absent horror of what needed to be said about New Orleans on January 16, 2006. All that will be left in your hands or mine after a rigorous analysis will be historicized cultural dust tracks and smoke. The jazz you will find in the transcript is not Louis Armstrong or Buddy Bolden or Papa Celestine. It is Sun Ra on a cosmic acid trip.

The speech does not give me access to Mayor Nagin's consciousness, but it does permit me to hear alarms, the sounds of sustained stress which live in the minds and vocal chords of all of us who have been intimately affected by natural disasters. We are displaced physically and mentally. We meander in whatever version of silva rhetoricae we find familiar. Some of us have become preachers, invoking the Church to help us with matters that are material and very secular and very remotely related to any proof that we are sinners in the hands of an angry god/God. We seek salvation in the tenets of a popularized, faith-based African American history that makes a quantum leap over the fact of enslaving Puritanism (then and now) and shelters itself amidst the Hebrews in pyramid-building Egypt. Time-damned by our vernacular tradition, Nagin commits political suicide in the guise of leading the children out of bondage by the means he deemed necessary into the funk-fantasy of Chocolate City. The Uptown Other (the business barons and their Republican cousins who have all the plans for insuring that "urban removal" and "genocide" shall prevail) is thoroughly delighted with Nagin's performance on January 16.

There is a name in French psychoanalytic philosophy for what the Uptown Other champions: barbarian socius. Read carefully the chapter on "The Barbarian Despotic Machine" in *Anti-Oedipus: Capitalism and Schizophrenia* by Gilles Deleuze and Felix Guattari. In New Orleans, we are not in the hands of an angry god. We are in the paws of the despotic barbarian formation for which President Bush serves gleefully as Commander-in-Chief. It is impossible to understand the psychological crimes that are committed daily in post-Katrina New Orleans without understanding how our country's elected leaders, either blindly or with full knowledge, support the growth of fascist imperialism in the context of international globalization. Please urge your students, Howard, to see through the smoke of sentimentality and platitudes manufactured by state-controlled mass media. Please encourage them to think critically about what a political and psychological swamp is or has the probability of being. Nagin's speech was fox fire.

What much disturbs Mayor Nagin, I suspect, is his impotence. He can not fight FEMA, Governor Blanco, the military, and the hired merchants of death

78

who may have murdered approximately 1,500 African American males during the early weeks of our post-Katrina aftermath. If you want to know where their bodies are, ask the American Congress to investigate why there is a sealed morgue in Gonzales, Louisiana. The bodies that have bullet holes in their skulls want to speak, to tell the stories of what we thought would never happen in the United States. In the context of the barbarian machine, he is a mere factotum. He can vent his and our [black New Orleanians'] deepest frustrations in black-flavored language, but he can not prevent the process and progress of bleaching the city. Cleansing is the priority. Toxic waste has to be removed from the city. Vermin must be exterminated. Hilter's children are having a holiday in New Orleans and the holiday is not Mardi Gras. The Uptown Others and their cousins will pretend conservative political correctness as they criticize Mayor Nagin for being racist, crazy, and unfit. Many of them helped to put Nagin in power. Now they will take anything like real power away from him and other elected African Americans as New Orleans suffers like a woman in the hands of a sexist god. After all, in their perverted Christian minds, New Orleans is a whore in need of behavior modification. Gliberals of all complexions will contend that Nagin's speech was a blatant violation of the fine spirit of Dr. King's dream of democratic transracial cooperation, for they would like very much to have Dr. King be the mirror reflection of their secret god Booker T. Washington. I hasten to say they understand Washington as much as I understand the Holy Trinity.

At some point very soon, Howard, black people who do want to return to New Orleans and to participate in its physical and cultural reconstruction must stop hiding behind dreams, their own and those of Dr. Martin Luther King, Jr. The stone I cast with alacrity is not at Mayor Nagin the man, the human being, who is as frustrated about reality as I am. I cast the stone at language that would have me believe that dreams are more effective than razing fire. I cast the stone at language that gives me no reason to believe large numbers of African Americans will ever be free of self-hatred or other Americans will cease to hate and seek to injure us or that the United States will ever rescind its variously inscribed racial contract. I have a real quarrel with St. Paul, but I think he used language accurately when he or somebody wrote "It is better to burn...."

TKP, February 3, 2006

9110182905

People are equally apt to confuse their organs of cognition and germination with ideas about massive destruction.

An anonymous philosopher

After Katrina, we seek centering in two states of being: reality and actuality.

Reality is brutally uncooperative, especially in such areas as preparedness, emergency, natural disaster, rescue and long-term recovery. Actuality is a gazillion particles of sense-data. Reality is always appropriating actuality. The mistranslation of the actual into the sign language of the real seems to be an activity born at the very dawn of human cognition.

February 10, 2006

Tribute for Ishmael Reed

Since 1969, Ishmael Reed's writing has been an essential tool in my equipment for living and doing in this world. I first read *The Free-Lance Pallbearers* in Vietnam and laughed in an alien landscape of horrors. Almost four decades later, I live in a landscape of massively destructive horrors, read his writings, and smirk. His words have made me too wise to laugh.

Just as I have an existential kinship with Richard Wright, I have a filial kinship with Ishmael Reed by virtue of the less than overt imperatives in his life work. Reed's primal role as a thinker and writer is to provoke recognitions. Unless one is a confirmed dunce, one welcomes and embraces the provocation.

For me, Reed's work is in a canon that is not one. I read him along a line stretching from African oral community management speech acts through the classic Chinese novel *Monkey* by Wu Ch'eng-en, Voltaire's *Candide* and Swift's "A Modest Proposal" to Ngugi wa Thi'ongo's *Devil on a Cross*: the probity of probabilities clears the mind of crap. Reed helps us to see a bit of the actual that "reality" wants us to evade.

Thus, I say to Mr. Reed, "THANKS." Thank you for helping me to help younger people– who are the future– to think through the wasteland human beings have made of their planet.

TKP, February 21, 2006

Edward Rothstein's "History Illuminates the Rage of Muslims" [www. nytimes.com/2006/02/20/arts/20conn.html] implants ideas regarding religion as a virus or worm that promotes bizarre behaviors in the name of supreme beings. In theory, the virus might also promote sensible behaviors in response to devastating occurrences. Writing *The Katrina Papers* has opened doors to strange perspectives on the universe.

Today is the 41st anniversary of the assassination of Malcolm X.

TKP, February 22, 2006

A Brief Defense of Richard Wright and Other Writers

Robert Lashley, whom one might call an angry critic, wrote a blistering review of Richard Wright's *Lawd Today* (1963) and posted it on his blog [aliterarythugsart.blogspot.com] on July 18, 2005. Had the review not been attached to another blog located on www.nola.com, it might have remained relatively unknown. The review, however, now circulates in the public sphere. It must be treated as an item in the reassessment of Wright prior to celebration of the Wright Centennial in 2008. *Lawd Today* does not satisfy Lashley's aesthetic expectations; the novel contains structural flaws. That is a fair judgment made on the basis of taste. What is unfair in the review is Lashley's poorly nuanced and racially problematic flagellation of Wright's misogyny without any mention of Wright's critique of misogyny in *Savage Holiday* (1954). Even more unfair is Lashley's excoriating other male writers, who may share some of Wright's assumptions about the functions of art, for bringing dishonor to African American literary tradition. As a critic, Robert Lashley must bear the onus of dishonor, because his vision of our literary history is at best myopic. He is a critic who has not been violated by scholarship. Had he acknowledged that the manuscript of *Lawd Today* was originally entitled "Cesspool" (c. 1934-35), he would perhaps have understood the folkloric and psychological accuracy of Wright's unflattering portrayal of Jake Jackson. Such an admission would not have changed Lashley's aesthetic conclusions; it would have moderated his passion for hasty generalizations that insult cultural literacy.

Lashley's diatribe fails to acknowledge that our literature is more than the expression of individual talent or the lack thereof. Literature is part of a historical process of reflecting prevailing attitudes as well as personal visions; literature is an integral part of the practice of everyday life. Our responses to what we believe literature represents may often reveal more about our personal desires than about our genuine concern that literature continue to delight and instruct us. By our use of literature and literary figures shall we be known.

Lashley has perfected the art of writing rants, and rants sometimes do deserve a reaction. His negations (or spoors of self-hatred) are such that I surfed the Internet to discover more about him. I did find some of his remarkable postings on http://www.beatrice.com/archives/000636.htm. In response to Ron Hogan's "Stanley Crouch Is a Punk," Lashley wrote on July 21, 2004, that Crouch has "been coning and getting over on people by kicking Black artists [sic] ass since 1979." He ended his posting with "Sorry for the rant, I just hate Crouch." He thought that Crouch is the contemporary version of George Schuyler and announced in a separate posting that after Schuyler's initial success as an iconoclast, his credibility was diminished when a "more liberal generation came along and saw that George was completely full of shit." On July 23, 2004, Lashley provided more commentary on Crouch along with remarks about Charles Johnson, Ellison, Bellow, Morrison, and Baraka. Lashley was truly on a roll. We find a posting from July 29, 2004, in which he rants about sexism in literature, replete with a spleen-flavored remark about Ishmael Reed: "I have never seen a male writer turn into a babbling incoherent sociopath in the prescence [sic] of strong women as I have seen Reed." And he ends his outburst with "Sorry for the rant, I just fucking hate Reed." Lashley's railing is quintessentially post-reason rather than post-modern. His use of the Anglo-Saxon profane as grace notes should warn us of something, and I think the warning has much to do with Lashley's refusal to recognize that he is in the tradition of speech acts committed by Schuyler and Crouch in deodorized English. He has fashioned his critical persona as the hip-hop reincarnation of Schuyler.

In other postings on his own blog, Lashley generalizes about writers, literature, and music to the max. It is his right to do so. Like Candide, he has the right to cultivate his garden. He has the right to distribute toxic commentary on everyone, but he should also expect that his commentary might be greeted by some readers, especially those from New Orleans, with spore remediation.

I would offer Lashley's review to my students as one example of how poverty-stricken criticism can be without scholarly information. If Lashley wants to persuade his readers that "Wright's worst aesthetic flaw" is "his tendency to pad a story for length's sake," he should note that one of Wright's probable models for writing the story of Jake Jackson is James Joyce's *Ulysses*, a novel that is stuffed with padding. Wright's failure is that of the young writer who is still in the apprentice stage of his career, and *Lawd Today* is one of the touchstones we might use to measure the failure or success of early twentieth century efforts to adapt modernism in the African American novel. Lashley's own flaw is his demonizing of Wright and other black male writers without necessary and sufficient cause, his ranting. A rant is to genuine cultural criticism what a matchstick is to a blowtorch.

Lashley is most annoying in the penultimate paragraph of his review. He finds "incoherence and downright evil" in the work of Chester Himes, "crass sexual and racist realpolitik" in the work of John Oliver Killens and John A. Williams, and "maddeningly brutal misogyny" in the work of Amiri Baraka, Ishmael Reed, and Cecil Brown. Lashley speaks ex-cathedra as he puts all of these writers under his "dark cloud of animosity." *These men are neither saints nor demons. We can not ask them to be more perfect than we are.* They are writers, who for whatever faults they possess, have struggled with the situated necessities of African American and American literatures and with how language constantly resists our efforts to utter a "truth." They are not, to borrow a phrase from Countee Cullen, "immune to catechism." They are, like Richard Wright, significant players in the game of literature, bearers of various parts of our cultural memories and re-memberings. They deserve better than Lashley's reductive hysteria and his hatred. What I suspect Lashley hates is the discovery that more than one grain of truth is contained in literature and that literature is often a brutal mirroring of who and how we black males are as we participate in endless and

82

unrelenting historical processes.

February 27, 2006

Poem 227, or Change, change, change/change of tools
"Yeah," he said.
We raw primitive.
My pants ain't ne'er been
proper
linchbequed."

"Hush," she said.
"You putting
your mouth
in your foot."

March 8, 2006

Last Friday, my friend Lolis Eric Elie, whose journalism is always flavored with caveats, wrote a fine paragraph in his column "'Big one' turns into big blunder" [*The Times-Picayune*, March 3, 2006, p. B-1]. I have sent him an email warning that I would quote the paragraph in *The Katrina Papers*.

The paragraph:

I propose that we refer to the president's inability to comprehend the potential danger of Hurricane Katrina as a failure of the English language.

My response:

Mr. Elie directs attention to... excuse me, the dirty clothes have announced they wish to be laundered... your president's failure to understand plain English. I propose that your president does much better with Spanish. Otherwise, he would not have seen the delicious wisdom of inviting Mexican guestworkers to invade New Orleans by invitation. I have no objections to Mexican citizens earning a living. They have to eat. My envy stems from knowing that American citizens have yet to discover a part of the planet where they can earn three times as much for their labor as they might at home. I propose that your president establish by Executive Order an initiative to study the feasibility of an expedition to discover such a location. Obviously, those who have been displaced in the construction and service industries in New Orleans by our guest servants should be able to migrate somewhere and earn sufficient money to feed and clothe their families. Your president also does not seem to comprehend the potential danger of allowing selected Arabs to have access to six major ports in the United States. One must note that all the ports are located east of Texas. I leave it to your imagination to decide why San Diego was not one of the ports. I propose that your president be required to take Arabic 101 and 102, so that he will begin to understand Arab nuances. He is your president. You selected him with much help from the criminals among us. You should want him to have mastery of language and cultural literacy.

Two columns over I notice that a "9th Ward evacuee back for Mardi Gras is slain." At least murder is normal in New Orleans. The aftermath of Katrina bids me to make a medieval distinction between Murder and Death. The unfortunate 26-year-old Katrina evacuee does not occupy the same box in my mind with Octavia Butler and Gordon Parks. Last night Maryemma Graham notified me that Mr. Parks was the most recent of our treasured geniuses to die. Mr. Parks was 93 years old. My boxes for the dead are not segregated on the basis of age. They are segregated on the basis of contribution to human culture. I do not know what Mr. Nameless 26-year-old contributed, although we should believe that he contributed something of value to the lives of his friends. I do know what Ms. Butler contributed to speculative fiction and what Mr. Parks contributed to photography, literature, cinema and music. They were escorted to another plane of being by Death. Murder, the bastard bridegroom of destruction, dragged Mr. Nameless to another plane of suffering. Perhaps I have not yet decided to go on record against the death-penalty because those guilty of murder (when self-defense was not needed) should have an opportunity to commune with their victims.

TKP, Returning to My Pre-Katrina Self on March 17, 2006

Aime Cesaire's *Journal of Return to the Native Land* (1939) is extremely modernist, brutal, and surreal in its treatment of returning to homeplace. He slashes through the jungles of civilization to alarm and enlighten, to reclaim what is small, original, and his own. Metaphors of illness and decomposition brand the legacy of the slave trade and colonization. His surreal poetry jolts me into recognition. Anger mounts. Drink the bitterness. Tattoo of historical abuses disguising the body, my body, your body, everybody. His brilliant accomplishment plasters the walls with envy. Reality is a museum of errors.

How smart and contemporary he is in condemning evil with tears chartered in Liverpool and the burnt brain cells of Leopold, genitals and forecasts of genocide, amputated limbs exported from Congo to California penthouse, excremental stench on a cruise ship, premeditated rape on the trail to glory. Cesaire's work wears a Janus face, looking backward to horrors past and forward to the conception of greater horrors. He would not have been read, I think, from such an ambivalent perspective in the 1940s. If we respect the integrity of Cesaire's work, we are not free to recast its meaning to suit our tastes. We are at liberty to appropriate its significance for our own purposes, thereby announcing our dependence.

Cesaire tosses me into the bloody pits of the Archive, in the discourses of colonialism, in the baptismal founts of the Fourth World. Somewhere among the documents and debris hides the hand and needle that can sew my wounds. New Orleans is the Church of the Never Ordained. Perdido. Olmecs make pyramids of Asian flesh and alien bones. The Gulf Coast is wiped clean. Perdu. The poet and the poem will not return me home. I must return me home.

TKP, Saturday, March 25, 2006: Relief and Disbelief in New York City

One typical New York Saturday begins with breakfast at the Manhattan Diner (Broadway and 77th). New Yorkers do not greet the morning as New Orleanians are wont to do. They rush through their first meal as if they were trucks headed for a five-alarm fire. The eggs are real. The bacon is real. The wheat toast seems authentic. The frantic motions of their mouths as their eyes drill the *New York Post* or the *Wall Street Journal* or the *Village Voice* is disconcerting. This is not how people eat. This is how finely tuned robots mimic eating in a spec-fi city-state. Potatoes trump grits as the blues have a confrontation with Euro-tech noise, and everything goes black to the future.

Something of greater substance must be engaged you think. Do you want to take the subway to the Strand? Do you want to walk over to the New York Museum of Natural History? You decide to do neither, because you notice the New York Historical Society has a "Slavery in New York" exhibit. Slavery is still a living issue. It is more important than butterflies or used books.

The exhibit is instructive. The slave trade in New York City, which is and has always been a site for multiple and continuous immigration, was more disruptive than the long dance with demons in, let us say, Natchez or New Orleans. In Southern places, people have longer memories. The timeline in the exhibit would have you believe that 1827 marks a terminal point for slavery in New York. There is something wrong with that impression, a bloody slicing of memory that should thrive and pass from one body to another in organic refashioning. New Yorkers do not recover the African Burial Ground until 1991. In New Orleans, drums or the percussive tongues of Africans have spoken since Congo Square/Armstrong Park was known as Congo Plains. In New Orleans and other parts of the South, African American character depends much on the retention of sounding. This is not the case in New York. The confluence of disasporas in that city created a whirling of culture where the center has never held. The focus on commerce and capitalism encourages people to buy cultures but not to make one that has its own integrity. People in New Orleans also buy cultures, but they devote more energy to making artifacts and rituals that are difficult to co-opt. Perhaps as one result of what slavery was in New York, it is now necessary for those who wish to be most Afrocentric to purchase an imagined Africa. In New Orleans, people do not traffic in Africa, making spectacular displays of the bogus and the authentic. They proudly live their neo-Africanity. The exhibit helps you to sharpen your critical vision of diasporic differences. It is easier to live with the loas of Hurricane Katrina than it is to accommodate the trickster gods of 9/11.

But you do not wish to outweigh your day. After a typical lunch in a typical Broadway eatery, you take a nap in your very efficient room (518) in the very efficient On the Ave Hotel. You know you have a long evening ahead. Your hostess, Dr. Andree-Nicola McLaughlin, will take you to a discussion of Octavia Butler's works at the Hue-Man bookstore. You will catch only the end of the discussion. That is sufficient to remind you that you do need to reread much of Butler's work. Spike Lee's *Inside Man* is showing next door at the Magic Johnson Harlem Unit 2304. You can only get tickets for the 8:30 p.m. show. You, Andree-Nicola, and two of her friends return to Hue-Man to have coffee and cheesecake and to murder time in pleasant conversation until you can go back to the Magic to see Lee's recent work. Andree-Nicola's friends are from California. They happen to know your former Dillard colleague Cheryl Dixon. Our vast planet is a small world.

After seeing the film and laughing at Denzel Washington's cool, cool humor, you decide that *Inside Man* is not a blockbuster. Yes, it will make more money than earlier Lee films. But it has flaws. One New Orleans movie critic put his finger on a not-too-serious flaw in noting that Spike Lee relies "at least once too often on Hitchcock's favorite technique to change spatial perspective in a scene and suggest psychological distress [Michael H. Kleinschrodt, "Bank on Success," *Lagniappe*, *The Times-Picayune*, March 24, 2006, page 4]. The minor flaw magnifies the major flaw: failure to focus on the implications of the war crimes that the bank executive tries to hide in the vault. What truly needs to be exposed about the Holocaust is repressed. Jewish betrayal is lost in the bifurcated duel between Clive Owen as the bank robber and Washington as the detective (a quite lovely cat and mouse game, I admit) and the secondary duel of gendered racism between white ice (Jodie Foster as Madeline White) and black fire (Denzel Washington). The social mission of commercial film is wonderfully expressed in *Inside Man*, although the mission is a disappointment. The mission is to say so much that the spectator does not comprehend how devastating the message would be if it were clearly stated. The film is the equivalent of a speech by President Bush.

Your mind has had an exhausting workout. It is more than ready to crawl into the luxury of a bed in the On the Ave Hotel, to let its post-Katrina aches dissolve in sleep.

TKP, April 1, 2006

Men are charmed by the displacement of persons and purposes. That is one of reasons fiction has not ceased to amuse us.

TKP, April 4, 2006

On April 3, 2006, you had to contemplate emptiness, the oddly bounded space of air in the Grand Canyon. You have been near the Grand Canyon. You did not have time during your last visit to Arizona to have the eyegasm of viewing this natural wonder. You view it in your head. The spacescape is composed of memories of *National Geographic* photographs and frames from various films. Your visual recall is superior to your memory of the steak you had in Chicago for your 22nd birthday. Yes, taking out debris from your house yesterday dredged up the young you and your solitary celebration of being 22. If you want to know why that should have happened, ask God. Do not ask me. I have little patience when it comes to explaining emptiness to people. Most people can not deal with the topic without assuming a fatal fetal position.

The house is almost completely empty of contents. The workers have begun to tear up the ruined floors. They will attack the mold-infested walls next. They will destroy closets in order to make them new. They will destroy the smell of dying in the house. The house is being robbed of its integrity, its personality. However good it might look in late summer— providing, of course, that the hurricane season does not finish what Katrina, Rita, and inadequate levees and floodwalls tried to accomplish in August 2005— it will not look right. However good it might look, it will only be a costumed ghost of the home you first slept in, in June 2003. The new walls and new floor and new electric wires will have no memory of the jubilation when 50 or 60 friends came in 2003 to warm the house. The new walls will speak post-Katrina, a language of emptiness that is intimate and vulgar. They will address, in late summer, the most dysfunctional aspects of the transforming New Orleans and their anger that the wrong person was elected mayor. They will only speak if weather does not make you homeless and houseless yet once more.

A friend reminded you on Sunday that nature will continue to sponsor hurricanes in the Gulf Coast region. He said those of us who rush to repair may live to regret.

Please. May we have one regret now and deal with regrets to come when they arrive?

Yesterday, I regretted discarding five boxes of LPs. These were choice albums I spent more than forty years collecting. With dry eyes and a wet heart, I consign my music to the curbside. My music is trash. LPs, cassettes, and many CDs have become trash. Emptiness pains like a fishbone caught in the throat. You can have more CDs, but you are not fond of CDs. Aretha Franklin does not sound right on a CD. She sounds corrected. So too do Stevie Wonder, Duke Ellington, Louis Armstrong, and Stevie Ray Vaughn. "Cold Shot." Perhaps classical music sounds very good on a CD. Classical music is, after all, hypercorrect. But Clifford Brown, Buddy Guy, Esther Phillips, Lynn Gold, Cassandra Wilson, Jerry Butler, the soundtracks of *The Color Purple* and *For Colored Girls* and *Shaft*, and Tommy James and the Shantells are not hypercorrect. They, the recorded traces of their creation, are human in the grooves. When you want to hear Roland Kirk's *Oleo*, you must hear the grooves and scratches. It took you twenty years to begin to understand the musical structures of *Oleo*, and you do not want to have that pain and pleasure cheapened by a CD. Only the original recording of "Crystal Blue Persuasion" can evoke the heat, sweat, terror,and comrades of Vietnam. It was in Vietnam that you first hear the song. And you were so overjoyed when you found the recording for $5.00 at a flea market in Jackson, Mississippi. All you have now are aurally unsatisfactory CDs.

Damn you. Grow up. Admit only live music is really worth the listening.

Today you regret that yesterday you threw away all the volumes of poetry you had collected since 1969. You are deeply hurt that all the signed copies of books by Margaret Walker were destroyed. I suppose you can live on the memory of having had long telephone conversations with Margaret about *Dæmonic Genius*. The rare and valuable sit in disgrace on many curbsides in New Orleans. Fanon's title *The Wretched of the Earth* (it sounds so much better if you translate the original French title as "The Damned of the Earth") wounds you again and again. Some of your neighbors are more wretched than you are. Remember that.

To hell with memory. Memory does not recover your collection of OBSIDIAN. Memory does not restore your issues of *Negro American Literature Forum*, *CLA Journal*, *African American Review*, *Negro Digest/Black World*, *New Literary History*, *Southern Quarterly*. You will never again have your precious *Black Box* cassettes. It is strange. Emptiness fills you. It is strange. As you dump one load of the poetry chapbooks and poetry volumes from the wheelbarrow, two chapbooks fly to the sidewalk. They are works by Dudley Randall and Audre Lorde. You lovingly gather them up for deposit in a safe, dry place. There is a message here. The English language needs a new word: **MISSAGE**. The second message is this: For several years you had considered starting the Project on the History of Black Writing database by using your collection of hard-to-find or totally limited, self-published poetry books. *The dream deferred is now your dream destroyed.* Live with the emptiness.

Katrina and the Army Corps of Engineers (who had very weird notions about what New Orleans deserved). They laugh at hubris. They laugh at you. Water invades your eyeballs. Man and nature have conspired to leave a grand canyon in your person. They have stolen years of investment. You are 22 again in the plenitude that is not. *Now, go and find comfort. Given that you find hope meaningless and disgusting, hang on to charity and faith. You were able to write this in the emptiness of your house. Have faith. It will be an act of charity when something slouches into New Orleans to fill your grand canyon of emptiness.*

TKP, April 4, 2006/Part II

"Mr. Norris the son said nothing, but he made a wry face and dusted his fingers as Hamlet might after getting rid of Yorick's skull, just as though he had that moment touched a Negro and some of the black had come off upon his hands."

Charles Dickens, *Martin Chuzzlewit*, Chapter 17

"He said nothing, but he grimaced and washed his fingers as Pilate did after dismissing the case of Jesus, just as though he had touched a Caucasian and some of the white had stained his hands."

From the unpublished essay "Triangle of Imitations"

On April 4, 1968, Duke Ellington announced from the stage of Carnegie Hall that Dr. Martin Luther King, Jr. had died. He announced the result of political assassination.

In the cool distance of now which was then the future awaiting an opportunity to become the past, I think of Nat Turner, Medgar Evers, John Brown, Abraham Lincoln, Malcolm X, and John F. Kennedy. Lunar and solar cycles realign. In a novel that is not beloved, Dickens speaks in the vicinity of truth. We want to pretend that thirty-eight years after King was removed like a thorn from the American body politic that colors (black and white in especial) do not matter in the United States. Color, we tell ourselves, is insignificant. Caste and class are all that counts. But the British author would remind us that we lie. Dickens describes a habit that is virtually encoded in the DNA of Americans and in the oath that naturalized citizens take. The very character of America depends upon race as a permanent category of social definition. It ought not surprise us when some much respected medical journal announces that dispassionate science has discoverd the racial prejudice gene. Our capacity for co-opting what the past predicts about the present is undiminished.

TKP, April 5, 2006

Teaching under adverse conditions in the aftermath of Katrina does have some advantages. My Shakespeare students bring information to my attention that rivals the latest discovery about outer space. According to them, *The Winter's Tale* is Shakespeare's most **sapphoric-clitorial drama**. I think my students may be touched by late feminist fantasy. In the aftermath of Katrina, our mental immune systems frequently fail.

Comment

The Caveat Onus: Book One is an act of love, a testament to Dave Brinks's respect for craft, invention, and humanity. Spun from lunar cycles, the poems here constitute the first stage of a reader's enlightenment about the Cave at Onus or the obligatory habitation of post-Katrina languages. By clever placement and displacement of language, Brinks offers us meditations that focus and transform our engagement with poetry. The poems heighten our sense of Brinks's aesthetic of necessity, his determination to give us twenty-first century moments of recognition. Under the influence of the caveat onus we move from anger and anxiety into proximities of acceptance, the mindscape of intimate estrangement. As moments both of recognition and recovery, the poems offer essentials for healing. Brinks knows that water must enter a reader before the reader enters the water. Let *The Caveat Onus* enter you, so that you can see more clearly how to journey into salvation.

Jerry W. Ward, Jr., April 5, 2006

TKP, April 6, 2006

The proximity of death justifies my right to sing the blues.

Hi Mr Ward,
Thank you for your very intriguing answers. I hope to meet you (relatively) soon and talk further. Did I tell you the exact dates of my trip. I'll be in New Orleans from June 6-20th. If you like we can schedule an appointment time (now or closer to June.) I don't have any contact info for you other than this email address. It might be easier for me to have a phone number to reach you at when I get to New Orleans. (It's something I'm asking all my interviewees. Just to try to make sure I can reach you.)

Thanks again. And I will certainly email at least once more before my arrival.

Yours truly,
Darryl Lorenzo Wellington

TKP, April 7, 2006

The drive from New Orleans to Vicksburg was pleasant. The dull route is I-55 (to Jackson) and I-20 (to Vicksburg). I-55 (to Brookhaven) and Highway 84 (to Washington) and Highway 61 (to Vicksburg) is more delightful in my eyes. This route allows me to pass by Roxie and takes me near Richard Wright's birthplace. It is tantalizing to imagine what the place was in 1908. When I turn right on Highway 61, I am tempted to reverse course and go to Natchez. Dinner at the Eola Hotel might be interesting. But I am rushing to get to Vicksburg before AmSouth Bank closes at 5:30 p.m. That is a priority. As I pass through Port Gibson, I try to see what was so beautiful that the Union Army did not pillage and burn the town. Recreating nineteenth-century thought is a good exercise. No one in her or his right mind would burn the churches in Port Gibson, especially not the First Presbyterian Church. At the pinnacle of the steeple is a hand, the golden index finger pointing straight up to the heavens. How should you read that sign? Does it tell you something about man's inevitable end? Is it a gesture of unpardonable disrespect? The sign leaves you dumb in the middle of possibilities. I think the Union Army dared not torch a riddle.

Highway 61 dips and rises, enhancing the visual rhythm of clover and other weeds on the median and the roadsides. On this road, the thistles seem to have ingested steriods. They look abnormal. Thank God the road is not flat. I am sleepy. Variety keeps me alert. I arrive at the bank at 5:28 p.m., lucky to be the last customer.

As I stand at the counter to cash a check, a teller asks me to remove my cap. I do not think my cap could conceal a weapon of minor destruction, but I do as I am asked. Bank rules post-9/11. Homeland security anxiety has successfully invaded most of our institutions, and now we can feel 96% safe. Or can we? Answer unknown. Yet, the answer is known in New Orleans. We feel 99.9% unsafe as we count the days before hurricane season explodes.

From the bank I go to Kroger's and have an encounter with parsnips. They have parsnips. Last week my body was screaming for parsnips. I have not seen them on any menu recently in New Orleans. Today my body can calm down and satisfy its desires. It also wants fresh spinach cooked with walnut oil. I realize how New Orleans I am becoming. In that city we do not eat for nourishment alone. We eat to sharpen our arguments about the choice and preparation of food.

My brief trips to Vicksburg do matter. They are escapes into normality. The air in Vicksbug is not perfect. It is far purer, however, than what we breathe in New Orleans. What seems to be fresh air is essential. It brings respite from the pollution of recovering.

Sunday, April 9, 2006

Although I have been to Mass and communion, I can't resist transgressing. Well, I don't want to resist. I want the thrill of criminality. Because it is radical and criminal to say it, I will say it: the increase in McCarthy-like attacks on the so-called liberals in the academic world is sponsored by the devil or by the politically correct conservatives who volunteered to be devilish.

Tuesday, April 11, 2006

Judas did to Jesus what Katrina did to New Orleans. He put him in a trick bag. Unlike Katrina, Judas had the dignity to kill himself.

From: "jerry ward" <jerryward31@hotmail.com>
To: profhcl@aol.com, ctmountain@cox.net, drjohnso67@yahoo.com, cchitman@cox.net, eaboll@hotmail.com, gduskin@aol.com
CC: dtaylordu@earthlink.net
Subject: Faculty Meeting, April 11, 2006/Notes
Date: Tue, 11 Apr 2006 21:21:01 -0500
Dear Colleagues:

1. We will have no "election of officers" until September 2006.

2. President Hughes emphasized that DU chose not to cut any tenured faculty after August 2005. Other New Orleans universities did. DU, however, must begin a visioning process and ponder whether student enrollment and the cost-effectiveness of majors can justify continuing this policy of retaining tenured faculty. The warning is that DU may not be able to avoid some reductions; criteria for program and faculty reduction will be decided with the visioning process for the new Dillard University. The curriculum will dictate cuts.

3. The DU mission statement will have to be revised to be consistent with the new vision. President Hughes believes the mission statement should be brief enough to fit on a business card.

4. Faculty may be asked to become more active both in retaining students and in making special efforts to recruit freshmen and other new students for 2006-2007. Faculty members may also be asked to write more grant proposals to support programs within their disciplines.

5. President Hughes believes that the strongest, most viable institutions have not focused broadly on comprehensive liberal arts but have identified the one or two programs that create a signature for the institution. Identifying the SIGNATURE may be a part of the visioning process.

6. We were asked to read the story about Bill Cosby and Dillard University in USA Today, April 11, 2006.

7. Contracts have been issued to 100 faculty members. The worst projected enrollment for 2006-2007 is 1,000 students. The best projection is 1,500 students.

I suggest that the seven items be reiterated within the context of Division of Humanities planning for 2006-2007.

I do not think my colleagues should panic now. I do think they and I should plan. All of us need a Plan B that may not involve Dillard University.

4/12/2006 10:44:29 p.m.

Had an anxiety crisis episode this morning and asked to be taken to the hospital. Felt incapable of dealing with ongoing depression. Tomorrow I am to talk with a psychiatrist. Will he use DSM IV? Am not anxious to have anyone tampering with my thoughts.

Tony King was very helpful today. He accompanied me to East Jefferson General Hospital Emergency Room. This evening, he, Danielle Taylor, and I had dinner at Lola's on Esplanade.

April 14, 2006

The final paragraphs in an editorial entitled "Houses of Straw" from today's *NY Times:*

> Have we learned any lessons from Katrina if the plan is to move back into the same houses and the same neighborhoods and trust the Army Corps of Engineers? Just like the mayoral campaign, the rebuilding process has been blurred by racial politics, especially the accusation of a bias against rebuilding African-American neighborhoods. It will fall to the state body— the Louisiana Recovery Authority— to use its buyout and reconstruction money to build a safer city. If it doesn't have the will to do so, we could see another disaster like Katrina.
>
> Nature will make no distinctions by skin color when it sends its next blast of wind and water at the city. It will not yield to good intentions. New Orleans should surpass what is adequate and expedient. It should be built as a model for how to protect our cities in the future, not a cautionary tale about trying to dwell in the past.

Reflect on common sense. In New Orleans, common sense can not prevail and it damned sure will not endure.

Holy Saturday, April 15, 2006

I quote the full text of Hank Lazer's email:

```
From: hlazer@bama.ua.edu
To: jerry ward <jerryward31@hotmail.com>
Subject: Re: Comment on Dave Brinks's new book
Date: Sat, 15 Apr 2006 12:54:26 -0500
Jerry—
Thanks for passing along your fine words on Dave's Caveat Onus.
Here's what I sent along:
Written figured re-configured – hallucination dream nightmare
```

meditation – balm petition judgment & redemption, Dave Brinks' Caveat
Onus arrives in the post-Katrina post-apocalyptic New Orleans tragedy
called by the government a "recovery." Brinks, though, locates a
source: "a voice speaks to you / from oblivion / whose mouths are zero-
shaped / and all in the key of blue." From this ancient tune, Brinks
makes use, as poetry must, of all available wisdom and engages in the
difficult discipline of considered attention so that "out of this dead
city / you carved yourself free and awoke." In a city where shortly
after Katrina "grey line passengers / are paying $35 to see the
destruction," Brinks believes "this slender hour comes forward / to see
what can be salvaged." Caveat Onus comes forward to help show us a
way onward for a city and a nation in peril.

—Hank Lazer

I think it is noteworthy that Hank and I both end our remarks on Dave's book
with ideas concerning the onward, the trip into a new state of being-in-the-world.
Both of us still embrace the human will to invent a solution.

Over a late lunch at the African restaurant, I remark to Kalamu ya Salaam that
it is very disappointing that not one of the candidates for mayor has said anything
about the future of labor in New Orleans. Not one of the candidates, including
the incumbent Ray Nagin, has an intelligent vision of how to induce companies
to create new jobs in the metropolitan area that would encourage pre-Katrina
residents to return. If one returns to New Orleans and takes such jobs in the
service industries that are not already filled by Latino workers, it is doubtful that
the person and his or her family could live at more than a third-world level. The
cost of living in New Orleans has increased alarmingly above the level that existed
before August 29, 2005. Only middle class and leisure class workers whose
jobs were not totally destroyed can still afford to live in pre-Katrina comfort. No
intelligent plan for housing for laborers who do not own property, the renters,
has surfaced. Given that the Cresent City (the new New Orleans wishes to be an
international tourist trap) is not lacking in power to invent or re-invent, perhaps
the solution shall be the construction of Brazilian slums for workers. The future
of labor, housing, and education in the City of New Orleans is an issue that
politicians have quite deliberately mumbled mumbo-jumbo around. They assume,
I suspect, that voters are zombies, voodoo robots. In certain folk cultures, when
we assume incorrectly, a twisting of sound and orthography and semantics results
in the case that you and me (ume) are asses (ass/ume). New Orleans is one of the
few cities in the United States where the cultivation of ignorance is thought to be a
part of its charm.

Easter Sunday, April 16

You stand on the levee in Convent, Louisiana, the southern breeze keeping you cool in the blazing sun, and survey the property that has belonged to your family since the beginning of the twentieth century. You turn 180 degrees and survey the Mississippi River. The levee on which you stand is a very good one. It has a compact with the river. Even in 1927, the levee and the river maintained civil respect for one another. Here in St. James Parish, they are more reliable than people, more reliable than the Army Corps of Engineers.

Seven years ago, one of your youngest cousins, who was then five, said you should go to the top of the levee with her to look at her river and her boats. Her river? Her boats? That such innocence prevails should induce gratitude.

Should Katrina's kindred decide to visit New Orleans in 2006 and finish the destruction of the city, you have an option. You can build a modest house in Convent next to a levee that promises not to fail you. But you should also remember the plain warning in the title of a poetry chapbook by Julius E. Thompson— HOPES TIED UP IN PROMISES. You should remember that promises are kept and promises are broken. You do remember as the evening breeze blows in from the river flowing past the Hilton New Orleans Riverside Hotel. I applaud your wisdom and understanding of a truth written in wind.

As I reread portions of William Bradford's *Of Plymouth Plantation*, I wonder why America is so God-riddled.

Monday, April 17

Morning Meditation

USA Today reports we have a housing purgatory in New Orleans. What catches your eye is the wording "the housing purgatory that has gripped New Orleans for more than seven months remains. And it won't ease soon." [Mindy Fetterman, "Replacing lost housing is off to a slow start."*USA Today*, April 17,2006: 1B,3B.] Purgatory used to be a state of mind or a spiritual estate, state or estate being reserved exclusively for Catholics. Now Fetterman, making an accidental tribute to Poetry Month, transforms purgatory into an entity, a being or person that grips. If the Trump has his way and builds an overwhelmingly phallic (circumsized) steel and glass tower, seventy stories high, in New Orleans, we shall have trumped purgatory and sent it back to the invisible whence it came. But as my late friend Tom Dent said, "New Orleans is a weird town." The ultra-wealthy who invest in Trump's tower or Spectrum Capital's Tracage should know that capital can be looted and burned. It is always possible for purgatory to return to purge what is imperfectly holy or downright corrupt. And return it shall with the fire next time.

Evening Meditation

The people of this country are begetters and spenders in the hands of a happy god. Such vices as moderation and thrift are unknown in this land. The inhabitants practice the virtues of prudent excess. They have mastered the bland art of consumption. They eagerly fill the coffers in the Holy Temple of Wal-Mart and other places of state-sponsored piety with billions of pieces of green paper boldly stamped IN GOD WE TRUST. Theirs is a commerce of contradictions. Their sacred constitutional documents speak of separation of church and state, but they ignore this organizing principle of the body politic. They are not incapable of managing the double consciousness of the secular and the sacred, but the majority of them opt not to do so. By reason of continual abuse, their minds have persuaded them to believe that their brains are too delicate and fragile to endure the disciplines of logic. The wealthiest of them vegetate like contented swine, certain that the damned of the earth will eternally bring aid and comfort to their sty of bliss. The less wealthy eat patriotism. They salivate shamelessly at the mere mention of the Gospel of Anti-Terrorism; they willingly offer up their young as sacrifices to end a human plague that only the much delayed Doomsday shall bring to an end. Their happy god, a green trickster wizard, has forbidden them to elect a philosopher-president who might succeed in leading them out of the cave into the sunlight. Unlike their mythic first parents, Eve and Adam, they are very, very obedient. They have gone so far as to tell their god that he can use their proxies to elect presidents who think that democracy is an institutional disease that should afflict the human race. In the name of homeland security, their happy god abridged their Constitution. They knelt and prayed, "Thank you, Judas." As we move among them and observe their virtues, we can reach but one conclusion: all of them, the guilty and the innocent, must be subjected to a rigorous program of behavior modication. We must send Hurricane Katrina and other natural disasters to set the process in motion.

Signed: The Sons and Daughters of the Third Universal Reconstruction

TKP, Tuesday, April 18, 2006: Letter to Dr. Julius E. Thompson

Jerry W. Ward, Jr.
Division of Humanities
Dillard University
1555 Poydras Street, 12th Floor
New Orleans, LA 70112
April 18, 2006
Dear Julius,
Here are recent entries from The Katrina Papers, an indication of where my mind is floating these days: [Note: entries for April 15 and April 17 were inserted here.]

Nothing's easy in the Big Easy. I had a stress-related anxiety attack last Wednesday and had to go to East Jefferson General Hospital for observation. That was followed-up on Thursday with a visit to one of the psychologists at Tulane. I quite bluntly informed the good doctor that I was not a devotee of long-term psychoanalysis, and that rattled him a bit. I am to see him again today at noon. Dr. Lee seems to be a cool human being, but I was not pleased with our session. Indeed, talking with Kalamu on Saturday was more therapeutic. Dr. Lee simply has to refer me to a good male psychiatrist— if one with whom I am willing to develop a trust level can be found in New Orleans. I refuse to submit my intricately crafted mind and personal history for the inspection of a female psychiatrist, because I do not wish to play gender games [I think I used the phrase "gender gymnastics" during our session]. It is much easier to tell another male that he is a son of a bitch than to directly accuse a female of being a bitch, if it comes to that. Otherwise, I shall discover "home remedies" for my ongoing depression and infrequent volcanic eruptions. Our stress-afflicted ancestors seemed to get along fairly well without psychoanalysis, so I should be able to hang on to a socially acceptable amount of sanity until I die.

If a person as privileged as I am has begun to have mental problems, consider the plight of the very poor who have quite limited access to counseling. There is more in the post-Katrina arena of suffering and recovering than meets the ear. And I do not think there is a psychiatrist— alive or dead— capable of dealing with my mind.

My patience continues to dwindle, and the sense that I am swimming in molasses increases. There are so many paradoxes to accommodate. I am becoming nocturnal again, finding great satisfaction in reading late at night and writing in the early hours of the morning. But that routine is not good for teaching. I am usually fatigued by 2:00 p.m., and my late afternoon classes this term met at 4:00 and 5:30. I do a good job of teaching American literature at 9:30 a.m. and a lackluster one of teaching British literature at 4:00. For some reason, I do come alive in the last class— Shakespeare. Perhaps the reason is located in my having enjoyed doing Shakespeare with Henry Knebler at Illinois Institute of Technology. Another problem I have to contend with is the disappearance of things. My memory of where I have put things is shorter than it was last August, and I become frustrated easily. Age and Katrina are doing me in. Kalamu said I should stop worrying overmuch about "small" things and even about the "big" issues in New Orleans that I am ill-equipped to resolve. And Joanne Gabbin reminded me in her email yesterday that I should worry less about others who really do not need to be worried about. [Note: Gabbin actually wrote— I want you to stop taking care of the world and take care of yourself. You have been so wonderful to me even in the midst of all of your uprootedness.] Nevertheless, Julius, worry is not an easily discarded piece of trash. And I don't have an address for the landfill of emotions.

Fraternally,

TKP, April 19, 2006

Today's classes are better than those we had on Monday. As students respond to my question about certain words and phrases in William Bradford's *Of Plymouth Plantation,* Anthony Lynn confesses uncertainty about the meaning of "body politic." So, I launch into explanation, recalling as much as I can about the concept from Hobbs and Rousseau. I assumed that students were familiar with the phrase, that it was a small item in our cultural literacy. Apparently, it is not. The alacrity in my explanation is quickened by the subconscious dynamics of the body parts in *Titus Andronicus.* In the British literature class, Erin exhibits the fatigue that has hit a number of Dillard students. All that seems important to her in Beowulf's fight with Grendel is Beowulf's twisting off Grendel's arm. "But Erin, you miss important information about the Christian ideas in the poem and Beowulf's confidence that God's will shall be done, if you do not apply close reading. You miss the Germanic grace notes." Erin stares blankly as Charlotte says, "Yes, you miss a lot." The remark is not, I suspect, a mean-spirited public condemnation of Erin's reading habits. It is an indirect call for the class to attend more carefully to the swerve of meaning in the translation. In the pre-Katrina days of my teaching, I would have been upset that a senior English major read so carelessly. Now, I worry more about the emotional congestion that may lurk in the eyes of my students. Perhaps I ought not worry about reductiveness being a sort of defense mechanism against the overwhelming complexity of living fully in the ambience of Katrina. In the final class, we fall into a kind of Thomas Morton response to the bloodiness of revenge in *Titus Andronicus.* We taunt the Puritan aspects of revenge tragedy. The extreme horror of the play becomes an object of laughter. I suggest to the students that laughter is a sign of my defiant pleasure in the evil strategems of Aaron, that a proper reading of the play would involve tears for the permanent cycle of evil that revolves so effectively in Shakespeare's apprentice work with tragedy. Being inside tragic conditions that have to do with Katrina's aftermath and the world's rapidly increasing disjointedness, we are disposed to react to literature in ways that do not conform to reception theory. Our post-Katrina practice of reading demands some revision of theory. We laugh at mere words. We reserve our sense of shock for the horrors that breathe in the streets of New Orleans. Katrina has forced some of us to taste the poverty of conventional explanations. We have to bathe in the small water of pre-future conventions.

As I passed Le Pavillon hotel after lunch, an indigo slave beckoned to me and whispered something about Jesuit slaveowners and the open secret that the spirits of our slave ancestors are waiting for the ideal moment to teach New Orleans the history of fire. If I am ever asked why I broadcast the violence that slave spirits are configuring for the United States and other portions of the New World, I will be obligated to say that I do not practice cutting off the tongues of the spirits. If New Orleans burns with a hard, gem-like flame, I am sure the religious pundits shall confirm that the phenomenon is the will of God.

Meanwhile, the spirit of the Lord certainly and obviously mounted the person of the Reverend Otis B. Moss, III, who preached the fabulous meaning of the story of the prodigal son at tonight's *Message in the Middle* in the Hilton New Orleans Riverside Versailles Ballroom. *Message in the Middle* is Dillard University's midweek worship service, a very popular service where we acknowledge that God gives us His Spirit to instruct us and does not withhold manna from our mouths.

Reverend Moss reminded us that he pastors Tabernacle Baptist Church in Augusta, GA, the home of James Brown. Reverend Moss is a better preacher than Reverend Jesse Jackson. My ears applaud as his voice does a praise dance on molecules of air, illustrating that no person need live below his or her destiny. I am pleased that our University Chaplain, Reverend Gail E. Bowman, invited Reverend Moss to chastise the darkness with light. As I descend from the ballroom to the restaurant, my soul is full of manna, but my stomach is demanding French Market pasta.

TKP, April 21, 2006

I agree that labor does not get its fair share of the wealth it creates. The Sermon on the Mount, the Golden Rule, the Declaration of Independence, all require extensive reforms to the end that labor may be so rewarded that the workingman can, with temperance, industry, and thrift, own a home, educate his children, and lay up a support for old age.

Rutherford Birchard Hayes

Synogogue in a mustard seed.
Small. Powerful.
Church spires were invented to impale falling angels.

People who live in New Orleans are being required to absorb many new words and concepts quickly. The public discourses about the city's future are liberally sprinkled with such words as charette, community master planning, and base flood elevation. You may hear very technical descriptions about aspects of hurricanes and expectation moments in the mathematical abstractions that scientifically describe a flood cycle. You have to learn what GSI means and how to use the data. You have to learn why the flood zone maps issued by FEMA are beta models which are designed to encourage political squabbling. Such maps are confusing even to ACE experts. As you try to exercise some intelligence in clarifying the welter of language wherein planning is wrapped, your emotions may drive your blood pressure up to the danger zone.

I am very interested in knowing why the French word *charette* was chosen to describe an American planning exercise. The word means cart, the cart used in the 19th century to collect assignments from art students. The *charette* is associated with anxiety. The word, thanks to its inappropriate appropriateness, fits in New Orleans, but it is a disaster when it is used in Mississippi. There is gossip that the governor of Mississippi was not pleased with the word, and that he informed someone the only French word he knew was bourbon. The governor is a very patriotic American drinker.

The Department of Transportation provides more information about *charettes* than one can easily digest.

April 22, 2006

I performed one obligation of civic duty today. I served, from 5:15 a.m. to 8: 30 p.m., as an election commissioner (Ward 7, Precinct 16) in the primary elections. There are 613 registered voters in this precinct; 136 people voted at the University of New Orleans polling site. I do not have exact figures for absentee ballots and for the number of early votes. It was a pleasure to certify the eligibility of voters, a simple process except in those cases where the precinct register demanded that a voter complete an address confirmation. It is pleasing that Ray Nagin (39%) and Mitch Landrieu (28%) will face each other in the runoff in May. Both candidates for mayor stress reconciliation. I suppose that is why Jesse Jackson walked through the UNO polling place to have his picture taken by the international press and by common people.

It is time for us to stop the bickering, according to Nagin, who believes he represented the displaced. It is time, according to Landrieu, to make New Orleans a great city with the cooperation of the African American, white, Vietnamese, and Hispanic voters. We shall focus on two candidates rather than twenty-three in the general elections. One candidate is nearly bald. One candidate is bald by choice. Class and race shall be inevitable factors in the May elections. Class and race are children that kill each other daily for dominance in New Orleans. Even in hell one is obligated to perform civic duties, trying desperately not to be rained on by clouds of suspicion.

April 23, 2006

Advice to New Orleans voters for the runoff scheduled for May 20: The only thing between L and N is M. M is for Marie Laveau. Let her decide the election.

Monday, April 24, 2006

American literature, British literature, Shakespeare– so runs the pedagogic liturgy. Anne Bradstreet's poems, *Sir Gawain and the Green Knight*, and *Hamlet*. And what has any of this to do with a surplus of water, the wetness that quite took possession of our lives, our minds, our souls? Absolutely nothing.

You did not like the premier of Wynton Marsalis's "Congo Square" in Louis Armstrong Park yesterday. Except for the African drumming, Marsalis's orchestration was so New York, so Lincoln Center, so Broadway, and so borrowed from Duke Ellington and Billy Strayhorn. A judicious tribute to the spirits who may choose to help us rebuild and heal New Orleans it was not. Even you, with your obvious lack of musical talent can hear the difference between commerce and commendation.

Tuesday, April 25, 2006: Brutal Blessings Blister Beautifully

W. E.B.DuBois was one of the most brilliant thinkers of the twentieth century, his mind as awesome in scope as his arrogance. And his arrogance was justified. The tapeworms of his world did not know how to measure his depth, and his putting great distance between himself and people of good intentions and merely ordinary intelligence was a powerful defense mechanism. DuBois could also be brutal. Was he not party to the undermining of Marcus Garvey? As we swim again and again in the sea of his words, we soon forget that razor-sharp rocks bide their time under the surface. We forgive his memory all his flaws. Stricken by awe, we are cowardly in our measure of his humanity. A little bit envious too. We are, of course, equally cowardly in the resurrected presence of Einstein and Freud and Marx. We shall not deny DuBois his due.

Like DuBois, Dr. Lucius Turner Outlaw, Jr., Associate Provost for Undergraduate Education and Professor of Philosophy and of African American and Diaspora Studies at Vanderbilt University, is a graduate of Fisk University. He delivered the keynote address at Dillard University's 2006 Honors Convocation. The event is one of Dillard's great traditions. The students dress in somber black. Faculty members don academic regalia and become, for a brief time, peacocks and peahens of higher education. A calculating philosopher, Outlaw chose to remind us of DuBois's sentiments regarding the work of the Talented Tenth. He reminded both students and faculty members that they do not have a right to be stupid in the twenty-first century. Outlaw walked the pathway of the negative to assault the negativity that students use as an excuse for poor performance and ego-worship, that professors often adopt in proclaiming what students are now too attention-limited to learn. In the tradition of DuBois, he gave us the brutal blessing of a scorpion. We do need to be severely wounded and reawakened about the field and function of the famed HBCUs in America. They are something better than cafeterias of certification for the world of work. Students are not customers or clients. Teachers are not clerks. And HBCU administrators, in the words of Outlaw, should behave like statesmen rather than seedy corporate executives.

The body language of the audience, especially that of the Dillard undergraduates, indicated that Outlaw's message did not win favor in their ears. His convocation address shall be as soon forgotten as was DuBois's brutal blessing at his alma mater in the 1940s. Nevertheless, I much appreciated Outlaw's being a man of principle, a man who is brave enough to conjure the corrective spirit of W. E. B. DuBois. After the convocation, I shook his hand and informed him that "DuBois is very much pleased with what you said." I think Professor Outlaw was complimented. I now feel a bit more at ease with dispensing brutal and blistering blessings among my students in the aftermath of Hurricane Katrina as I close my ears to their cries of confusion, loss, and pain. DuBois, Outlaw, and uncommon sense ordain my becoming a Puritan again, the kind of Puritan DuBois would never admit he was. I can close my ears but not my heart.

Wednesday, April 26, 2006

The sky is rain grey this morning. You hear thunder, and it is not in your soul. Thunder is anger in the upper worlds. Walking through the breezeway between the older and newer sections of the Hilton New Orleans Riverside Hotel, you note how grey segues into grey, lighter and darker in random harmony. You think of Ernest Gaines's story "The Sky is Grey." You think of the word "grey" (or did he spell it "gray"?) in the opening of Melville's "Benito Cereno." You remember something you are supposed to do, and you quickly forget what you have remembered. Why do you think so automatically of grey in literature and not of the same shades in guns and ammo clips? Why do you not think of grey as the color of people waiting in nursing homes for the mercy of dying? Grey is the color of your hair. Grey is the color of your Lexmark printer and your Kensington mouse. It is the color of your memory. Grey is the color you see when someone asks if you asked Denzel Washington for his autograph last week. No. If Denzel Washington wanted you to have his autograph, he would mail it to you. Grey is grey, Ms. Stein. Grey is the canvas painted by the blues.

You remember that April is Poetry Month. But what has poetry to do with the rising cost of gasoline or the retrofitting of democracy? Is poetry a lame excuse for trying to deal a death blow to what is repulsive? Is it literature that sponsors the sense that progress in a recovering New Orleans is like a deranged elephant? Is that what poetry is about— elephants who need therapy, purple grass and golden plastic, grey skies, minds that make excursions into forbidden zones? Is rain a poem, a liquid sonnet that refuses the covenant of conventions, sliding down the greasy pole of alliteration? And how can a poet recognize when she has crossed the line, like Katrina, and stolen the identity of her muse? Katrina, Katrina. You are a horror that has taught us the poverty of anger. In the black days and grey mornings of Europe, they lied and called you Grendel's mother. In Africa, my ancestors called you what your are: a she-haint from unholy land.

Thursday, April 27, 2006

Things to be remembered invade your mindspace like overnight mushrooms blighting a lawn.

I reviewed the final draft of the SAT Literature examination again this morning, typed out a brief note, and mailed the materials prepaid UPS. Task one done. Although I got up and showered early and had my morning cup of Starbucks-cloned coffee, it is already past 10:00 a.m. when I finish the SAT material. Not time enough to deposit a check in the bank and get up to Tulane for my 11:00 a.m. appointment. Task two undone.

You and your body navigate the Toyota up St. Charles Avenue, and you are amazed that this much applauded thoroughfare looks like a brat.

People in New Orleans do not pronounce CALLIOPE correctly. When it comes out of their mouths it almost rhymes with ALLEY OOP. If you used the phrase "Calliope in the Calliope," what would you be talking about? Ask Chakula. He would tell you you ain't talking about nothing, his face assuming the mask of mock anger that always inspires you to laugh. You are the only one who knows that the streetsign CALLIOPE inspired the phrase. You intended a keyboard instrument in the Calliope Project not a Greek Muse in a musical instrument. The possibility that you intended a Greek muse in the project is very much out in left field. You could, you know, go far afield and use the phrase in a poem and keep all your listeners (except those from New Orleans) very much confused about what you are saying. It might be healthy for you to create confusion. What rare confusion you could create in a restaurant if you ordered sunny-side up apricots with a cup of hot Alaska or freshly squeezed Florida.

Friday, April 28, 2006

Our bodies are sometimes wiser than our minds. Last night at 8:00 p.m. I wanted to make a quick trip up to Vicksburg.

My body said "NO. I WILL NOT DRIVE 234 MILES IN THE DARK OF NIGHT, JUST SO YOU CAN CHECK YOUR MAIL, PAY A FEW BILLS, AND *RESTORE YOUR BALANCE* IN WHAT YOU CALL A NORMAL ATMOSPHERE. NO. YOU AND I ARE STAYING IN NEW ORLEANS TONIGHT."

The tone was so harsh and deliberate that I made a concession to my body and allowed it to crawl into bed. Had I defied it, it might have fallen asleep at the wheel, and I would have to make a permanent visit to _____ [place unknown].

My body slept until 5:00 a.m. It did not sleep like a log. It slept like a body that has been functioning nonstop for 62 years.

Saturday, April 29, 2006: The New Orleans Word Festival

Breakfast this morning with Ernest Jones and Lolis Edward Elie was a reminder of the last breakfast the three of us shared in July just before Katrina and the levees altered our city. We were at Le Richelieu at Lolis's favorite table being served by Michael, Lolis's favorite waiter. We were discussing the New Orleans Word Festival, Ernest's brainchild, and planning events for the second festival in October 2005. We were painting wonderful dreams.

The lawyers Lolis Edward Elie and Ernest Jones became a part of my extened 62nd birthday celebration in July 2005.

We were having breakfast at Hotel Richelieu on Chartres Street, spending a leisurely Saturday morning to discuss the fate of the world and the forthcoming New Orleans Word Festival (September 25-October 2). I had noticed a copy of *Guns, Germs, and Steel* in the back seat of Ernest's SUV. I asked him what was the subject of the book. He launched into an extended explanation, telling me about animals, climates, domestication, and the formation of cultures. I began to think the book might be worth reading. When we returned to Lolis's house in Treme, I announced that Sunday would be my birthday. Ernest immediately said I must have Jared Diamond's book. He signed it "Happy B'day/From Ernest/7/05." Lolis gave me two bottles of white wine. The book and the wine were compatible. I spent the late hours of Sunday getting acquainted with the extraordinary work of Jared Diamond in evolutionary biology.

Dreams drown and recur as déjà vu or nightmare. Today it is déjà vu. Lolis, Ernest, and I are having breakfast at Le Richelieu at Lolis's favorite table being served by Michael, Lolis's favorite waiter. We are discussing the New Orleans Word Festival, Ernest's brainchild, and planning events for the second festival in October 2006. We are painting wonderful dreams.

The new dream is different. Lolis still insists that we invite a writer who has a national reputation. Someone like Walter Mosley. Ernest worries that we will not be in a position to partner with literacy groups. He worries too that money that might have been available through a grant from the State of Louisiana has now been allocated to take care of more immediate problems than the celebration of the word. I am concerned that we should invite Dave Brinks to participate in the festival on October 7, because the first anniversary of the revival of the Seventeen Poets Series at the Gold Mine Saloon will be October 13, 2006. I think it is only right that Dave's heroic efforts to keep poetry and other art forms alive in the city be acknowledged.

Ernest asks my advice about the focus of this year's festival. I propose that the broad theme be DISASTER AND USES OF LANGUAGE. There are two aspects that warrant attention. The creative use of language to project possibilities that may help people to put disaster into perspectives, into frames that suggest disaster does not render life hopeless. The second aspect is a practical use of language to describe features of disaster and preparedness for disaster that ought to persuade likely victims to be prudent. The creative and the practical uses also have a negative side. **They can serve to secure stereotypes.** I suggest that the festival should explore the synergy between the creative and practical uses of language in the contexts that exist in the aftermath of Katrina. A light bulb illuminates Ernest's mind. The glow brightens his face. Ernest, who is displaced in Baton Rouge, who drove an hour and a half just to have breakfast, describes conversations he has had with James Borders about the language used by the various tribes of Mardi Gras Indians. It seems to be a combination of Creole with various West African languages and some vocabulary borrowed from Native Americans. This language, in its origins and use is at once creative and practical when it is examined within the evolution of urban life in New Orleans, within the evolution of African Diaspora traditions. If the territory has not already been explored by cultural anthropologists, it should be investigated through a project sponsored by the New Orleans Word Festival.

After breakfast, as I drive to the Jazz and Heritage Festival, anxious to make use of my Brass Pass, I worry about omens. I am happy that our communal meal reminds me of old New Orleans. Nevertheless, I am discomforted by my clear memory of the past. Suppose our breakfast is a prelude to a repetition. A good sign appears. On my way to the Southern Comfort Stage I meet Louis Edwards, a VP for Festival Productions, Inc. Louis Edwards is also a novelist, one of the underread male writers of our region. We had wanted him to participate in the Word Festival last year. Perhaps this year he will.

April 29, 2006: Email inspired by experience at the Jazz and Heritage Festival

> Subject: S.O.S. People of no color out of control in New Orleans

Please encourage African Americans who lived in New Orleans before Hurricane Katrina to return as quickly as possible. The black numerical minority now in the city is swiftly discovering that people of no color (the current majority) behave badly when we have too many days of absence. We need reinforcements.

For example, as I was waiting for Etta James's performance at the Jazz and Heritage Festival today, I could smell marijuana (of a very good quality I must add) being smoked behind me. I turned around and saw a man and a woman of no color freely sucking on a shared toke. About thirty minutes later, the wind blew a fresh stream of marijuana smoke into my nostrils. When I turned this time, I saw a group of six people of no color freely passing around a large roach in a silver clip. Two, whom I assume were the grandparents of the children playing nearby, were sending a very bad message about freedom to the children. They sent the message that people of no color can break the law with impunity in New Orleans and smoke marijuana in the public space of the Fairgounds. Please imagine what might have happened had the smokers been members of the numerical minority.

Earlier in the afternoon when I went to one of the men's restrooms in the Grandstand, two policepersons— a female of no color and an African American male— were asking someone to come out of the restroom. A female of no color emerged, and the African American policeman informed her she could be arrested. He said, some man will do something and you will begin screaming. A second female of no color was still in one of the stalls, and the policeman had to ask twice that she come out. The males of no color seemed astonished. I proceeded to the urinal and did what a man had to do. But I was mildly shocked at how females of no color acted out their boldness and obvious lack of breeding. They were exercising the tyranny of the majority in a very dangerous space. And being the historically conditioned person that I am, I thought of Miss Ann slipping down to the slave cabins after midnight and screaming at the top of her lungs, when the overseer almost caught her in the act, that she was "raped."

Please encourage African Americans to return. People of no color are rapidly turning the Big Easy into Babylon.

Sincerely

Jerry W. Ward, Jr.

Chakula Cha Jua responded to this email by noting his disagreement with the contents. As he put it, the characters were not new. There was no discontinuity in their behavior, no U turns. "The people of no color were acting the same way, if not worse, even before Katrina. I guess it just has something to do with having no color. In the words of Bill Cosby's character Fat Albert, they are like teachers out of work. 'No class.'"

Sunday, April 30

Since February I have been participating in All Congregations Together [ACT] activities to organize communities in New Orleans. I have been asked to read the ACT announcement about "The People's Interfaith Mayoral Run-Off Forum" scheduled for May 7, 2006 at St.Gabriel the Archangel Church. The page I have been given to perform is a call and response sketch. It is not right for our first 8:00 a.m. mass since Katrina. I had to rewrite it, especially since I was at one point to say, "As it is written in John:xxxxx...." What a dunce I would have seemed. There is in no translation I am familar with in which John:xxxxx says, "Faith without works is dead." What a typo. What a misleading reference. Why have I been given a bad script? Catholics tend not to want to be Protestants at 8:00 a.m., and they certainly do not want to be directed to non-existant Scripture.

No more than forty people attended this early mass at St. Leo the Great, or, as we now call it as a result of a temporary merging of under-populated parishes, St. Leo the Great Cluster. Although the date and time and place for the forum are printed in the Sunday bulletin, it is important that I amplify the message. I feel odd being a political messenger in church, because I have antique notions about the sanctity of the altar and the pulpit. I am a reluctant prophet according to the psycologist I have been talking to for the last three weeks. But given that the new Catholic Church ignores many of the traditions I came to love during my childhood, I suppose God is going along with the changes and ordaining my role. I suppose I am a strange tool of the Divine Will. I have to suppose my standing in the pulpit is evidence of things as unknown as the purposes of Hurricanes Rita and Katrina. The last hurricane before Heaven turns out the lights of the universe will be named Jesus. Now, that is evidence of something that I do know. I speak plainly to the congregation. I avoid the shout-chant I deem more appropriate for Sanctified venues.

Good morning. My name is Jerry Ward. As a member of the St. Leo Cluster Action Group, I have been asked to draw special attention to the announcement in today's bulletin regarding THE PEOPLE'S INTERFAITH MAYORAL FORUM sponsored by All Congregations Together next Sunday at St. Gabriel Church Complex. This forum is an excellent opportunity for us to put our faith to work and ask the run-off candidates— Ray Nagin and Mitch Landrieu— those hard questions that agonize us in this period of recovery.

AS A PEOPLE OF FAITH, we believe ALL THINGS ARE POSSIBLE! As it is written in the Epistle of James, 2:17, however:

Even so faith, if it hath not works, is dead, being alone.

As we seek to rebuild our neighborhoods and our homes and our lives, and to help our families and friends return to New Orleans, time is crucial. NOW IS THE TIME for us to REINFORCE OUR FAITH WITH WORKS. NOW is the time for us to

WORK as a faith community to ensure OUR VOICES ARE HEARD AND OUR
ISSUES ARE MET.

The major purpose of the forum is to send a very clear message. WE WANT
TO ENSURE THAT NO MATTER WHO IS ELECTED MAYOR, THAT THAT
PERSON KNOWS WITHOUT DOUBT THAT ALL CONGREGATIONS
TOGETHER AND THE ST. LEO CLUSTER ARE BACK AND FULLY
COMMITTED TO REBUILDING OUR COMMUNITIES. That person must also
know that we will no longer serve time on the cross of dysfunctional politics.

We need all women, men and children in the St. Leo Cluster to represent their
church and community and themselves at the forum. IF YOU DO NOT REPRESENT
YOUR FAMILY, YOUR CHURCH, YOUR COMMUNITY, AND YOURSELF AND
YOUR ISSUES, THEN WHO WILL?

Thank You!

I am much relieved when I have finished the message. My eyes twinkle as I
envision the crucifixion of citizens on the cross of dysfunctional politics. Is the
bitter taste of humor yet one more sign of things unseen?

Monday, May 1, 2006

Troy "Trombone Shorty" Andrews's stellar performance at Jazz Fest
yesterday is still playing in your head. The future of jazz in New Orleans resides
in the creativity and brilliance of Troy Andrews and Jonathan Batiste, in Kermit
Ruffins when he is most black and blue, when he is most the legitimate heir of
Louis Armstrong. You know that the only sin of jazz in New Orleans is in its
skin. Yes, the music. Hip-hop zydeco swamps back to the origins of jazz in a
normativity. As the last musical note on earth dies, you will see the fire burning
black and the water crying blue, God's voice tattooed on a human face. Listen: an
abbreviated cosmic contraction.

TKP, May 2, 2006 : Part I

May 1 was once an international Communist holiday.
May Day, New Orleans. May Day. Write a Whitman paragraph. Write a
Kaufman poem.
New Orleans: the Communists did not promote today's nation-wide rallies
for immigrant rights. Polish Socialists did not bellow in solidarity. Only those who
would inherit the earth made noise. Un dia sin Latinos. It must be love.

2 May 1945: Soviet Union announces the fall of Berlin. Ashe.

New Orleans, No consumas productos Gringos. Ashe. No consumas productos. The bread you eat is slave labor. The salt in your meat is slave sweat. Oil. It is all about oil. In Vietnam it was about rice futures. A change is gonna come. It will not be a nice change. It will be a loaded dice change. No consumas productos diablos.

2 May 1945: Nazi troops surrender in Italy and parts of Austria.

Un dia sin nada, amigos. Mayo. Go, sell flowers to the dead who ride the streetcars of desire. They will write a part for you in the *Masque of Whiteness*.

New Orleans, Vincente Fox does not know how to make common cause with Wal-Mart. The Fox walks hand in hand with the Bush. The Fox knows how to insult people of African ancestry. He will not apologize, Mr. Joyce. The lost ethnicities of Africa shall scratch out his eyes. The Bush does not have eyes. Don't matter. St. Christopher shall lead him down the path to redemption through the valleys of Mexican revenge.

New Orleans, the Chinese are on top of their game. They do become political and economic bedfellows with the Sam Walton clan. The Indians will follow and give nuclear club membership to Aboriginals. The North and South Poles shall warm the earth.

New Orleans, tell Africans to beware. Immigration quotas do not allow you to border hop, even if you have visa in hand and money in bank. Be smart. Stay at home. Vaporize neo-colonial gluttons with ju-ju. Practice loving your neighbor and yourself.

In less than a decade the current Latin American leftists will become ultra-conservative. Smoke smells, New Orleans. They will butcher nuns, rape priests, torture liberal spokespersons for human rights. And missionaries. Uncle Sam will learn to dance and change his name to Harry Sam. The rain forests shall burn. Let us then sing *Nuestro Himno* in Swahili.

New Orleans, the Asian Islamic militants are rising. 9/11 was their initial Saudi holocaust. The Bushes and the Saudis have a common ancestor: Papa Adam Abraham. Latina/Latino beware. Ben Aladin will put you in his lamp. Euro-Americans be a dangerous people. Ask the Choctaws. Ask the gay man who hangs like a crucifix on a barbwire fence. Ask the Pima, the Hopi, the Aztecs. Ask the lesbian the softshell Baptist will not give a drink of water.

Katrina make gumbo, no? The color-blind and ethnic-deaf Communists did not concoct today's march for human freedom, for making the United States the melting-pot the most patriotic of patriots used to claim America the Beautiful is. U.S. has no U.S.S.R. scapegoat. U.S. is responsible to U.S. The world is becoming an unadulterated pile of merde. What deity will give you a kiss to build your dream on? Only Armstrong knows. Gossip has it he did not want to be buried in the Crescent City.

Human freedom breeds in a pile of sacred *merde*. In the University of Hardknock Katrina, you got to learn fast.

Beware. Apocalypse is not a folk tale.

The British "royals" have the faces of Trojan horses, living memorials to the sins of Catherine the Great and Queen Victoria.

Your time for meditating at Fons Sancti Joseph in Plaza D'Italia is limited, New Orleans. A fallen angel flaps like a flag from the steeple of St. Louis Cathedral. The curtains in the temple tear every five minutes.

You must learn new habits, New Orleans. Embrace your illegal immigrants. Do not shoot them with forty-one bullets like New York. Gather your illegal self into a ball and roll with the good times. Say prayers to the Dafur saints the Holy Roman Catholic Church will not be able to cannonize for several eons. Pray for those who sin in Tel Aviv, Gaza, Iraq, the mountains of Tibet, and Jerusalem. Pray for Haitians the loas have abandoned. Flush rats from penthouse caves.

Beware, New Orleans, the United Nations is becoming a global ghetto, a FEMA for disasters. And King Leopold never left the Congo.

TKP, May 2, 2006: Part II

I was not able to attend yesterday's rally for immigrant rights, but I did answer the call of the Greater New Orleans AFL-CIO to march and rally for the creation of a workers' rights commission. The proposed workers' rights commission would "investigate and issue findings about how workers should be treated." [The New Orleans Agenda, <vincent@sylvainsolutions.com> April 30, 2006]

I am a worker (teacher) and Louisiana is a right to work state. People do have a right to work without joining a union. Employers, however, can take advantage of the right-to-work and cheat workers by hiring scabs at lower wages than should prevail. Union workers and non-union workers have a right to be paid equally for equal labor. I understand why some workers do not trust unions. Unions do not have the cleanest record in spending union dues. I understand why some workers think the union is a safety net. It really does not matter much whether union leaders are honest men and women. What matters is that union leaders set in motion negotiations that protect rights. Health care plans, workman compensation, safety in the workplace, fair hiring practices, and several other rights have to be protected. The proposed commission would investigate and issue findings. Findings often sit in files as the real conditions of labor worsen. Is that all I shall have marched for? Dead files?

During the march from the Hilton New Orleans Riverside Hotel to the Hale Boggs Federal Building two blocks away, I carry a loud red and yellow sign: REBUILD WITH JUSTICE. Like my fellow workers, I want my voice to be heard. Lawyers are workers. Of the approximately 220 people involved in the rally, I would guess that 110-140 of them were AFL-CIO lawyers. In the current scheme of American life, it is difficult to know with certainty that anyone who can make a substantial difference is listening to your voice. Making an unheard noise is better than remaining silent. In the current scheme of things, it might seem that one has to have a leisure job in order to take off and demonstrate at 3:00 p.m.

TKP, May 3, 2006

Adventures with Children of the Bipolar Gods is an extraordinary book. It should be required reading for all English graduate students.

I was not sure where the May 1 entry was going, so I sent it to a few friends. C. Leigh McInnis sent this brain-blessing on May 2:

Doc,

First let me say that I've never considered *TKP* merely a prose document. It has always read as something in the technique of Toomer's *Cane* or Whitman's *Leaves of Grass* where forms and genres are precisely bent and manipulated to raise the intensity of the subject as well as to make the familiar unfamiliar— reference the segment on Kwanzaa where you call poetry into the service of prose. This is what gives *TKP* its weight and its clarity— the understanding that all language is, at the base level, poetic (symbolic) and that we write to make sense of the fragments of our lives. Katrina has hurled us into the chaos and reality that all of our lives are merely one pulled thread away from being fragments of chaos and on another level, we are given the understanding that life is but pieces of fragments that we glue together. This piecing together of life is our poetic attempt at meaning.

So, the latest entry is more of the same great writing because it understands that the line between prose and poetry is often arbitrary and always shifting— shifted by man to make meaning of his life. Take *The Souls of Black Folks*. I've realized that what makes it difficult reading for freshman students is its poetic nature. Du Bois was a poet in the same way that Shakespeare was a poet who simply had an excellent understanding of staging. The young reader simply wants Du Bois to "get on" with his point. But Du Bois knows that he is making meaning, and only poetry can complete the point that prose begins. The listing in the latest entry is brilliant because it forces us to list, not just the Katrina events but all of the events that lead to meaning in our lives. And then the cultural cross referring is prose in its analysis but poetic in the meaning again when these varying lives are laid upon or beside each other. "Katrina make gumbo, no?" This statement shows how you are creating a gumbo technique to deal with a gumbo situation. And isn't that what African American art is always about? Isn't that Jazz? Isn't that Funk? Isn't that the quilting/sampling of Hip-Hop? Isn't that was makes Prince the supreme alchemist. With *TKP* it is inevitable that the prose will not stay where it belongs because it is seeking a new medium and a multi-layered medium to express this multi-layered issue.

Candice Love-Jackson thought initially that it resonated something of a poem by Derek Walcott. Toomer, Whitman, Walcott– that's indeed good company. I will not allow myself to believe too soon that **TKP** is, as they say in the changing vernacular of the young, "all that." **TKP** is just a simple effort to tell the simple story that is mine.

I would like to reread *Pilgrim's Progress* and the *Confessions of St. Augustine* before I die. I think I have time to do so.

I had lunch today with Marshall Stevenson, Dean of the Social Sciences at Dillard. We had to discuss what selections we should use for the 2006-2007 supplemental in-house text for African World Studies 100. I like Marshall because he is brilliant and modest. He asked if we should try to find an article on Katrina for the course. "No," I said. "It is too early for us to begin assessing anything about the impact of Katrina on the African Diaspora." He concurred.

Marshall gave me a copy of Thomas H. Benton's "The 7 Deadly Sins of Students" from the April 14, 2006 issue of *The Chronicle of Higher Education*. It will help me think about what is embedded in the topic for the National Symposia on "The Millennial Student" that the NYU Faculty Resource Network will have in Puerto Rico. I do plan to submit a one-page proposal for a paper on "Pre-Millennial Teachers and Millennial Students," emphasizing that our thinking must be tempered by considerations of class, caste, institutional composition, and race. The literature on millennial students that I sampled today is grounded in theories about generations. I suspect the theory has some merit. I also suspect the theory may be used as an ideological tool, and it must be opposed by the commonsensical evidence that many students in HBCUs (they were probably never considered in shaping the theory and its models) do not conform in the least to the splashy description of the current generation of undergraduates. They may share many traits and behaviors with their peers in other institutions, but I do not sense that many of them exercise the arrogance of freedoms. When I asked students in my British literature course this afternoon what is a "millennial student," a few of them thought he or she would be a student who entered college in 2000. Thank God. They have not yet been infected with the virus of generational wisdom.

I mentioned to Marshall that some of the "millennial students" who have been recruited by the extreme right to monitor the speech of liberal professors are threatening. They do not know enough of history to know that they are being encouraged to behave like Soviet agents or Maoist agents during the brief Chinese cultural revolution. Our extreme sensitivity to the operation of conflicting discourses in the United States is possibly one result of tensions caused by natural and manmade disaster. We know more than may be good for us of terror and trauma. Historical perspectives on terror and trauma fit appropriately in our teaching of African World Studies just as trying to purchase an angle of vision on the aftermath of Katrina and Rita is an obligation as we deal with our immediate lives.

Thursday, May 4.

As I hurry across the Tulane campus for my appointment with Dr. Marshall Lee, I am soaked by the heavy rain. Do I need these frequent baptisms? The three books I plan to return to the Tulane Library after my weekly session of probing the edges of my psychological condition do not get wet inside my briefcase. One of the books is *My New Orleans: Ballads to the Big Easy by Her Sons, Daughters, and Lovers* (New York: Touchstone, 2006). Rosemary James edited this anthology. I met Rosemary and her husband Joe DeSalvo several years ago in Natchez and then again in New Orleans one day when I was having lunch with Violet Bryan in the French Quarter. They run an independent bookstore in Pirate's Alley. A nice eclectic bookstore, the kind it is increasingly difficult to find in urban areas. Unlike the mass-produced Borders, their bookstore has character. Characters are a penny a dozen in New Orleans, but **character**, one of the secret ingredients of the city, is in dwindling supply. The briefcase was a gift from Tom Dent, so I assume whatever is inside can expect to be protected. My assumption is verified when I place three dry books on the circulation counter at the library.

Rain. Water in Kampala, Kiev, Katmandu, Kent, Kansas, the whiskey stills of Kentucky– all the K-places. *We are preoccupied with water.* Rosemary James notes as much in her introduction for *My New Orleans.* The twenty-nine authors who contributed essays, poems, and sketches to this post-Katrina collection give us many clichés and a few insider insights about the Crescent City. Despite the laid-back habits of native New Orleanians, the city was never the Big Easy in a literal sense. The city is merely relatively large (measured against other towns in Louisiana), and it was easy only in and on the eyes of tourists. The second line always saw the other side of town. Ethnic coexistence in this city never was and never will be easy. I have never liked the moniker **Big Easy**. It sounds like the title of a hardboiled detective novel. **Crescent City** acknowledges that we have a peppercorn of respect for cartography. At any rate, the contributors tell us about nasty water, magic, Creoles, community, characters, Mardi Gras krews, Tchoupitoulas Street, the cuisine, a cassaway, the Columns Hotel, a Yoruba orixa, pungent air, and why New Orleans musicians can be impersonated but not duplicated. Not one writer, however, mentions one of the great living testimonials in the city: the homeless lady on the corner of Canal and S. Claiborne. If Troy Andrews can "immortalize" Orleans and Claiborne on a CD, some writer should immortalize the lady. She is an emblem of urban survival pre- and post-Katrina. She epitomizes why New Orleans still exists. In this city, people do not die until they choose to do so. That, however, is a delicate theological point that must be handled somewhere.

Each time I see the lady on the corner, she seems to be confident, dignified, Spartan. She does not beg. She is a negative, an undeveloped photograph. She keeps her earthly belongings in two neat bundles, bundles that stand next to her like bales. She is black. Her clothing is black or grey or the color of accumulated grime. In all seasons she is prepared for eviction or evacuation. Summer and winter, she is layered in dark clothing. I wonder that a person layered in so much clothing does not suffer heat stroke. She does not smile. Poverty does not smile. Her plump face is clean and stoic, marked by resignation to things as they are. She has seen much. She has stories of the New Orleans that was, that is. We do not know if she will ever tell her stories. She may have legitimate reasons for keeping them under wraps. She is the epitome of something for which I have not found a name. That something entwines survival with spirituality. It is an unlicensed caduceus. One day the corner will be empty. She and her unarticulated stories will have disappeared. Perhaps, despite the absence of her sign, the something she symbolizes will be remembered, will be collected as a ballad to the Crescent City.

Dinner and conversation with Kalamu ya Salaam at the Marigny Brasserie is the most pleasant experience of the day. The Marigny is upscale. Neither lunch nor dinner is cheap. But who can worry about bargains in New Orleans?
The poor, of course.
But the poor have not returned to the city in large number, and those with comfortable incomes really do not give a damn if they never return.
That is only partially true, and that is why you think so frequently of the homeless lady on the corner of Canal and South Claiborne. You may have a comfortable income, Dr. Ward, but you must recall that you have spent much of your life fleeing from the foibles and mean-spiritedness of the middle class. It is the flight, intensified by your disgust with the glee that some members of your reputed class take in condemning the poor for being poor, as they aggressively support all the ideological mechanisms that perpetuate poverty worldwide... it is the flight that agonizes you. So, when the psychologist tells you the "giant inside wishes to break out," he is telling you (without knowing very precisely what he is telling you) that the futile aspects of your lifelong flight are calling in the chips.
That is not the way Kalamu and I talk about the conditions of now. Our speculations are generally substantive; they are based on public data.

And if the two of you were as clever as you think you are, you would be more skeptical about the reliability of data.

It is not about us. The sad condition of our planet is the damnation of all classes; it is a signal that the American Empire shall gnash its teeth.

That is a laughable conclusion, my friend. Humorous but not convincing.

Friday, May 5, 2006: CINCO DE MAYO.

The Commander-in-Grief has made us tough. He put the possibility to love in a body bag.

At today's Jazz and Heritage Festival [Week 2, Day 1] you tried a Cuban sandwich, and you did not resist getting a Southern Comfort mojo daquiri and a rum praline. The sandwich was tasty but not extraordinary. The daquiri did precisely what it was intended to do. The praline delivered sweet satisfaction. You are disappointed by the music you sampled today. The Brooks Family Project was loud and lively in the Jazz Tent; they were followed by Jeremy Davenport who plays a good trumpet but who should avoid singing. Stephanie Jordan, whose wonderful notes and almost-too-perfect articulation of syllables captures the ear, was best in her tribute to the late Shirley Horn– it was "Here's to Life". In general, her singing does not make it to the level of memorable interpretation– the bar set by Cassandra Wilson, Betty Shirley, Diane Reeves, Carmen McRae. Ms. Jordan is undeniably beautiful; today her profile is one that would have inspired Degas to do some of his very best work in sculpture. Would that her ability to truly do something to a song matched her physical beauty. Marva Wright's competent shouting drove you to the Southern Comfort daquiri. Koko Taylor usually gives you hard, whiskey-flavored blues; today all she serves is a watery martini. Even the opening remark about her entrance– **She's coming with either her black drawers on or no drawers**– falls flat. She came in silver lame. All that was once gold is reverting to base metal.

Saturday, May 6, 2006: An Interview

Kalamu ya Salaam came to my hotel room shortly after 9:00 a.m. to videotape an interview about the idea of community in New Orleans. The interview is a pleasant conversation, a typical example of how easily Kalamu and I can weave our various ideas into whole cloth. There is much agreement about New Orleans having become a place of agony as a result of the "community" we assumed would last forever coming to a halt in August 2005. Kalamu mentions inertia. The train has stopped but the passengers continue to move in the direction the train was headed. I admit that we will try to continue pre-Katrina social bonding in the city, but the city of the future will be such that multiple problems will retard the velocity of bonding. We talk about why New Orleans unlike Atlanta has not recognized itself as an international city. For most of the people who lived here, it was an international destination parallel to some islands in the Caribbean that are international tourist destinations. That is what Kalamu believes. The business community in New Orleans seems very much aware of the international potential. The ordinary citizen is blind to such potential, blind and content if things appear to be looking as they looked in the past. The more I talk, the stronger becomes my sense of the city's retrogression. The telling of bald lies about how fabulous and magical our recovery is. That is tourist garbage. We haven't recovered a damn thing. We are making something new that seems to be old, but it is just not "The Real Thing" as Henry James portrayed it. We talk about our late friend Tom Dent, who was so pivotal in our lives, and the need for people from New Orleans to travel, to see more of the world in order to be appropriately critical of their birth city. The musicians did it. Kid Ory was in Chicago when he sent for Louis Armstrong, for example. Andrew Young, a native New Orleanian, gained credibility in the Deep South as a result of his work in civil rights, and he was excellently positioned to continue what Maynard Jackson started, in nurturing Atlanta into international stardom. No native daughter or son has so blessed New Orleans by way of making the little people in the city aware of their international importance. Kalamu and I have both traveled. He has traveled more than I. We ask ourselves where is New Orleans in relation to Abuja (Nigeria) or Tokyo or Athens. We do not ask self-consciously. Comparisons are automatic, almost instinctual. If our talk means nothing to the larger world, that is OK. We refresh our bonds to each other and our links to New Orleans by way of talk. Our post-Katrina survival is our priority.

After our interview, I walk with Kalamu back to his car on Girod Street. He tells me that Nicholas Payton has cancelled his gig at Snug Harbor. The morning air is warm. It is a relief from the hotel's air conditioning. I decide to take a walk down Girod. It is a fine morning to reward my eyes with some of the charming remains in the Warehouse District. I see that the NOPD has been busy. Many illegally parked vehicles have traffic tickets. I see the sign that lets me know where National Fruit Flavor, Inc. was once located. Apparently, the company made ORANGE SQUEEZE. I stick my head inside the shell of what might have once been a packinghouse. The gutted space is open to the sky. It looks so inviting, so ready to be photographed.

Our policepeople have more freedom to attend to small crimes now, because the crime rate from January through April has decreased. Police Superintendent Warren Riley has announced that New Orleans is safer than it was before Hurricane Katrina. We had said something about the second line and the Mardi Gras Indians during the interview. And I just happen to see Cherice Nelson, the daughter of the late Big Chief Donald Harrison. She is buying flowers at the open air market. She lost her job at Tulane, so she is now pursing a Ph.D. at UNO. Being inside the tradition, she wants to focus her research on the African aspects of the Mardi Gras Indian phenomenon in New Orleans. Cherice is aware that some indigenous peoples are confused by what African Americans have been doing these many years in calling themselves Indians. The academic world would like to put evidence of African continuity under erasure. I suggest that she has what needs to be said in her head and that she should say some of it at this year's New Orleans Word Festival. I think that the Mardi Gras Indian groups have not had real attention since they were invited to participate in the American Folklife Festival in Washington, D.C. back in 1985.

At the open-air market I buy five tomatoes. They are so red, so firm. They are from a farm near Covington. I have one of them for lunch when I return to the hotel. In a sharp and unfair comparison with yesterday's jazz festival, the tomato must be rated *excellent*.

Sunday, May 7, 2006

Another New Orleans Sunday of obligations conflicting with wishes. My promise to serve as timekeeper for the ACT Mayoral Forum this afternoon at St. Gabriel the Archangel at 3:00 p.m. overrides my desire to catch some early acts at Jazz Fest [Week 2, Day 3]. I can only catch the end of Jazz Fest, the closing hour. Were I able to erase all sense of political, social, and civic responsibilities, I would have a happy life of chilling with the vibes. I could repeat yesterday's experience of attending a cookout at my cousin Joyce's house in LaPlace. Just family members and neighbors eating and drinking and talking trash on a hot Saturday afternoon. Such experiences are necessary but momentary escapes. Too soon I am thrown to the ground by obligation. Yes, I have to be a witness of the early days of how corporate politics accomplished the removal of African Americans to clear space for a new New Orleans.

Prepare your notes for tomorrow's class discussions. Send an abstract to the Faculty Resource Network at NYU for a paper you want to present at the Seventh Annual National Symposia. Discard the papers and newspapers you do not need. Your hotel room will make a better presentation of itself. Respond to the email from Robert Butler. Buy the Times-Picayune. Try to purchase a copy of James Materson's The Search for the Real Self at a bookstore.

Listen, imp, I am not sugar on the floor.

No, you are no sugar. You are black pepper, and most of your options are six feet underground.

Thus, the other voice, the italicized me, provides copious backtalk in my mind. I am prepared to think the other voice is a work of fiction.

I enjoyed serving as timekeeper at the ACT Mayoral Forum this afternoon. Neither Ray Nagin nor Mitch Landrieu shall remember who I am; they shall remember confronting a stern timekeeper at one forum.

Monday, May 8, 2006

Stefan Wheelock mentioned on Saturday how enthralled cutting-edge scholars seem to be with Slavoj Žižek's outpourings on Lacan and abstruse matters of representation and interpretation. Stefan resists the temptation to trot behind the latest academic fashions of thought. If I taught Stefan one valuable lesson, it is to be grounded. I am well pleased that his pursuit of scholarship is grounded by questions about the ultimate significance of scholarly productions. We are, all of us, components of a mega-ideological machine. Some of us are less dependent, thank God, on external help to liberate ourselves from the mechanical. We maximize how organic we can be.

Tuesday, May 9, 2006

"Why is it that any technological and scientific achievement reached in the Middle East region is translated into and portrayed as a threat to the Zionist regime? Is not scientific R&D one of the basic rights of nations?"
Mahmoud Ahmadinejad's diplomatic letter to George Bush

You had a very rewarding conversation this morning with Carolyn Vance Smith regarding the planning for the NLCC outreach activities for 2007 and for the 19ᵗʰ annual Natchez Literary and Cinema Celebration that will focus on Richard Wright in 2008. The conversation highlighted, on the other hand, certain difficulties you have in functioning well under the post-Katrina cloud. You are still capable of generating good ideas, but your ability to execute them has slowed down considerably.

You will at some point have to write about New Orleans as an allegory. That is why you picked up Josh Cohen's Spectacular Allegories: Postmodern American Writing and the Politics of Seeing *at the Tulane Library after your visit with Dr. Marshall Lee. It is all very corny, but this New Orleans allegory has footnotes, and the feet that make the footnotes wear shoes. In short, the personifications of abstractions in the case of New Orleans are embodied, not verbal.*

You had lunch today at Tulane University. You ordered a wheat bagel and small coffee at PJ's Coffee at the plaza nearest Freret and McAlister. Your modest lunch cost three dollars less than it would have at the Hilton New Orleans Riverside Hotel. Lunch was pleasant, especially your visiting, after a long absence, with Rosemund Tuve's Allegorical Imagery. *There is something quaint about your post-Katrina habit of making friends with animals and inanimate objects. Your behavior is a candidate for investigation. An undergraduate passes under the breezeway. He sneezes. He sounds like an unidentifed species of duck.*

Wednesday, May 10, 2006

Why is Paul Rusesabagina being smeared as a criminal in the Rwandan press? And precisely what is a Hutu *de service*? Are there Tutsi *de service* behind this campaign to paint Rusesabagina as a false hero? Who is oiling the machinery of *Fortuna*? What lessons here have to be applied in political analysis regarding elections and day-by-day recovery efforts in New Orleans? Questions have become my enemies.

> **Our chicken, that art in the oven, baked be thy name.**
> **Thy doom has come, our will is done**
> **in the kitchen as it is on the table.**
> (a poor man's blessing)

A meeting this evening regarding the future of one Catholic school in New Orleans has only worsened my fears about what the Archdiocese is promoting in the city. It is very widely known that the Catholic Church is very comfortable with racism and that a few members of the clergy and an overwhelming number of professed Catholic laymen and laywomen are tainted with the diabolic dye of racism. Some American Roman Catholics accommodate these givens with ease. They simply believe in God and ignore the human manifestations of the Holy Mother Church. Holy Mother's prelates are too often what and where they ought not be. When her prelates begin to play games of Martian chess, using human lives as pawns, one does not need a terminal degree in theology to know something is awry in the practice of religion. Perhaps as some believe, Katrina was trying to serve notice. From what my eyes hear and my ears see, Katrina failed dreadfully.

Thursday, May 11, 2006, 3:05 a.m.

I am still desperately seeking ways to write in front of the day rather than behind it. Perhaps if I should abandon my sense of time, I might suceed. On third thought, that would not work out well. I would never know what I was behind or in front of. As I grow older, minute by minute, and become more tolerant of accidents and by-accidents, I appreciate very much more what infants can teach us about the blessings of life.

Friday, May 12, 2006

Uncoordinated Contents of Memory

Quite often, you have no recollection of what the note you find on a piece of paper is about.

St. Katherine Drexel, founder of the Sisters of the Blessed Sacrament for Indians and Colored People. 1915.

Is the note a reminder that the good nuns did little for people of no color?

Quite often you have no recollection of what was swirling in your mind as your hand and a pencil left the note on the page. On the same page you find "Beauty is a dunghill covered with snow" and "Complete essay on Pinter's speech." A saint, beauty, and Harold Pinter– go figure.

As you drove up to Vicksburg yesterday, you remembered fire. Walter Barnes, a clarinet and saxophone player and a band leader, was born in Vicksburg in 1907. He died in the famous Rhythm Club fire on April 23, 1940. How did Richard Wright transform the newspaper reports about the fire when he wrote *The Long Dream*?

A Truth Conceived on a Highway

In his youth he was naive. He believed people meant what they said. He believed there was a one-to-one mapping between words and intention or deeds. Even during his early college years, before he developed the capacity for cynicism, he thought that when Ruby and the Romantics sang "Our Day Will Come," something of a bright future was being promised. Had he listened more carefully to Ray Charles, he would have known Ruby was like a dream, never really what she seemed. The magic day he longed for went without ever coming. It is unfortunate when a male does not know at the age of seven that lyrics are only musical lies. His adult life becomes a difficult row to plow.

Saturday, May 13, 2006

365 Days in New Orleans: Katrina's smoldering comment

Yes, they live carnival each day of the year. Without carnival, they would have no reason for living. No, as far as I know, they do not have King Cake for breakfast. Robust and full-bodied, a cup of Community coffee sends their days off in the right direction. In this weird city, the hours criss-cross and double-cross as the spirits of the first line regain their blood and flesh in the second line. For a New Orleanian, merely walking down the street to make groceries is a parade. He or she is quick to manufacture an excuse to celebrate. In this city, parades and pretenses constitute the normal. Excess is normal. One might suppose that a sequel to *Da Vinci Code* might be shot in New Orleans under the title *The Secret Life of Christ*. It would be easy to bribe the Archbishop to ban the film and thereby increase sales at the box office. It will not be necessary to bribe the Archbishop. People in New Orleans are too weary to care very much about what nonsense Hollywood projects on a screen. They have to conserve energy for carnival.

People in New Orleans do not wait for Mardi Gras to display their pretended and real insanity. They act out absurdity on a daily basis, paying tribute to the Seven Deadly Sins. After all, the priest in the most convenient confessional will be generous and absolve them at a moment's notice of pride, sloth, gluttony, lust, greed, envy, and wrath. Only a few Protestants in the city dwell upon sin, the serious consequences of sin. Everyone else will honestly admit the only sin in New Orleans is in the skin. Sin is only a tin cup of gin. Without the Seven Deadly Sins, the tourist industry that is so necessary for the city to live would dry up and die. Only here does capitalism thrive on frivolity. New Orleans is a Bower of Bliss that temperance can not destroy. Its interstitial identity is always on time and off the beat.

365 Days in New Orleans: Jonathan Edwards meditates on Katrina's smoldering comment

> The wrath of God is like great waters that are dammed for the present; they increase more and more, and rise higher and higher, till an outlet is given; and the longer the stream is stopped, the more rapid and mighty is its course when once it is let loose. ("Sinners in the Hands of an Angry God")

The water is Lake Ponchatrain. It was dammed and is damned. Katrina knew herself to be God's instrument.

Hurricane Katrina created three outlets: the failure of the 17th Street canal, the failure of the London canal, and the breach of the levee next to the Lower Ninth Ward. In addition, water spewed from the Orleans Avenue canal. Had the Army Corps of Engineers been about its father's business, Katrina would not have created the outlets. Prudence prevents poor performance. But the Army Corps of Engineers did not consult the beavers. The beavers would have gladly taught them the secrets of damming. Rue the day these government employees behaved like

Puritans, believing they knew everything better than Indians. Lackluster in their damming of water, they damned the inhabitants of New Orleans.

New Orleans discovered how rapid and mighty the terror of water can be, for God withdrew His hand from the floodgates and let the city taste disaster. It is deadly for men to imitate God's wrath, for then their feet slid in the slime of sin. Wrath is mine, said the Lord. Men should not stain their hands with arrogance, for it opens the gateway to wrath. Such is the expensive lesson New Orleans learned. From time to time, the angry father decides to drown disobedient, deaf, and disrespectful children.

Sunday, May 14

What you consume and the circumstances under which you consume are important in the healing process. You want the repair of what has been damaged to appear seamless. It is obvious to everyone except you that you want to inhabit fantasy.

You went to Mass at St. Paul's today and found Father Patrick Farrell's Irish accent to be charming. The modulations, the rise and fall of voice, were so charming that you can not report what his sermon was about. Nor can you report accurately what you read today in the Spring 2006 issue of Louisiana Cultural Vistas.

Monday, May 15

Advocates of environmental justice have reason to warn us that landfills for debris have to be carefully located. The Vietnamese community in East New Orleans does not wish to have waste dumped near their homes. The Vietnamese are legal immigrants or naturalized citizens. They have rights. It has taken Mayor Nagin too long to recognize that they have rights which ought not be violated. He has been busy with turning a blind eye toward the influx of illegal immigrants who are helping him and us to make New Orleans ready for rebuilding. All of us— old citizens, new citizens, and non-citizens— are subject to poisons that threaten our genetic futures. Far too little attention has been given to health futures in those areas affected by Hurricanes Katrina and Rita, to the futures of people and the planet.

Tuesday, May 16: Dream Information

Ray Nagin supporters in purple shirts try to console Mitch Landrieu. They tell him, "We are neighbors. We will protect you." On the reverse of the dream, Mitch Landrieu supporters in green shirts try to console Ray Nagin. They tell him, "When the mighty have fallen, we are here to pick them up." My refusal to make sense of this dream puts me in deepest voodoo. But what the hell. My soul has always survived burnings. And a dream is only a dream, isn't it?

Wednesday, May 17

I believe Tom Piazza's *New Orleans Matters* has great insights. I will not read the book yet. I will not read the book until I have finished writing *The Katrina Papers*. I do not want Tom's words to incite me to think in ways that are imitative. I shall derive my own insights from the source. As Ishmael Reed suggested many years ago, if you are going to practice voodoo, you should be clever enough to make your own stuff.

Thursday, May 18, 2006

Home delivery of mail resumed today at 1928 Gentilly Blvd. The postperson delivers a large batch of election propaganda and only three pieces of what I think is necessary mail.

We have dinner this evening at Gumbo Shop (630 Saint Peter Street). Kalamu was supposed to meet me for our weekly intellectual meal, scheduled for 6:00 p.m., but he had not shown up by 6:15. I ordered my dinner and ate in reflective silence. The seafood okra gumbo bears a slight resemblance to what my mother used to cook. Katrina has not destroyed my ability to have fond memories. The next time I eat at Gumbo Shop, I shall try a cup of Gumbo Z'Herbes. As I leave the restaurant, I notice what is printed on a tee shirt hanging in a window across the street: JESUS LOVES YOU. EVERYONE ELSE THINKS YOU ARE AN ASSHOLE. It is funny to read such a message in the vicinity of St. Louis Cathedral. It was funnier still to have seen a hoary artist with magenta hair sitting in front of the cathedral. Extremes. Preach to me of extremes.

Kalamu phones me at 7:05. He is at Gumbo Shop. I am on the levee, watching the river. He had forgot at what time we were supposed to eat. We have our conversation at a fast-food Chinese joint as Kalamu makes do with fried rice, orange juice, and pound cake, a far cry from the alligator sauce piquante or crawfish remoulade he might have chosen earlier. It does not matter very much. Our conversation is better than food, better than the drugs my psychologist might suggest I take to retard depression. We talk about schooling today, after I proudly inform him that Dillard University will give an honorary degree to Mary Frances Berry.

Friday, May 19, 2006

I am up early this morning, and I sign the Southern Poverty Law Center petition to President Bush. He needs to be reminded, in the words of the petition, that large "corporations involved in the Katrina reconstruction process are getting rich while immigrants doing the dirty clean-up work are getting cheated. Federal agencies with the power to intervene are dragging their feet." Above my signature appears the sentence: "I urge you to order FEMA, the Department of Labor, and OSHA to ensure that Katrina workers are treated fairly."

> Estamos reclamando, nada más, los derechos que todos mercecen.
> **Si, Jorge. You are seeking the right to be paid,**
> **You want more than water for lunch**
> **and heartache for dinner.**
> **You do not want dried blood in your nose**
> **and broken promises in your pocket.** Si, Jorge.
> Estamos reclamando los derechos.
> **Si, Jorge. Si.**
> **Reclaim your humanity.**

I must reexamine what I have signed before mailing it. I have actually signed a "PERSONAL REPLY MEMO" to Morris Dees, Southern Poverty Law Center, thanking him [as the representative of the entity SPLC, I suppose] for standing up against abuse and injustice. Now here are the rules of the game. If I really want to stand with him and support him and the Center in this important new human rights struggle, I am to enclose a special contribution in the amount of _____. The minimum I can check is $50. Given the enormous expenses I have, in trying to recover in New Orleans, I do not have surplus funds to make such contributions. Perhaps not enclosing a check means I am **sitting in** rather than **standing with**. So be it. I shall make the historical gesture of sitting in, of reminding myself ironically that, more than fifty years ago, sitting in was a creative action to promote civil rights. As I seal the envelope that shall return the signed memo without contribution to Morris Dees, I think of my ancestors who were not helped by the intervention of federal agencies, who were indeed cheated of their citizenship rights with the blessings of federal agencies. How right it seems that in order to become real Americans these immigrant workers should taste the lash of injustice. Abuse is at the very core of the ritual of Americanization. Dysphoria.

Saturday, May 20: Mayoral Runoff

Having worked as an election commissioner at the polls from 5:30 a.m. to 8:46 p.m., I am tired when I return to the hotel. Performing an act of civil duty has rewards that only the performer can appreciate. One of them is a peculiar sense of neutrality: I have no passionate feelings for any political camp or krewe. Neutrality is the Marie Laveau factor in the voodoo politics of NOLA old and new. To hell with the empty promises and the slogans that insult anyone with more than a fourth grade education. Watch the track records; watch the process.

By 11:10 when I am writing this, it is obvious that Ray Nagin has 52% of the votes and Mitch Landrieu has 48%. Nagin will have four more years to either succeed or fail in accomplishing his **Republican/Democrat** pledges to ordinary citizens and to the business community. In his triumphant speech, Nagin beams on the television screen, stretching forth his hand and inviting unification just as Ethiopia has done for centuries. His speech resonates like a Baptist sermon. His supporters can toast and boast with glee. During the party, Nagin and Spike Lee (according to the television reporter) are having private talks.

The Landrieu supporters who had gathered at the Hilton New Orleans Riverside Hotel to celebrate a victory are compelled to celebrate a defeat. They are somber as Landrieu delivers a remarkably dignified concession speech. They celebrate stoically, as if small traces of hemlock flavor their drinks. They are neighbors in sadness, appropriately mourning the fall of their **Democrat/ Republican** champion.

Marie Laveau has indeed decided the election, and she decided in favor of destroying the security of racially-painted binary oppositions and of party affliations. She unleashed the loas of Mamon. She has also decided that, for the near future, politics and life in New Orleans will be determined by money, money, money. I shall sleep well tonight, for I know that Papa LaBas and the voters have opened the portals for a season of chaos. My neutrality is not to be equated with inactivity. Indeed, I shall have to double or triple efforts to put money in my wallet.

May 21, 2006: AN EVENING MOMENT

On the Riverwalk. Woman. Speaking. Expounding. Petitioning.
Addressing the Mississippi River. "I am better than you people."
Woman. Green eyes. Contact lens green.
Woman. Proclaiming. "I forgive. I always forgive. That's why Clem's wife is alive."

Speaking. On the Riverwalk.
Woman. Her hair mimics her words— wild, free in the wind, flame-coloured.
A flame. No. Just wild.

Water mocks speech
Speech on the rocks.
Rocks be silent. Rocks be still.

Wind kisses irony.
Words. I forgive. I always forgive.
"Me too," the river smiles. "Me too."

May 22, 2006: The Splitting

I first saw invisibility in Canada many years ago. While I was sampling exhibits at the expo in Montreal, I stopped in the little darkened theater to see the split-screen. Placid water was projected on the left-hand screen. On the second screen, perhaps three or six feet to the right, the bottom of a boat sits on the water. What is the point of disconnecting the water from itself? What is the point of splitting the screen? Suddenly, a hand holding a pink flower appears on the right-hand screen. The hand moves, tossing the flower upward. The flower moves upward and off the screen. My eye follows it trajectory into the darkness of the theater. A few seconds later, the flower begins its slow descent on the left, floating downward and making a silent splash in the water. Ah, the wonders of twentieth-century cinema technology. My eye has been seduced into following a path that does not exist. My eye did not have the pleasure of being so fooled again until I saw the movie *Close-Up*. There the tennis ball did not exist either, but with the help of sound I followed its moves back and forth over the net that did not exist. One point of splitting the screen was to make the absent palpable, to train our eyes to see the invisible.

Deja vu kicked me like an angry mule this morning as I looked at the front page of *The Times-Picayune*. On the left side of the page above the headline "Nagin upbeat after win," there is the color profile of a serene Nagin, eyes closed with a mysterious smile, holding the hand of a choir member at St. Peter Claver Church. Under the headline "FBI details Jefferson's dealings" on the right side of the page is a smaller-than-passport-sized, three-quarter shot of Representative William Jefferson. His mouth is slightly downturned, his eyes staring off into the unknown. My eyes play a wicked trick. Nagin's smile travels across the page into the vicinity of Jefferson's anguish. On the front page of the Sunday *Times-Picayune*, the same split layout was used. Under the very bold-fonted headline **IT'S NAGIN,** a four-column photograph of a broadly smiling Nagin upstages the small, somber photo of Jefferson that would be reprinted with a darker shadow today. The blunt headline reads "FBI raids Jefferson office in D.C." I wonder why I did not experience deja vu yesterday. Perhaps I did not then want to set the ugliness of the invisible in motion, because it would have suggested that a triumphant Nagin was laughing at the unwise choices that put Jefferson in the spotlight of shame. The technique of the visual split, whether in cinema or newspaper, encourages us to, at once, see and think of what is not there, very much not there. The layout editor at *The Times-Picayune* is clever. Readers in New Orleans will **see** a major difference in the political styles and fortunes of Nagin and Jefferson; they will **think**, however, how similar the two men are as the thorny crown of suspicion is forced down on their innocent-until-proven-guilty heads. This is better than a Greek tragedy. I feel a moment of pity and fear, and then I feel absolutely nothing. The ideological hegemony of the visual does the nation's dirty work.

Thursday, May 25, 2006.

Magazine Street. People once lived here, had normal lives here. When you listen to your friend Chakula describe his days on Magazine Steeet and his heroic efforts to keep the banana plants from dominating his backyard, as he puts his seventh spoon of sugar in his mug of coffee, you have visions of community and humorously coded conversations. Even before Katrina, commerce had succeeded in displacing residents with antique shops and God-knows-what speciality stores. Magnolia Street is a merciless reminder that in our country and in our cities property and profit are more highly valued than people.

Today you have a mission. You must drive to the Afro-American Book Stop (3951 Magazine) to purchase Harold Clark's first novel, *Chummy's Spirit*. The novel costs $16.95. The tax costs $1.53. You hand the clerk, Vicky, a twenty-dollar bill and two quarters. She gives you cash credit (in plainer days one might have said "change") in the amount of $2.02. The cash credit is not enough to purchase lunch from the salad bar at Sav-A-Center supermarket. God is good. As you walk toward the store, an elderly lady says, "Sir, did you drop this?" She scoops up a five-dollar bill from the asphalt and extends it to you. "I might have. I am capable of such things," you reply. Thank you, Lord, for sending lunch.

Kalamu ya Salaam brings me a CD of music by the New Zealand group MT Raskil Preservation Society, featuring vocals by Hollie Smith. The group has mastered the tempo and colorings, the exquisite sincerity, the voice rhythms, the insider-inflections of the African Diaspora vocal performance. Kalamu loves what they have succeed in doing. So do I. Despite objections from cultural anthropologists and others, I am convinced that the indigenous peoples of New Zealand are descendents of a very early dispersal from the continent of Africa. The Genome Project has not yet identified the gene that allows Africans, however dissimilar their cultural evolutions have been, to know when they are listening to kinfolk. Such a gift is an indication of how important my weekly dinner conversations with Kalamu are for my healing process.

Friday, May 26, 2006

THIS MORNING:

Had an intense and productive conference call with Tom Piazza and Jack

Davis about the *Rebirth: People, Places, and Culture in New Orleans* conference and the panel on which Tom, Irvin Mayfield, and I will address the topic "What Makes Community?" Our conversation was an undressed rehearsal for what we will say on Wednesday, May 31, at Tulane University. Tom and I were on a panel earlier this year at Xavier, so we are "known quantites" to one another. I enjoy bouncing my skeptical pessimism off of Tom's objective optimism. I can't predict how that literary working relationship will be altered by Irvin. I have had any number of pleasant conversations with Irvin, and I did serve on the advisory board for the Institute of Jazz Culture he established at Dillard University. I do sense that Irvin's savvy and musical genius will help us to turn up the volume.

Unsent email to Kalamu:

Dear Kalamu,

I usually do not comment on dialogues regarding what ignorant white poets say about brilliant black poets, and I try to get on with encouraging the literary historical documentation that exposes Billy Collins and his ilk. In this instance, Professor Daphne Muse's personal witness regarding Hayden's personality struck me and forced me to recall that an Army buddy and I (we were stationed at Fort Knox) had to defend Hayden at a conference in Louisville when very militant young black men verbally crucified him. Hayden was grateful for our intervention; we spent a pleasant hour in conversation with him, a simple act of trying to help a black man and artist who had a more global vision of being-in-the-world than many of his contemporaries. We respected his right to be different. I thank Professor Muse for reminding us that understanding African American literature demands our close reading of both Robert Hayden and John Oliver Killens.

Peace,

Jerry

A computer malfunction prevented my sending this message for the dialogue on Billy Collins's remark that Hayden did not write about race. It is less than amazing that writers who write exclusively about the white race are exceptionally blind to the fact that writers who write about the human race are writing about race.

Just finished a half-hour conversation with Dave Brinks. I agreed to introduce him at the booksigning for *Caveat Onus* on June 8. This is very much a day of manufacturing ideas. The red message button is blinking on the hotel phone. Exodie Roe, one of the most brilliant of this year's seniors at Dillard University, has called me about a critical matter that involves our fraternity. I listen very cautiously to his explanation. The case he describes is not simple. It is very complicated, involving, as it does, the century-long history and endangered ideals of our fraterity, convoluted legal considerations, Roe's frustrations, and my fraternal uncertainties. Surviving Katrina's aftermath is marked by a daily layering of new problems. This case, which is to be subjected by the University to a rehearing at 4:00 p.m., is a new problem. After I finish my conversation with Mr. Roe, I immediately call the father of another student who, like Roe, is being threatened with suspension. The content of this conversation is privileged, because I invoke the construction that can be placed on my talking with a friend who is a lawyer, one of my fraternity brothers, and the father of one of the undergraduates accused of misbehavior, namely being present while potential fraternity brothers were hazed. Lord, why do You send me new problems that I am powerless to resolve?

THIS AFTERNOON:

I walk from the Hilton to have lunch at the Catty Car Corner (1340 Poydras Street). To give my body some respite from what feels like an eon of unhealthy food at various New Orleans restaurants and cafes since January, I decide to have the vegetable plate. That is a better choice than the Fried Shrimp Plate or the Fried Catfish w/Crawfish Sauce. As I wait in line to pay for my meal, I talk briefly with Carolyn Harrison, a lady who stayed in the Vicksburg shelter with me during the first two weeks in September 2005, about evacuation plans for the coming hurricane season. As we wish one another a blessed day and a good weekend, the pleasant sensation of comradeship evelopes my body. I do hope my body appreciates the message.

I check for mail at my Dillard office. There is none. I now find myself walking to the main post office on Loyola to mail a contract to Cambridge University Press. Halfway there a very short Latino asks me for a cigarette and for directions about how to get to I-10. He needs to go to Biloxi, Mississippi. Some employer there has not paid him. The man is weary. He tells me he is thirsty. He needs water. I don't have a bottle of water in my briefcase to give him. He says he is hungry. His eyes tell me he is not lying. And even if his eyes are lying to me, it does not matter. My evil angel says he is playing me for a fool. My good angel utters one word—charity. I listen to my good angel, reach into my wallet and give the man five dollars. "This will help you get food, amigo." He thanks me. In a reflex action, my hand touches his cap as I say "God bless you." As I am leaving the post office, Lolis Eric Elie drives up. We have a heartwarming chat. I jokingly tell him not all of my friends can afford to drive a new convertible. He replies that I should select better friends. "All of your friends should be able to afford a new car. It is very affordable when it is six years old." An unexpected meeting of a friend who writes for the *Times-Picayune* is so New Orleans. He says we should break bread soon. I suggest he should join his father, Ernest Jones, and me for one of our always delightful Saturday morning breakfasts at Le Richelieu.

As I walk back to the hotel, interesting thoughts accumulate. Perhaps the little Latino was Jesus Christ. Perhaps he was Christ testing how genuine my humanity, to say nothing of my Roman Catholicism, is. I remember that, yesterday, five dollars magically appeared for my lunch. Perhaps I actually passed on to one of my brothers in need God's gift to me. One question remains: would I have performed the same act of charity for a North American? *The K Moment* has left indelible stains on my life. Eric's witty remark about what people should be able to afford occasions a flashback. Did Tom Piazza not say this morning that many people are secretly glad that the poor will not be able to return to the city and that crime will diminish?

The K Moment (a mixture of melancholy and joy) is part of an evolving local vocabulary. The new New Orleans lexicon will include *hurrication* (a hurricane vacation) and *traumaticalize*. We may also begin to speak of people who have been FEMAed by the Federal Excuse Making Agency. It is doubtful that these nonce words and phrases have any agency beyond the borders of New Orleans. The historicized cant of survivors rarely does. And termites are repairing the roof of the Superdome.

THIS EVENING
Those of us who make our beds in New Orleans have learned to sleep soundly on the surface of water.

May 27, 2006: Corruption Must Have Style

Is it at all appropriate to mention that Glenn Haydel, former New Orleans Mayor Marc Morial's uncle, admitted in U. S. District Court that he stole slightly more than half a millon dollars when he managed the Regional Transit Authority? Yes, if one mentions the Enron scandal and the harm caused by Enron founder Kenneth Lay's commission of bank fraud and the help he received from Jeffrey Skilling. Skilling and Lay invested almost $70 million in their defense. And Skilling had to post a $5 million bond to be free. Haydel is a candidate for membership in the exclusive club to which Lay and Skilling belong. These men have invaluable lessons to teach the youth of America.

In the culture of corruption, it is easy to segregate the little fish from the big fish. The big fish steal enormous sums from investors and the American public. The little fish are only capable of stealing small amounts of money from the American public and blue-collar workers. The amount of money Haydel diverted and the amount Representative William Jefferson is alleged to have handled in the iGate episode is paltry in comparison to the fortunes salted away by crooks at the pinnacle of American free enterprise. New Orleans is full of little fish who swim poorly in little ponds. A corporate or political thief who steals less than $200

130

million is either lazy or brain-damaged or not well informed that, in the twenty-first century, theft must be committed with elitist decorum and objective absence of conscience. We must reduce the magnitude of stealing by petty thieves. If we ever create a world class school system in New Orleans, students should not be allowed to graduate until they successfully pass a course in the etiquette of corruption. And that course should be a model for public schools nationwide.

Sunday, May 28, 2006

I am eating Graham crackers. Ralph Waldo Emerson did not give a public lecture on Graham crackers. He did allude in one essay, however, to the Mr. Graham for whom the crackers are named.

The Filmworks: Entering Another's Dream of One's Own

In Issue #1 of *Black Film Review* (December 1984), David Nicholson wrote:

> Watching film is akin to dreaming. It is also a shared experience. We share a space with other watchers, and we enter another's dream– that of the filmmaker. If the film is to reach us (in other words, if we are to enter the dream created for us) it must be accessible: we must share the reality upon which it is based, or be convinced to do so.

I am watching *Juice* (Paramount/Island World 1992) featuring Omar Epps, Jerman Hopkins, Samuel L. Jackson, and Queen Latifah. I am watching parts of the film as it replays in my memory of the film. This activity is not dreaming. This sharing is real. My mind is sharing visual memory with my brain.

Memorial Day, May 29, 2006

I came up to Vicksburg to get some writing done, but a "spell of sickness" has forced me to abandon those plans. A stomach virus I think. My limbs ache. My body alternates between being too hot and uncomfortably chilled. I volunteer to remain in bed most of the day. I let the cell phone charge all day; I am in no mood to chat on the telephone. I feel dehydrated. I get only a modicum of relief from drinking water and cranberry juice. It is almost 9:00 p.m. before I feel strong enough to drive down to New Orleans. I do not like this dramatic announcement that I need to get more rest.

Tuesday, May 30, 2006 4:51:14 p.m.

The effects of the "spell of sickness" have diminished, but you don't chance having breakfast. You have a session with the psychologist at 11:00 a.m. and do not want to have to say "Excuse me" in mid-sentence as he eggs you on. Manners cling to you like barnacles on a pier, like rust on water-logged iron.

I do have a wheat bagel and coffee for lunch. Lunch and breakfast are interchangeable; so too are opinions and facts in the chaotic dynamics of everyday life. The mental tennis matches with the psychologist become more intense each week, so I take a nap when I return to the hotel to regain some energy. Dozens of volleyball players are checking in and checking out of the hotel. It must be a relief to be away from one's home and free of worry about hurricanes. Ten months ago, I enjoyed such freedom.

I will need energy for the AKRI Option III meeting and for the chat President Hughes has planned to inform us about the return to the campus in August. I have never been fond of meetings. In the aftermath of Katrina, my tolerance for meetings is low.

Wednesday, May 31, 2006: REBIRTH: PEOPLE, PLACES, AND CULTURE IN NEW ORLEANS

The three-day conference sponsored by the National Trust for Historic Preservation and Tulane University (Dillard, Xavier, Loyola, and the Preservation Resource Center of New Orleans are co-sponsors) began yesterday with pre-confernce field sessions. One session involved dinner, drinks, and music at selected restaurants, bars, and clubs. In the official letter, dated May 3, 2006, which I received from President Scott Cowan of Tulane and President Richard Moe of the Trust, the gentlemen mentioned the purpose was "[t]o energize and elevate the discussion about the important role arts and culture play in the reconstruction effort." I volunteered to serve on a panel because I wanted to be sure that the "people" component of "culture" did not get short shrift.

This morning, President Scott Cowen opened the day's meetings very effectively; his speech was crisp, concise, and economic. There was special warmth in his introduction of Irvin Mayfield. Irvin, accompanied by Ronald Markham (a mechanical engineer who is also a musician), set a very polished tone for the conference with his discussion of the blues and jazz, his playing of a blues piece, followed by his version of "Yesterday" by the Beatles, followed by a musical demonstration of "the first line" (march to the cemetery, the dirge) and "the second line" (every expanding celebratory return from the cemetery). The last selection underscored his mentioning that his father, who drowned in the flooding of the city, had given him the means to deal with such a tragedy: jazz. Irvin was at his elegant and eloquent best as he prepared the ears of the invitation-only audience. Irvin was very careful in placing his explanations and his playing within the context of American democracy. After his performance, President Cowan introduced Oliver Thomas, councilman-at-large who filled in for Mayor Nagin, and Richard Moe. Moe focused on the work of the Trust with places and cultures. His remarks provided a good opening for Jack Davis, publisher of the *Hartford Courant*, to introduce those who served on the "What Makes Community?" panel: Irvin Mayfield, Tom Piazza, and Jerry Ward.

Tom read from his prepared remarks about community. He said something about black and white that sent up the red flag regarding binary discourses. Had I not early this morning read the phrase "media malfeasance" regarding the coverage of the Katrina disaster? I have no prepared remarks. *I trust improvising.* When Davis asked for my comments, I began by suggesting that Irvin and Tom were very much a part of my community in the city. I noted Irvin's alluding to the blues, to the classic definition provided by Ralph Ellison— running one's finger over the jagged grain of experience. I added, "catching splinters and healing from the injury." I framed the remainder of my remarks with a quotation from *The Katrina Papers*: "Those of us who have made our beds in New Orleans have learned to sleep soundly on the surface of water." Community is about people being interdependent. It consists of relatives, friends who have returned to the city, and friends who are still absent, friends and colleagues at Dillard University. It is about our social communion. Rituals are important. I mention Dave Brinks and his efforts to reunite writers and artists, the October resuscitation of the 17 Poets Series at the Gold Mine Saloon; I mention the March 6 taping by PBS of a special reading in the series. I wanted the audience to know about the most democratic venue for arts in the city. I want them to note that kind of human spirit that Dave nurtures. It is important for us not to get bogged down by the classic oppositions of black and white. I remind the audience that the coverage of Katrina in the first weeks of September 2005 would lead to the idea that no Latinos/ Latinas, no Vietnamese, no Greek-Americans, no Asian-Americans inhabited the city. The media invoked the classic and reductive black/white template, a template that cherishes the black as victim. This habit is not to be tolerated. It will not serve us well in the future.

The audience has a special interest in restaurants and cuisine. I could not resist mentioning that Pampy's on North Broad may lose all of its former pretense to elegance and become an upscale fast-food joint. I emphasize that I am replaying Mr. "Pampy" Barre's remarks on a NPR program. Restaurants have been special sites for eating, for conversations, for political planning. That must be remembered. Food and politics are old friends. I do hope the audience will recall the political implications of what they ate during the pre-conference field sessions.

To recreate a sense of community that will support the rebirth of culture, we must have respect for the multilayered cultures of the city. We can have no respect if we turn our backs on the facts of class tension in the city, the enormous distance between the rich and the poor. Someone mentioned the Aspen Institute during the opening session. I picked that up by noting that those who ski in Aspen may have absolutely no perspective on the lives of successful people, poor and middle class, who lived in the much maligned Ninth Ward. I recounted the attitude of Gentilly Civic Improvement Association residents to a story about having raised five children in the Ninth Ward. Their negative dismissal led me to believe they

would willingly feed rat poison to everyone who formerly lived in the St. Bernard
Project. This genteel audience must hear something that is often unspoken, as
New Orleans puts on a daily Mardi Gras face for the sake of tourism. Tourism
is a vital part of the New Orleans economy, for the majority of the city's revenue
comes from tourism. Nevertheless, I feel a moral obligation to end my remarks
with a strong assertion. Rebirth demands Honesty, an honesty that may never have
existed in New Orleans or in America. *WE MUST STOP DOING WHITEFACE
FOR TOURISTS. THAT KIND OF MINSTRELSY WILL NOT AID THE
RECOVERY PROCESS.*

Irvin followed my remarks with a nicely packaged patriotic message. Jazz
teaches us that democracy is not easy, that we are always in struggle. The life of
community depends on constant stuggle. I confess that what Irving actually said is
now foggy in my memory. I was busy controlling the internal flames my comments
had started. I don't clearly remember what Tom said either. When Tom was
reading, I was pouring gasoline on the smoldering coals of what I planned to say.

I take a break after our panel and have coffee with Tom. He persuades me
that I should hear First Lady Laura Bush's keynote address at 11:30. I return to
Freeman Auditorium, Woldenberg Art Center, to witness the address. I catch the
end of the second panel on "Rebirth of New Orleans's Historic Neighborhoods:
Coming HOME AGAIN!" Kevin Mercadel of the National Trust, New Orleans
Office, is saying something important about sites and creativity, the shotgun house
and jazz. I think of where I write and how the quality of writing is affected. What I
write in a hotel room has a very different flavor from what I write in my Vicksburg
apartment or on the campus of a university where I am a guest. The writing I did at
home, prior to Katrina, was utterly different.

Notes from listening to Mrs. Bush:
Her timing is perfect. She began at 11:35. She ended at 11:55.

She thanks the sponsor for this summit. Cowan is a huge advantage for
New Orleans. Can I crack the code of what she just said? She mentions we have
the 40th anniversary of the National Preservation Act. It is important to protect
America's historical heritage for the next century. These discussions at Tulane
will help promote dialogues during the forthcoming Preserve America Summit. It
helps President Bush's Preserve America Initiative. (I don't want to misread the
code here.) Well-preserved history can revive local tourism. Katrina is a defining
moment in New Orleans culture and history. New Orleans can come back. She
thanks everyone for commitment to presevation.

Her timing is perfect. The measured words of her speech are perfect. I have
witnessed conservative perfection. All the insiders are pleased.

A Loss and A Promise
I opt not to join the participants and audience for lunch, although I regret

not hearing what Brian Williams, anchor for NBC Nightly News, has to say. I have obligations at Dillard, obligations that have much to do with its rebirth! I do plan, however, to attend all the sesssions tomorrow.

At St. Augustine's: 7:00 p.m.

After a rather heady discussion of *King Lear* in our Shakespeare class, I rush to St. Augustine's Church (1210 Gov. Nicholls St.) to see *Maroon: On the Trail of Creoles in North America* by the Quebec filmmaker Andre Gladu. This is the premiere. Gladu and Father Jerome LeDoux were scheduled to be present. Neither was. The film was rather long, but it was an eye-opening painting of rural French Louisiana, the Creole music that links the rural with urban New Orleans, the slow death of a culture. The film causes me to think about departure, refusal, what it might mean to be a maroon after Katrina. The film visualizes much about the role of faith in preservation of community and traditions. The information about a truly Creole Mardi Gras is striking, because a genuine Mardi Gras deals primarily with a people's culture, not their commerce. Wonderful contrast of a people's celebration with the pre-cooked celebration offered up in New Orleans.

Part II: CHTHONIC ENTRIES

Thursday, June 1, 2006: FIRST DAY OF HURRICANE SEASON

"How you be?" Kalamu greeted me and shook my hand as I got into his car in front of the hotel. "Tired from two days of the National Trust conference," I confessed. He gives me another CD of New Zealand music. "And here," I said, "is a copy of the conference program. Let's go to Mama Rosa's. I read somewhere that it's reopened." As we drive to one of the first restaurants where Kalamu and I began our weekly dinner and conversation ritual three years ago, I begin to talk about Andre Gladu's *Maroon.* How impressed I was with Gladu's not looking at the fragile glamor and pretense of New Orleans but at rural Louisiana and the reality of sweat. How much awe there was in seeing the film in St. Augustine Church. It was something of a triumph of the spirit over the machinations of the New Orleans Archdiocese. The showing had something to do with the spirit of the Unknown Slave.

Kalamu tells me he had intended to see the film, but other obligations had to be taken care of. Yes, that is always the case, isn't it? Other obligations. I want to do this but must do that. Frustration has become so comfortable. So normal. This is America. This is New Orleans. This is the new New Orleans produced by hurricane and water. The city is a black line of obligation. As we eat, I give a disjointed report on the conference, a string of moments I remember most clearly. The fine music we had after lunch from Michael White's quartet. Remarks by Ellis Marsalis, David Torkanowsky, and Tom Fitzmorris. A statement by a man named Voltz, about how those who are official city planners are prevented from demonstrating that they are capable of doing their jobs by the stream of outside consultants, whom the city council insists on hiring to produce expensive reports. Reports and dust. Reports gather dust like books of poetry in America. And I was the only person who did a second line dance as the jazz band played at lunch. Kalamu smiles as I talk on and on. He has lived in New Orleans all his life. What he is hearing sounds like a replay of what has always been.

Yes, these weekly dinners inspire me to think and rethink. Kalamu is an "ideal" reader/listener. His is the sympathetic but critical ear to which some words in *The Katrina Papers* address themselves.

Second Day of the Conference

Slept late. Missed Lt. Gov. Mitch Landrieu's talk about "Louisiana's Role in Reviving Cultural Heritage" and the panel on "Striking a Balance: The Important and Delicate Role of the National Critic in Reviewing Cultural Entities in New Orleans." Enjoyed the aliveness of the panel Dr. Michael White moderated on

"Rebirth of New Orleans Music Culture." Most of the panelists agreed that New Orleans was going in the economic black hole long before Katrina. They seemed not to disagree with Ellis Marsalis's idea that musicians depend on people's having disposable income. There was consensus that teaching music in the schools could help young people develop discipline, that music should be put back into the public school curriculum. There was remarkable non-reaction to Marsalis's mentioning that home economics and trades were once important in schooling. There was civil disharmony between Nick Spitzer, the host of *American Routes*, and the pianist David Torkanowsky about the role of money in the preserving of music culture. Will the rebirth of music culture in New Orleans, I wondered, really be the birth of twins?

Walter Isaacson, president of the Aspen Institute, presided over the summarizing panel "Mixing the Gumbo: Reactions and Responses." Isaacson dreams of rebuilding a magical city. What makes community in New Orleans may still be a moot question, but there is no doubt about the necessity of having a good system of public education in the long-term process of rebirth. There must be some balancing of downhome cultures and economics. Diversity in New Orleans culture must be preserved. Restaurants are stablizing elements in neighborhoods. Paradigm shifts will occur in how we think about values in neighborhoods. Tom Fitzmorris's irony-clad remark that outsiders neither think of nor want New Orleans to be a serious city and that insiders should not desire seriousness if they want success in the tourist industry— well, this bit of perverse and perverted irony caused my ears to burn. *Did such a remark come from the whiskey sauce one pours over breadpudding or from a pot of magical gumbo? Poor New Orleans. Damned for being good. Damned for being bad.*

Our lunch was light and refreshing. The final comments by Scott Cowen and Richard Moe were urbane and reassuring. By 2:30 p.m. the conference ended. It succeeded in nurturing optimism about **places** and **culture**. Preservation is probable; rebirth, possible. Handle this credo for the new New Orleans carefully. Double-edged razors must be handled carefully, especially when your hand thinks **people** received insufficient attention.

June 2, 2006: Weather and an Interview

Today was the second day of hurricane season. I barely noticed the ineffective attempt of raindrops to dampen the soil and the concrete of New Orleans.

Joshua B. Guild, a graduate student in history and African American Studies at Yale, interviewed me for almost two hours about New Orleans and the future of historically black colleges and universities in the city. Mr. Guild is amiable. I am relaxed as I talk with him. He asked intelligent questions. I hope I gave him intelligent answers.

June 2, 2006: A FILM IS A MATTER OF CULTURE

He arrived at 7:15 p.m., slightly more than an hour after the event had begun. A few hundred members of the New Orleans Museum of Art had gathered for the preview of the Ansel Adams exhibition. In the crowd he met a person whom he had known for seventeen-plus years. The person has some authority in making funding decisions about the preservation and promotion of Louisiana's cultures. He and the person had both seen Gladu's *Maroon*. Smiling, the person asked him what he thought of the film. Smiling in return, he said he had found the film instructive but too lengthy. It needs cutting. The person agreed. "It was about an hour and a half. It could be reduced to three minutes."

Three minutes! The person offered a salvo of opinions. Gladu did not know what he was looking for. Just got off the bus with a camera. Became fascinated with black people in rural Louisiana who speak French. [*Correction: Some speak French, some speak Cajun, some speak Creole.*] Gladu has no sense of history. Did you see how stupidly he presented history. He did not consult historians or books, just shot pictures. His work is not academic. "Such sloppiness disgusts me." His voiceover explanations are abominations. Gladu does not understand music. He does not understand the refinement of Creoles. What have maroons to do with Creoles anyway? *Gladu's film is an onion. The person was trying to mince it with an ax.*

You, who are he, insist that Gladu deserves some credit. The film was not totally bad. For Gladu, Creoles are people who came to Louisiana from Haiti, and he did frame his thinking correctly by opening with the lighting of candles and the pouring of libation at the Ancient Tree. That is a Haitian gesture. You praise Gladu's interrogation of the very concept of Creole. The term **Creole** is very flexible. Its meaning depends on whom is using the term at what time. Gladu is right to say that very black-skinned people were not accepted as Creoles until after the Civil War, because many who belonged to the third race between black and white rejected them. Gladu's getting the country musicians to talk has value. Those musicians do not think of their continuation of tradition to be a preservation of what is Cajun. It is Creole. *Whether it is good evidence or bad, Gladu's film provides raw material for historians to dissect. The film is not history. It is a lyric odyssey.* You are adamant in your belief that maroons have a lot to do with Creoles. Some maroons, you remind the person, were the parents of Creoles. You must not dismiss genetic fact. A tarbrush is powerful.

The person smiles broadly. "You are very generous. You have a big heart." Our post-Katrina experiences should teach us all to have big hearts. That is what your eyes say without speaking. "Isn't discourse wonderful?" the person asks. "Yes. It helps to think deeply about this matter of what is Creole." *You can see the wounded humor that rides your voice.* Turning in opposite directions, you

138

and the person bid each other good night.

At that moment, the person, whom you have no legitimate reason to hate, reminds you of what you resent about people who think God ordained them high priests of culture. The person reminds you of what you most dislike about the arrogance of some people who live Uptown. Charity demands that you pray as your anestors would have prayed for the person and the neocon priesthood. They must learn that culture is deliquescent.

June 3, 2006

Language. The *DSM* (*Diagnostic and Statistical Manual of Mental Disorders*) or DSM-IV-TR. The superior skill the human brain has in designing desires which the mind allows the body to write, to write with ink, lead, other people's blood or silver nitrate. The images that float across the back of my eyes are like the sculptured photographs of Ansel Adams, a species of saturated brilliance that dazzles when it saunters into view. Perception is capable of complex motions. And deceptions... don't forget the deceptions.

As I reread Chris Rose's article "WHITE FIGHT: Mining the cultural landscape for humor can expose land mines," (*Lagniappe, Times-Picayune,* June 2, 2006) the rightness of the metaphor is like the song of a gnat in the ear. Irony is the dominant flavor in humorous and serious communication about Hurricane Katrina and all that has followed in its wake. The gnat sings a loud truth, a truth about the permanent impossibility of believing anymore that human beings can utter truth. Consider the opening paragraph of Rose's article:

Let me tell you, people: Writing gently nuanced and adroitly astute racial commentary is a thankless task.

That hook does land the fish. Rose, however, is not really interested in fish in this moment of truth-telling. He is interested in warfare. [See www.nola.com/rose]

He wills not to be, in the good Christian sense, a fisher of men, but a reporter on a Civil War battlefield. All racial commentary in America is about the War Between the States, an event that the children of immigrants do not get immediately. The remote kindred of those who migrated to Jamestown in 1619 against their wills get it. The remote kindred of those whom indigenous peoples discovered in 1620 in Plymouth get it. Immigrants just don't get it. Thus, Rose pretends he writes nuanced and astute racial commentary. In actuality, he writes munitions that explode in his face. Why should he believe anyone would thank him for doing that?

Given that Rose participates in the tragic drama of New Orleans, he should know that his gentle and adroit uptown humor is destined to boomerang. In this city, what goes around comes around. Metaphors shaped by the contexts of Vietnam and Iraq do explode in ordinary ways. When Rose suggests that the funky habits of white people should replace the culturally grounded rituals of black New Orleanians, he has become a racial traitor. And it is not even his race that he is betraying. Irony fails. Truth triumphs. Whites who hate blacks recognize that Rose has exposed what they would prefer to keep in the closet. If Rose deserves thanks for anything, it would be for stumbling over the truth. Nevertheless, I find it impossible to thank him and obligatory to school him. Thus, I sent him an email message this evening.

Dear Mr. Rose: Your "White Fight" article made me laugh. Had you known that pre- and post-traumatic disorders in New Orleans are identical, you would have understood why many readers responded to you as if you were an African American male.

Rose and other writers who swim in humor will eventually recognize that if truth lives, it lives at the bottom of the oceans.

June 4, 2006: Post-traumatic Stress Disorder on Pentacost Sunday

According to the bulletin at mass today:

The sending of the Holy Spirit takes place on the Jewish Feast of Pentecost, the harvest festival celebrated fifty days after Passover. The readings from the Jewish scriptures that the Lectionary uses for the Vigil of Pentecost are all present in the background of Luke's account. Luke evokes the tower of Babel from Genesis 11, the fiery appearance of God to Moses on Mount Sinai from Exodus 19, the gift of the spirit in Ezekiel's vision of dry bones, and Joel's prophecy of the spirit being poured out on all flesh. [Copyright 2006, J. S. Paluch Company, Inc., 3708 River Road, Suite 400, Franklin Park, IL 60131-2158, 1-800-621-5197. With Ecclesiastical Approbation.]

It is refreshing that the Roman Catholic Church is at last admitting that it is a pork-eating branch of Judaism.

The color of choice today is red; the saints are wearing red. I am wearing a green shirt and blue trousers. I am not ecclesiastically correct and shall receive neither approbation nor absolution. It is just as well. I'd look funny walking around with a tongue of fire dancing atop my head.

Monday, June 5, 2006: SWAMP NEW ORLEANS: A Meditation on Allen Ginsberg's "Howl"

That's your blood down there in the landfill, your luminous blood mistaken for foxfire. That's your blood dripping from the world's largest clarinet embedded in the side of the Holiday Inn that used to be the Howard Johnson, the site chosen by James Mark Essex for his last stand. Essex is not exactly a hero. He is a dead man, a memory that refuses to die. What Essex was defying was the myth of a society that paints its future backwards. And our blood down here heard Essex howling in the winds of Hurricane Katrina. That's not all that our blood heard. It heard the shrieks of Spanish and French masters and mistresses, their vampire teeth gleaming in the moonlight over the Vieux Carre, fashioning tools to torture their human property into birthing unnatural capital. Human property screams back, spitting ground glass, burning fields of sugar cane, and nuclear bullets. Our blood surreal. The anguish of whites enslaved because they looked too Southern to be white found voice in the tree-breaking August winds, winds that prayed for Bras Coupee, for what chased Buddy Bolden into a fine madness, for the industry that transcends history and boils life down to jazz. The winds prayed that the sin of not being sinful enough would be forgiven. The winds prayed for the sin in the skin. The august wind prays for Chinese drugs in the laundry. That's our blood down here in Swamp New Orleans, here where after the howling abates we elect leaders to conspire with federal demons to blast us with eternal confusion and illusions. Our blood joins the second line with Essex, defying the logic of the river and the cognition of the lake. It digests its Americanness. Our blind blood hears everything. It sees nothing except the fool's gold of a dry future. Swamp New Orleans is not hell, although our deranged blood believes it is. Our blood is determined to stay the course whatever the cost, our blood— our awe-filled creature of habit. Our blood rebuilding, making the old more perfect than the new. Swamp New Orleans is a quite normal trashpile of humanity doing what trashpiles of humanity have done since Time began to measure itself in hourglasses, sundials, clocks, watches. Sunshine, always optimistic, breeds cedar-strong hope and medicinal herbs of beauty. We stay the course because we have no choice. We are, I guess, molecules of myth looking for mythology.

June 5, 2006: Notes on a Minor Epiphany in a Hotel

Under the pressure of globalization, the sense that readers have a shared community of values has disappeared. Globalization is a curse. Why measure literary works by assumed standards of goodness, excellence, or utility? Why have standards? Why, indeed, make gestures of helping groups of people to reach consensus? Do we do so only because we dread chaos? Doesn't practice deconstruct standards and the futility of belief in absolutes? Why should a teacher attempt to be a saint, to maintain faith in a conversation that doubting students no longer believe ever existed?

These questions are acid. I bathe in agony. My flesh slowly dissolves. Soon the skeleton will appear.

As Mr. Lawrence Seagull wrote in his commonplace book, it is obvious that intellectuals and crackpots share a common passion to change things. That is

*where the acid came from. It spewed from the passion. After all these centuries, we
have not yet accepted a fact: the world can not be changed.*

The contemporary university provides enormous opportunities for failure.
Often, teachers who encourage students to imagine what does not exist end up
with remarkable wounds. It is not that they have failed to teach something. The
more quantifiable the information and skills they help students to learn, the closer
they come to having success. Where they fail most remarkably is in the realm of
values. Undone by their own enthusiasm, these well-meaning teachers retreat
for a moment and curse the day. Like holy fools, they never learn. They are at it
again the next day, wounds forgotten, preaching beautiful, empty sermons that
change nothing. The innately thankless and fatally romantic qualities of life, if we
remember anything from Machiavelli, lead to ruin. When teachers attain a grain of
worldly wisdom, they change themselves. They flush compassionate bullshit down
the toilet.

For many years, I have been generous in writing recommendations for
undergraduates who are seeking jobs, scholarships, or admission to graduate
and professional schools. Without lying about their shortcomings, I simply
highlighted their hidden potentials. I have been hanging on to a rope and fighting
a monster of negativity with one hand. Today I reached the end of long patience. I
released my hold on the rope. The monster bit my heart with glee.

It is standard procedure in my department for students to use MLA
documentation style. We expect them to master that style by reading the *MLA
Handbook for Writers of Research Papers,* and by following its models. We
expect our majors, especially our seniors, to demonstrate mastery. Despite my
pleas and warnings, one senior, who is also a Mellon Fellow, showed no evidence
of having studied the *Handbook.* Or, if she had consulted it, she either could not
or would not follow directions. Today, I snapped. This senior forced me to see
the foolishness in hoping that students have hidden potentials.

*What a cheap epiphany to have in a hotel. Did you have to be in a hotel to
have such a simple recognition?*

*Don't chase rainbows. Don't chase impossible dreams. Live outside the
illusions and limits of an academic box.*

Take a tip from Hurricane Katrina.

I wrote at the end of her revised paper on *Beowulf* and *Sir Gawain and the
Green Knight* that she should not ask me to write a recommendation. After more
than thirty-some years of caring too much, of wanting to be supportive as my
brilliant or competent or always struggling students move ahead with their lives,
my will to support students who lack simple discipline came to a halt. I do not have
to hurt students by writing negative opinions in letters of recommendation that
have something to do with their futures. It is enough to say everything by writing
nothing. That is the ethical thing to do. Tough love is a beautiful thing. It puts

excessive generosity on a diet. Probability ensures that I will have other students who truly deserve very positive recommendations. Should probability fail, I can still spiral into death without a suitcase of foolish worries.

Tuesday, June 6, 2006: D-Day and Greatness at Dillard University

My colleague V. P. Franklin, Revius Ortique Endowed Chair in Politics, History and Social Thought, gave a lecture on "From Slavery to Freedom and Beyond: The Meaning and Significance of the U.S. African American Experience" at 7:00 p.m. Franklin is also the editor of the *Journal of African American History*, and Dillard's persuading him to join our faculty last year was a coup. The achievement led me and many of my colleagues to have great expectations. Out of the ashes of complaint and disputes, the usual fare for faculties, the phoenix of greatness might arise. The Humanities Division was courting Jessica B. Harris, offering her the Ray Charles Chair. Great expectations inspired Henry Lacey and me to plan a very special program involving Harold Batiste last August for the Jubilee Scholars (Dillard's freshmen, or "freshpersons" in the parlance of the ultra-correct). Great expectations drove those of us who teach African World Studies 100, a required course for Dillard students, to have an inspiring two-week conversation in May 2005 regarding content and pedagogy. Franklin's lecture enlightened me about the fragility of expectations. They can be interrupted by August hurricanes. They can be seen for the treacherous webs that they are from the perspective of impecable scholarship in history. What a fortunate accident it is that Franklin gave his lecture on the anniversary of D-Day. The academic greatness I desire for Dillard University is indeed a deferred dream. When the dream is manifest, I shall have long ago joined other dead particles in the cosmos. Such is man's fate. Such is the African American future in New Orleans.

Wednesday, June 7, 2006

The book the psychologist asked me to read as a part of bibliotherapy is not in the main library on the Tulane campus. It is in the medical library at 1430 Tulane, Room 2520. I can't find the address on the building, so I take a wild guess— following my sometimes perfect intuition. The sign on the door indicates those entering must display their Tulane ID at all times. But this is New Orleans. I ignore the warning and walk directly to the reception cage. I have no visilble ID. I ask the receptionist if the library is on the second floor of this building. *Yes, but you can't use the elevator to your right. You must use the stairs or one of the three elevators at the other end of the building.* I say thanks and climb the stairs. The fellow at the circulation desk informs me that my Tulane guest library pass has expired. *You can, however, use the books in the library.* Thanks, I say again, and descend the stairs to the stacks. I find the book, sit at one of the desks which brings a flashback of the stacks in the old library at the University of North Carolina-Chapel Hill in the summer of 1964, and finish reading in less than an hour. And what was it the psychologist hoped I would discover from the reading? That SAFE stands for Safe, Abusive, Feelings, Empty? Or that the cure consists of admission, restoration of belief in God, an humble request to God that my shortcomings be removed, making amends to those whom I might have hurt, praying and meditating, and transporting myself into a spiritual awakening? Frame those questions within comments the psychologist made yesterday. When I suggested the title of the book alluded to Plato's cave, he said that the book referred to ideas far older than Plato, ideas that led Europeans to claim that Africans were primitive. If I pursue that idea to its illogical extreme, I must conclude that only primitive people have an unfiltered belief in God. The civilized are condemned to walk up twelve steps to possess belief. Should I accept that conclusion, I shall also be accepting the possibility that I am playing a chess game involving reality and actuality. A sentence from Toni Cade Bambara's novel *The Salt Eaters* flies by: Are you sure you want to be well? I shall recommend that the psychologist read Bambara's novel. After all, bibliotherapy should involve reciprocity.

Thursday, June 8, 2006: The Invasion of Paper

Today was a busy-ness day. This morning, Lynn Strong, Dillard's Director of Undergraduate Research, gave me my copy of the Judge's Manual for the 2006 Undergraduate Research and Creative Works Competition. Between 9:30 a.m. and noon, six faculty judges used a four-point scale to assess projects ranging from Jolisa Singletary's "The Unexpected" (original song that assures us "there is still hope when the unexpected come") to Bryan J. Conyers's impressive research on "Jet Formation in Granular Media: Relationships between Ambient Pressure, Gas Density, and Impact Energy." The judging is difficult, but there is some reward in talking with students who are exceptionally articulate about their projects. We salute these students for being determined to do important work despite all the disadvantages our displacement has brought. It is almost 1:00 p.m. before I complete my scoring and leave the exhibit area with the manual, the competition program, and additional explanatory documents the students so eagerly handed us. Paper has only begun to invade the day.

In the afternoon, I read the newspaper and deal with the new worry that approximately 85 million gallons of drinking water leaks into the ground because of the unpredictable breaks in the New Orleans water system. Obviously, Conyers's research on jet formation might be used to explain just how dangerous these unfortunate fractures are. I will have to save the newspaper for several days, because the report on our city's leaking water needs a more dispassionate analysis than I can make today.

I have promised Dave Brinks that I will introduce him at tonight's reading and booksigning of *Caveat Onus* at the Gold Mine Saloon. I insist on keeping my promise, despite having threats from the Provost that I simply must attend tonight's Sixth Annual Faculty Awards Ceremony. Otherwise she will suffer embarrassment. I have to become an artist of time management. I leave a voice message for Dave, telling him that I must make the introduction at 7:30 p.m. so that I can attend the second half of the awards ceremony. I need sunlight, the warmth of the sun. The air conditioning in the hotel has chilled my body. I skip lunch and go to the Spanish Plaza and take a nap in the sun. That is a bit dangerous. Panhandlers and other shady characters haunt the area, and a sleeping man is an easy target for a daylight mugging. I need sunlight. I consign my fate to my guardian angel and enjoy a warm nap.

Around 3:00 p.m. I allow paper to invade my life again. I have to write and print out two copies of my introduction. I return to my cell and the computer. Writing introductions is hard. If they are long and decorated with inflated praise, the audience will be bored. If they are too short, the audience might think the speaker is being stingy. I had already written a note about one of the poems in Dave's book back in December, so I let that note be the germ for today's remarks.

December 20, 2005: His mind is the gift

Today my friend Dave Brink sent me "the caveat onus:: twenty-six." His words dance a gift in my mind. "Thank you Dave." "Thank you, Dave" is too formulaic to bear the weight of my gratitude. Why does this poem astonish me?

June 8, 2006: The gift is a truth

Let me try again. Dave Brinks is a well-published and respected poet, a husband and the father of two children, a citizen and a voice of conscience in New Orleans, the editor of YAWP, a publisher and the founder of 17 Poets reading series, and the only barkeeper in the city who smashed the wall between Apollo and Dionysus. His gift-giving is a gesture of caring, a manifestation of his big heart, a sign of his unique skill in crafting links between words, but more importantly links between people. Those of us who know him or know his works testify automatically to his generosity, his giving of himself.

What astonished me in December was how well Dave's poetry spoke to truth. His desire for resilience was his desire for everyone else. His gift of poems furthers the bonding of intellect, imagination and humanity, those of the receiver and the giver. The pleasure of his work on and off the page is surprise. For him the intangible counts.

What we celebrate about and with Dave Brinks tonight is his yoking of his words and our memory. It is true, as one poet wrote, that in Dave's language a force of nature meets a poet of equilibrium. * Dave's gifts to all of us are tokens of salvation, tokens of balance. The wit of recognition in the lines of the book

145

Caveat Onus mocks post-trauma depression. Gloom becomes bright laughter and widsom. The burden of recovering is made lighter by Dave's insights:

O Felicity you can't have it both ways
I don't care what street it is

It is my pleasure to ask Dave now to let us walk with him through the tough geography and geometry he has discovered.

*Maureen Owen's exact wording was "Sometimes a force of nature meets a poet of equilibrium."
[Comment page on Caveat Onus from Lavender Ink, the publisher of Dave's book.]

I finish writing the introduction at 4:10 p.m. and then begin walking from the hotel to Bennachin, where I am having dinner at 5:00 with Kalamu. Time is not treating us kindly today. Kalamu does not arrive until 5:30 p.m., because he has obligations to students at the Center. I sip a cool glass of *wonjo* (red zinger) until he arrives. I jot a note: the language on the menu at Bennachin comes from the Bassa people of Cameroon and the Mandinka people of Gambia. I read Wednesday's *New York Times*. I contemplate the difference between *gingero* and *wonjo*. I glance with an old man's lust at the very attractive young woman who makes a production about her take-out order of plantains not being cooked to her satisfaction. Being given a fresh box of plantain seems to satisfy her. Kalamu arrives. Then we begin our meal of steamed fish, plantains, and spinach and conversation about leaking water and escaping time. Kalamu and I are like two characters from Ernest Gaines's *A Gathering of Old Men*. Kalamu is beginning to think that success is damnation. One gets asked to do more and more as one tries to reduce the number of commitments one will make. We speak of the futility of trying to have a freedom school without a freedom movement, an independent school without a supportive community. The latter, Kalamu rightly claims, would really be a private school with all the problems private schools inherit. Despite everything, Kalamu and I celebrate how painfully well things are going for both of us, with our teaching and writing projects. We confess our weariness. Our creativity forces us to carry many burdens.

Kalamu drops me off at the hotel at 6:35 p.m. I take quick shower, get dressed, and walk up to the Faculty Awards Ceremony. I have a quick glass of white wine and one small piece of cantaloupe dipped in chocolate and assure the very anxious Provost that I shall return by 8:30 p.m. She refuses to believe how very important it is to me that I keep my promise to Dave. I repeat that it is important for the umpteenth time. Lots of exercise for me. I walk the approximately ten blocks to the Gold Mine Saloon. I chat hurriedly with Lee Grue. She gives me a gift— *New Laurel Review*, Volume XXIII, the long-awaited Cuban issue. Time is at my back. I remind Dave of my plight as I toast him with a glass of wine. Time is at my back and the second glass of wine swims in my brain. I congratulate Valentine Pierce on her residency at the writers/artists retreat near English Turn. How did you know that she asks. *I have ways. I know things.* I then confess that Lucianne Carmichael, the founder of A Studio in the Woods, told me at Tulane last week. Only a small audience has gathered by the time I begin the introduction. I preface it with a brief apology for not being able to stay for the real festivities. Dave is pleased with the introduction; he signs my copy of *Caveat Onus*; I hurry back to the hotel. Now, we have more paper. A book. A magazine. Advertising material from Lavender Ink. I walk into the awards ceremony with my third glass of wine just as President Hughes is finishing her remarks. It is 8:15 p.m. I sit on the front row, a gesture to reassure the Provost that I have returned ahead of schedule.

And why was it crucial that I be at this ceremony? I got two awards. The "Extra Mile" plaque that was given to faculty members who shouldered special duties in the AKRI (A Katrina Recovery Initiative) project and the "Higher Ground" Award "in Recognition of Actions in Courage During Pre and Post-Hurricane Katrina." I am the first faculty member to receive a "Higher Ground" award. Am I humbled? No. I am inspired, either by emotion or wine or both, to take the executive privilege of thanking Dillard University and reiterating my commitment to leading students from the freshperson year to graduate school and occasionally sitting on their dissertation defense committees and giving advice about surviving the "publish or perish" tenure process. I also mention that my journal is swimming.

More paper is on my hands: the awards program and letters of thanks from President Hughes and Provost Bettye Parker Smith. More paper and more obligations. Mine is truly a papered life, a life of words on paper. The poem still loves the page.

Friday, June 9, 2006: Heads

My early morning email duties and Internet surfing send me to E. Ethelbert Miller's blog. Ethelbert and I go a long way back, and it is always a peculiar pleasure to sample his odd way of telescoping the world. He comments on the display of Abu Musab al-Zarqawi's head in photographs, reminding his readers that war is not a safari and the taking of human heads does not belong to the same category of activity as the collecting of trophies. The AP photo chosen to provide us with visual instruction on the front page of today's *Times-Picayune* contains two heads: the head of Major General William Caldwell, which is securely attached to his camaflouge-clad body as he points to an artfully framed photograph of the head of Zarqawi. Zarqawi's head looks as if it has been bleached white to emphasize how dead it is, and it seems to be surrounded by a halo of blood. The eyelids seem to be sealed.

Will super-sensitive parents forbid their children to look at this item of news?
Is the head of a corpse too shocking for the eyes of American children? Who
knows?

It is alleged by Jonathan Finer of *The Washington Post* that Zarqawi was
the public face of the bloody insurgency in Iraq and that his death "was the
most significant public triumph since the capture of former President Saddam
Hussein in late 2003." ["Close adviser leads to Zarqawi," *Times-Picayune*, June
9, 2006.] The second head staring from the front page is that of Representative
William Jefferson. There is no logical connection between Jefferson and St.
John the Baptist, but my imagination makes an analogy between Jefferson and
St. John: heads on platters. One head is like a virus being examined in a culture
of corruption. The other is sanctified for religious adoration. The head of the
Congressional Black Caucus has vigorously objected to efforts to strip Jefferson
of his seat on the House Ways and Means Committee. The head of the Roman
Catholic Church, as far as I know, has not made any significant report on St.
John's head as a trophy for a Middle Eastern belly-dancer.

I remember a line from a poem by Elizabeth Sewell: "It was quite the season
for the rolling of heads." I think the poem was written in 1963 or 1964. Forty
years later, we are still dealing with heads. And I am quite too dumb to say exactly
what we are doing with them.

Friday, June 9, 2006: Water

Water. In Hindi with English subtitles. Written and directed by Deepa
Mehta. Showing time: 1 hour and 54 minutes. Starring: Lisa Ray, John Abraham,
Seema Biswas, and Sarala.

As millions of gallons of near-potable water waste beneath the surface of New
Orleans, you join the thousands of people who deny there are any life-threatening
problems in the city and retreat into the dry, cool quiet of Canal Place Cinema to
watch a highly publicized film about water and widowhood. Framed images of
people bathing in the unclean rivers of India are matched (in your head) by the
frameless images of people wading through unclean water in New Orleans to
escape the threats of post-Katrina deluge. The simple title of the film is absurdly
attractive. Normal circumstances disappeared with the winds of August 2005.
You can't view the film under normal circumstances. The Dada circumstances
of now will have to suffice. In violation of how the feminist mafia would direct
you to respond to Water, *you react most positively to Mehta's evolved sensibility*
regarding how subjective belief is the foundation of human tragedy in India and
everywhere else. Mehta's ideological correctness, like the self-justification of the
neocon Christians in America, is a tool of analysis. Her correctness is not a subject
for interrogation as you view a film. Foolish is the man who stands in a weed-
choked garden and asks the hoe for directions.

148

Rodneka Shelbia and Maria Hernandez, two of Kalamu ya Salaam's former students at Frederick A. Douglass HS, are very forthcoming about the subject of water. I have met these two young women. I remember Rodneka's responses in our Langston Hughes Reading Circle; I remember her intelligent conversation about her writing when I had dinner with her and Kalamu at Wasabi and her devastating smile as she hugged me at one reception for John Scott's "Circle Dance" exhibit and asked, "When are you taking me to the restaurant again?" Maria expresses her adolescent angers without self-consciousness. Her sandpapering, unadorned remarks in the Reading Circle took me by surprise the first time I met her. These are the outbursts of a woman three times Maria's chronological age, the anger of a woman who has suffered much. Maria read a poem at our memorial for Lorenzo Thomas at Cafe Rose Nicaud. She wore a dress and heels for the occasion; she was visibly uncomfortable in such costume, despite the presence of her obviously pleased mother and siblings. Her favorite clothing would be a tank-top and jeans. She doesn't need to keep it real. She is real.

Tonight, neither Maria nor Rodneka is real. They are images and voices that I recognize in a "Storm Stories" segment on The Weather Channel. I watch their images and feel... yes, feel pride that they tell their stories with confidence. The segment has been edited and shaped to gain coherence. I am not hearing their whole stories.

They speak of evacuation to Baton Rouge (Rodneka) and Tulsa (Maria). They speak of their ruined senior year, of how much they miss Frederick Douglass High School and their friends. Water ruined their immediate futures. Shock writes an essay on their faces as they look at their former homes for the first time. Rodneka will finish high school this year, and she has applied to three colleges. Maria will also graduate, but her future plans are uncertain. She is sure that she will not return to New Orleans. Rodneka shares her doubts about the value of returning and of reopening Frederick Douglass. Maria is bitter about how shabby the school system in New Orleans was. The school was failing, the students were failing. Maria feels New Orleans was saying to her peers "Steal cars. Sell crack." Her peers were not Uptown, French Quarter, Lakeview, Garden District. Rodneka is discontent but not bitter. She likes the peace and quiet of her new home in Baton Rouge, but she misses the noise, the New Orleans rhythms that added flavor to her life. The two of them look with dismay at what their former school's community garden has become— a dirt and gravel space where tomatoes and squash should be growing. Weather, water, death. Young dreams refuse to stay dead. There is an elusive something that Maria and Rodneka can teach us about Mehta's film.

Deepa Mehta urges us to recognize the primal use of water to satisfy thirst, calm tantrums, cleanse dirt, fleas, sin, guilt, and the body. Water sometimes equals redemption. Despite the many scenes of water in the film, I read the unfolding story as an allegory of ancient filth in the guise of religion. The life of modern societies depends as much on dirt as it does on water.

The Laws of Manu, in which some contemporary Hindus apparently still believe, are male-dominant and less merciful in the putting of woman in her place than the Old Testament. Mehta cleverly grounds her story in 1938, the year Ghandi was released from prison by the British, one of the many years on the Indian road to unification and independence. The theme of unification in suffering is illuminated by the lives of widows relegated to life in an ashram, especially after the women must come to grips with the sudden presence of an eight-year old girl who is a widow. In an alien eye in 1938, arranged marriage in India and inevitable widowhood are parts of a vicious economy; the condemnation of the widow who chose not to follow her husband in death or to marry his younger brother is man's ancient past inserting itself in a present with a twist: whatever the original rationale, it has been transformed into a money-driven ignoring of the spirit of religious justice. Cast out the widow and save money. An objective Western anthropologist in 1938 might have ignored progressive politics in India and argued, somewhat convincingly, that giving rights to widows in the 19th century had tainted the purity of Hindu cultures. The year could have been 1939, but the reference to Ghandi and his political triumph would have been less poignant, grand, and meaningful to the logic of the film. This film asks the so-called post-post-modern imagination to get off its butt and become pre-future.

Mehta knows how devious Western thought is in its romanticizing of the Orient and traffic in women's bodies. For this reason, she kills false romance with the romance of a fairytale love affair between a Brahmin law student, with Ghandi nationalist leanings, and a widow, who is prostituted to support her sisters in the ashram. The transgression of religious and caste law in their courtship is couched in beautiful images and words about water, stories in mythology about rain. Mehta forces her audience to walk through the gate of poetry in order to confront nasty realities in the rejection of widows. After learning that her husband-to-be is the son of one of her clients, the widow/prostitute commits sucide by walking into the river. I have reservations about this easy solution and about the suggested irony of the male lover's becoming a virtual widow. The saintly figure of Ghandi is used as a familar deus ex machina, coming late in the film after the child widow has been defiled, traumatized by her being used as a sex toy. Her betrayal was sponsored by the mother-superior of the widows' ashram. The bereaved student joins Ghandi's train and generously accepts the burden of taking the child widow with him to what promises to be life in an enlightened India. *Water* has no happy-ever-after; it has no ending. It concludes in that dark space where we are tantalized to grope.

"Water" is problematic and reductive and very effective in provoking us to think profoundly about the place of tragedy in daily life. In that sense, filmmakers and other artists who want to represent the tragedy of water in New Orleans will find Deepa Mehta's work highly instructive. The perpetual wonderment of tragedy is that we do not tire of looking into its fractured surface to see ourselves as we really are. Tragic dreams live in hope, despair, and gentle curses.

As millions of gallons of water go to waste beneath your feet, you conclude that genuine tragedy must always be a flawed presentation of an agonizing question that "history" confirms will always be the changing same. Ah, Katrina. You taught them better than you knew.

June 10, 2006: Hotel de L'eau Vivre

Darryl Lorenzo Wellington, a freelance writer for *Dissent*, interviewed me this morning. He asked good questions. I think I gave him decent answers.

When you have become a junior senior citizen, you have less certitude about things. When you have survived Katrina, you are prepared to believe that certitude is a panther that always runs faster than you can. Before the interview, I hurriedly read Darryl's review of *Target Zero*, a new collection of Eldridge Cleaver's writings. Does this review confirm my belief that I need not rush to reread Cleaver? But I must reread Cleaver for the sake of knowing African American literary history better, must I not? He was an outlaw who wrote well. There are many outlaws in the world who write well.

It is a no win/no win situation. Don't read Cleaver. Do reread Cleaver. What good is remembrance of things past? In 1968, I walked rapidly to a bookstore in Albany, New York, to buy *Soul on Ice*. Was I pleased or dismayed by Cleaver's boasting of his power as a rapist? Was his odd argument that his violations of women were ways of paying back America for its rape of Africans convincing? Who is paying America back for its rape of the people who discovered the Europeans? Terrorists? I do not remember when Cleaver's *Soul on Fire* was published, or when I saw it at a bookstore in Jackson, Mississippi. I chose not to buy the book, a sign that any positive ideas I might have had about the man had vanished.

I can't explain why Hotel de L'eau Vivre is an appropriate name for a hotel or Jazil is a good name for a horse. Perhaps the name of the hotel is a blind prediction of things to come. The name of the horse hangs on a corner in a dream of New Orleans, somewhere near a Cuban restaurant on Magazine Street. Perhaps the dream has nothing to do with the birth of Alberto, the anticipated first tropical storm of the season. On the other hand, it could be one of the odd desires that happen suddenly in the summer. Titles of literary works replace the language that belongs to the description of reality. Tennessee Williams had a way of stumbling over the right title. The titles, like God's agents, live closer to actuality. Survivors ebb and flow in actuality. Dwelling in insanity makes everything abstract.

I had a brief conversation this morning with Candice Love-Jackson, chair of the Department of English at Tougaloo College. Candice's comments on life at our alma mater make me laugh. Candice made me laugh before Darryl called to request that we meet for an interview. Laughter had something to do with my willingness to talk with Darryl. Knowing that he and I share an interest in Richard Wright had something to do with my being receptive to his probing, to this act of oral history.

I do not remember when laughter begins, nor when it ends. Is a plate of grits a subject for laughter? A clown who strikes out and loses a chance to be in the World Series? Do we have a catalog of things we must not laugh about? Who wrote the catalog? Junior senior citizens do not remember events in proper sequence. Often they do not remember the right way to make questions. Can people remember events in a perfect chronological pattern? Do people have answers for which no questions yet exist? Am I having questions about questions about questions?

We had lunch at Lucy's Retired Surfers' Bar and Restaurant in the Warehouse District. Afterwards, I show Darryl the Luzianne mural that is down the street from Lucy's.

ENTERGY did not turn on electricity at my house yesterday. I haven't had electricity at 1928 Gentilly for five weeks and repairs have slowed down. I do not have gas at the house either. This is depressing. The absence of basic services, as those who do not have them in New Orleans know, is depressing.

ENTERGY IS LIKE FEMA AND THE AMERICAN GOVERNMENT; IT IS AN AGENT OF MASS DEPRESSION.

ENTERGY's computer was down when I called, so the live voice was unable to check my account. This is depressing. I went to mass at St. Leo the Great at 4:00 p.m. Since I was really pissed off with ENTERGY when I entered the church, I am not certain that mass and Holy Communion had any spiritual effects. This is depressing. My perfect intuition tells me that I shall never again live in my house. It is saying I will die soon. I wish my intuition was a better liar.

Sunday, June 11, 2006

12:26:02 p.m.

My cell phone has been on silent this morning, so I missed a call from Stefan Wheelock. I call him back. Hearing his cheerful voice makes me feel better. In these troubling times, hearing a cherished voice from my past is reassuring. Stefan wants me to glance over his curriculum vitae before he sends it to Maryemma Graham at the University of Kansas and to read his cover letter and proposal for his first book. Yes, I am willing to do that. Stefan knows that I would not hesitate to send him feedback unless... unless I was incapacitated. He is one of the select few of my former students whom I would not deny immediate attention. He belongs to the elitist group of scholars, teachers, and writers called "Jerry's Kids."

2:35:39 p.m.

I have downloaded and printed Stefan's CV, but I have not scanned it for errors or unfortunate wording or any feature that would make it unattractive. I have been inspecting the errors on American Literature Survey I papers. One paper is good. Another has many careless errors and poor development of ideas. A third has great ideas that have been murdered by the overblown language that students are wont to imitate. Academic writing is killing civil communication as the grandiose diction of pseudo-theory beheads the human voice. I do want my students to possess and use a rich vocabulary, but I want them to use that vocabulary with more than a modicum of common sense. It is folly to dress yourself in a $2,000 suit if you have not taken a shower and your underwear is not fresh. Common sense should govern the presentation of self and the presentation of ideas in academic writing.

Much of life, however, suffers from a surplus of nonsense. The same is the case with writing in the floating, deconstructed profession of English.

8:36:14 p.m.

**Brother man, if you insist on playing God,
do study your script. Yesterday
you put your divinity on backwards.**

Monday, June 12, 2006: The Greeting "Good Morning"

"*GOOD MORNING.*" How many times in your life have you greeted parents, siblings, neighbors, friends and co-workers, almost strangers and total strangers with "*Good Morning*?" How many times have you uttered this innocent lie without guilt, indeed without thought or feeling?

You have a world-class hangover.

"*Good Morning.*"

Lightening severs the sky like electric scissors; dark, dangerous clouds eyeball you; rain falls and splatters like minature turtles. Wind screeches that a Category 3 hurricane is gathering force in the Gulf of Mexico.

"*Good Morning.*"

Your father died without a word of warning last week, and yesterday you got the news that your youngest son has a rare type of bone cancer.

"*Good Morning.*"

We have said "Good Morning" so many times to so many people that the words are devoid of intent. Forms. Just civil forms of habit, convenient gestures to convince others that we are not confronting them with hostility or evil thoughts. We do not discover the hidden danger until someone says "*Good Morning*" and immediately sticks a gun or knife in our ribs and demands money.

In the nine months since the coming of Katrina, I have grown weary of the polite lie. Today, one of my colleagues asked if I was having a good morning.

"NO. I AM HAVING A VERY BAD MORNING. ENTERGY HAS MADE ME VERY ANGRY. I AM TIRED OF SAYING EVERYTHING IS GOOD. I AM ANGRY AND THE MORING IS BAD. BUT I DO HOPE YOU WILL HAVE A GOOD DAY."

09:03:21 p.m.

I hear thunder. The sky over the Mississippi River is mauve grey. Alberto is practicing how to make jazz.

Tuesday, June 13, 2006: Email to Kim

Dear Kim,

Work on the house is going at a snail's pace. The electricity was off for five weeks as the contractor and I negoitiated with ENTERGY. Much of what could have been done in that time is delayed. I'll be lucky if I can at least move back to the unfinished house the first week in July. Naturally, as I fear that recent entries in The Katrina Papers show, I'm just on the edge of being totally mad. Mad in the sense of angry, and mad because everything seems unhinged.

I sent the early warning because I'm not at all certain what access I will have to the Internet when I leave the hotel. It takes a lifetime to get telephone service in New Orleans, and I may have to switch to some kind of cable service just to use the computer.

One of the more remarkable things about New Orleans, at this moment, is how certain those of us who live here are about uncertainty. We are like passengers on the Ship of Fools. Here, however, it is the Ship of Lies. The tourist industry says crime is down in the city. The police department, which is mentally unstable, says crime is up and its ability to control the city is down. People who talk "POSITIVE NEW ORLEANS" deny that any of us who are having negative experiences exist. It is all such a nightmare.

Wednesday, June 14

Fame has no value if it does not pay your daily bills.

I worked out the daily crossword puzzle in *The Times-Picayune*, a trivial feat which was a larger than average surprise. During the calendar year 1985, I enjoyed working out the crossword puzzle in the *Washington Post* each morning, before beginning my more meaningful tasks at the National Endowment for the Humanities. Those puzzles were a step above what I dealt with today. They helped me to keep certain words in the "active" category. Not having dealt with crossword puzzles for many months, I was surprised to discover that they and newspapers belong to the same genre.

Had dinner at Lola's.

Using the phrases "fiction and autobiography," "politics and writing," and "sensibility and guilt," I put together a rather good commentary on Nathaniel Hawthorne's "The Custom House" for my American literature students. What Toni Morrison named the Africanist presence in American writing is neatly buried in the introduction to *The Scarlet Letter*, but I was more interested in having students understand that Hawthorne's description of the American eagle on the Custom House was a mediation between Puritan governance and contemporary government.

Thursday, June 15: Email to José Torres Tama

Dear José,

I am really deeply affected by your commentary, because it reaffirms my belief that those who serve steaming platters of POSITIVE NEW ORLEANS have base motives, whether they admit it or not: they want everyone who is not upper-middle class (except underpaid laborers) to die or disappear. Thanks, José, for your fighting words, for using art in the service of humanity. Thanks for steadfastly being in the words of the poet June Jordan "a menace to my enemies."

José had sent an email to members of the arts community regarding the escalating cost of housing in New Orleans. *The Last Madam* opens today at Southern Rep. As this play about Norma Wallace, a dashing French Quarter madam, will help audiences rediscover that New Orleans has long been a smart whore in a nun's habit.

Meals with Friends

They are my colleagues and friends. They need to talk. They are convinced that talk goes better with food. One colleague and I have lunch at Cafe Adelaid. I can have martinis for a quarter. Never pass up a good deal. My friend who is a workaholic is fond of the food at Bennachin, the only African restaurant in the city. The food is extraordinary, always at the right temperature with the right flavors. For dinner, however, I'll want something Oriental.

Conversation at lunch revolves around divorce and other choices. His divorce final, my friend has to make decisions about staying in New Orleans or moving to the east so he can be closer to his granddaughter, the pineapple of his eye. Whatever he decides, he will have to sell his house and split the profits with his ex-wife. Although neither he nor his neighbors had major hurricane damage, property on his block is not selling fast. He is considering the limited options that he has. I twirl the olive in my second martini and look at the pieces of his bruised

155

life as they fall on the table. My colleague's speech is calmly animated. He is, after all, a distinguished scholar and teacher. I am a good listener. I am obligated to provide advice about a future. His prospects for a new job sound good. I advise him to explore the possibilities and to insist that he be hired with tenure.

Dinner conversation flows and stops and flows over bites of Thai cuisine. The restaurant sits without pretense in the Marigny, about two blocks off Frenchmen Street. My workaholic friend and I are pensive. Searching in the debris of our daily lives for small treasures. Searching for bright moments to bring splinters of light into our coal black universe. He tells me the success story of a student, who, after some prodding, wrote a brilliant essay about her father. I tell him why I am pleased with some of the thinking and writing that students have done in my American literature course. We share the most recent news about mutual friends, about our own writing projects, about the hidden agenda of demolishing housing projects in the city. I suggest the plan came from *Alice in Wonderland* without rational supervision from Lewis Carroll, who was a mathematician. He laughs. I find the lemongrass tea is a refreshing change from Southern sweetened ice tea. The meal and the talk end too quickly. We look at each other, all too aware that what we see is the way a weariness of coping with the aftermath of hurricanes has added a patina of gray to our skins. With proper Hollywood lighting, we could pass for the wretched of the earth that we have become.

June 16, 2006: Another Version of Yesterday's Dinner

Dinner with Kalamu at a Thai restaurant in the Marigny is a relief. Speaking with the authority of his cinematic eye, he calls this the golden time of day. Even if it were raining opaque sheets of water, Kalamu would find the gold. His optimism brings relief.

We find it relaxing to summarize the week's events. Top on our list is HUD's promise to demolish four public housing projects within the next three years. The plan follows the logic of nonsense. Asked to resolve the problem of housing for people who do want to return to New Orleans, the Mad Hatter would devise a more canny solution. But what can we expect? Washington is outside the beltway of reason. It is dedicated to the proposition that American citizens should be kept in permanent uncertainty.

I tell Kalamu that the 1,000 units HUD promises to have ready by August will be used to house Latino guestworkers. The Latinos did not displace black workers in New Orleans. They are responsible insofar as they help employers to ensure that black workers remain permanently displaced. This fact does not constitute sufficient grounds for anti-Latino sentiments. It does, however, arouse suspicion about whose side AFL-CIO is on.

Kalamu and I admire the work José Torres Tama is doing as a performance artist. José shares our affinity for art that confronts politics or demands social

156

justice. What a sharp contrast there is between José's attitude about the functions of writing and that of an African American poet who recently sent an email to Kalamu. The poet congratulated him for noticing that most of his poems were in iambic pentameter. He then lectured Kalamu on how dangerous it is to be anti-academic. He contended that Kalamu will never get the credit he deserves, because he offends too many people in the academic world. I suspect the poet is still very bitter about being excluded from the *Norton Anthology of African American Literature*. Now in his seventies, the poet wants recognition. Unfortunately, he did not play his academic cards with the flair that Michael Harper did to win the game. Many of the writers who are associated in greater and lesser degrees with the Black Arts Movement complain that they do not receive recognition.

This excursion into what I suppose is literary gossip brightens my Thursday. I have little sympathy for writers who carp about recognition. After all, Fame is Fortune's first-cousin. Fame is only important if it helps you to pay your bills. Fortunately, I can pay my bills without whoring after Fame.

June 17, 2006: Reading a Novel in Vicksburg: Notes for a Review

I once asked Tom Dent if he could write a story about an ordinary New Orleanian. Without hesitating, he said no. Tom was a very skilled writer. He studied people the way some students study for their Ph.D. comprehensive examinations. Tom expected me to know that the ordinary New Orleanian does not exist.

Literary characters who persuade us they are New Orleanians must be portrayed as stereotypes. Fiction writers keep them real by making them fake. It should be obvious that the idea of New Orleans is a distortion of the actuality of the city and the daily lives of its inhabitants.

Harold Clark's manuscript is now a novel, *Chummy's Spirit*. Harold let me read the opening chapter before he found an agent and a publisher. He writes well. This is his first novel. He does not experiment with characterization; his characters are immediately recognizable if the reader lives in New Orleans, and recognizable as a character type if the reader lives in New Mexico. Outsiders will appreciate the larger story Clark tells, the story of an older woman's determination to stay the course and achieve her mission. Insiders will listen for accuracy in the dialogues and look for parallels with their everyday lives. Indeed, both outsiders and insiders who want to read a life-affirming story will be pleased with the novel.

Although I have lived in New Orleans for more than three years, I am reading *Chummy's Spirit* as an outsider. I am not yet an expert on the people and rituals of the city. I am a Vietnam veteran, so the parts of the novel that deal with our war there and the minds of the Vietnamese pull up old memories. If I find myself fighting the novel, it may be that my repressed memories of the killing fields would like to stay repressed. But I have to remove myself from that subjectivity for a moment and try to deal with what the novel contributes to African American fiction. Once I finish the book, I conclude that Clark has contextualized the desire to know "the truth" about how loved ones die, in a way that is different from the run-of-the-mill African American story. Chummy wants to know how her husband died in a brothel and how her son died in Vietnam. For Clark, context is everything, and his yoking black female desire with stereotypes of domesticity and the discourse of Vietnam makes the novel innovative.

It is the repetition of what has already been done with the subject of female desire in African American fiction that challenges a reader who is familiar with much of our fiction. The reader who reads novels without any special knowledge of literary history has the freedom to be less critical, the freedom to enjoy a good tale. For those of us who are damned by knowledge, the novel forces us to consider whether we have yet another portrayal of the strong black woman, a stereotype that Trudier Harris has judiciously critiqued. It does seem, however, that the sweetness and promise of Clark's novel are contained in breakthroughs of inclusion. Chummy is not politically correct. She voted for Bush the father and Bush the son. She is culturally literate. These features of her character help to smash the walls of stereotype. They prepare us for what is to be most admired about Clark's fiction: the inclusion of Vietnam from the angles of love and reconciliation. There is no tiresome complaining about how African American life experiences are reduced to the status of unacknowledged presences in American fiction.

Two passages may serve as touchstones. In the foreword, which is a part of the fictive machinery, the editor makes a telling remark about jazz funeral revelers:

> Despite the kindness they had shown me, I knew that most of them would never be welcomed into my immediate or remote circle of family, friends or associates. (ix)

Jazz people may not be welcomed, but it is peculiar that editors, news reporters, oral historians, and others who live inside their skin privileges are so anxious to fill the gaps in their lives by exporting the black stories (in which they find kinship) to immediate or remote circles. Clark ensures that the black story will be understood as the American story.

In Chapter 41, Mai, a Vietnamese woman, writes to Chummy:

> My parents have been living in America for just over twenty-six years now, and I have not seen or spoken to them since the day the Vietcong destroyed our village. My father, however, has written to my sister over the years, and still believes that Phong

brought bad karma to not only our lives, but to our entire village. He is still ashamed of me giving birth to a baby for an American, and believes that more bad things are to come for me. He never wants to see me again. (208-209)

Mai's letter sets off an alarm. We must not assume that Vietnamese Americans are forgiving of how the American presence disrupted their culture and brought the bad karma of biracial children.

I like Clark's mixing what we know well with what we are only now beginning to consider about the multicultural aspects of our society, because his novel deserts the ghetto of pity without abandoning the imperative that literature be a situated artistic response. It is right that *Chummy's Spirit* ends:

"The book is all wrong."
"Why?"
"Because my story is just beginning."

When the novel stops, we are left to ponder the impossibility of finishing a story or of predicting what can happen in our culture. Therein lies Clark's ability to smell the wind in the bird's nest.

June 18, 2006: When a President's Mind Speaks from a Mirror

you hear, for example, oil,
which of all things, when benefits are calculated,
can read my father's lips: hire cheaper labor wherever

redistribute the burden of life
more fairly

read my mother's mouth in the Astrodome
as she tells new democracies to fill their own body bags

read my tongue as I preach
the faith-based gospel of trublem

June 18, 2006: Recycled

Life after August 2005 pushes words from underground. Back in October, LaVerta Lundy wrote to her Dillard colleagues: "I have put all the brokenness, the ugly, the smelly behind me and I am pressing on. I have gained new eyes in which to see people better and nature differently." It would be a good thing if filmmakers had such new eyes. The best we can expect from them are the same old outrageous film narratives. There will probably be no footage of Mr. Robert

Davis, age 64, a retired teacher, being knocked down, handcuffed, and restrained by the NOPD on October 8, unless Michael Moore is directing. The unreliable camera will probably record a Bollywood lie: in New Orleans the victims of police brutality generally are very wealthy with mistaken identities. In New Orleans, my own new eyes allow me to see how much justice is criminal.

Monday, June 19, 2006: DEATH IN NEW ORLEANS

It is not unthinkable that life in New Orleans after September 2005 involves, in the words of José Torres Tama, "a master plan in the dark shadows." The plan isn't new. It was in place and operating back in January 2005 or March 1876 or any random date from the past that pounces upon the mind. Prior to the coming of Hurricane Katrina, the plan was less visible. Within the matrix of our first-class culture of corruption, it seemed absolutely normal. It is amazing what a little wind and water can reveal, the cancered bones and tainted blood under the skin of beauty displaying themselves without shame.

The phrase "dark shadows" invites me to remember a popular Gothic television series from the 1960s (and, apropos of nothing, a series from Boston titled "What's Happening Mr. Silver?"). In New Orleans, the Gothic competes with the voodoo for attention. Anne Rice is an expert in the Gothic qualities of New Orleans, but you will not find the plan depicted in her novels. She is daring but she ain't crazy. Full disclosure would bring together scions of the best families and the most vicious thugs in a dance of death. Death will have none of that. He prefers to tease us with hints in the daily obituaries and matter-of-fact stories about murder and mayhem in *The Times-Picayune*.

Crime has flourished in New Orleans since at least January 2006; it is becoming more obvious, even to tourists who are discouraged from inspecting the poorly policed areas of the city at any time of day. Streetwise citizens do not inspect those areas either, because they do not want to be caught in the crossfire of our quite normal underground economies or to be dragged into the deadly swamp of bling. The NOPD is baffled, or at least that is the stance that it is politic for the NOPD to take. It would not be cost effective to spill the real beans.

POSITIVE NEW ORLEANS assures the world that crime in the city has diminished since "those people" got banished to Houston, Mobile, Atlanta, Utah, and other points on the FEMA compass. POSITIVE NEW ORLEANS is reluctant to say, however, that those people are killing those people.

Those people are not killing, thank God, are not killing people unlike themselves. That is the sigh of relief one hears in the more upscale restaurants. It was the sigh of relief the Uptown housewife expressed to her husband over coffee this morning. "Honey, I told you those people are pests. It's really good news that HUD will tear down those wretched projects and keep many of them out of town."

The demographics of New Orleans are such that those people who traffic in drugs and kill those people they blame for deals gone bad and related insults or acts of disrespect– those hopeless criminals are condemned by demographics to confine their activities to the inner corners of the inner city. POSITIVE NEW ORLEANS became quite nervous this morning when it read the *Times-Picayune* headline "Police seek leads in 5 killings." It should have been nervous. The little maggots of benign genocide have doubled their birth rates on the inner corners.

Don't take my word for it. Ask a dead teenager, one who is black and male. Play chess with Death. In New Orleans we call the losers victims of suicide. The winners find comfort in varieties of mental disorder. I am a winner. Some days I feel myself moving from depression to psychosis. The journey is much easier than I thought it would be.

Tuesday, June 20, 2006: Moods and Murder

Some days I feel like a helium balloon
Some days I am a helium balloon one second before the string will pop that connects it with the earth.
Some days I feel like the earth– a space that is being stepped on
Some days I have no words to describe feeling

I hope POSITIVE NEW ORLEANS gets the message Mayor Nagin and the City Council might be trying to send by requesting that at least a hundred Louisiana National Guard troops and sixty State Police officers come to New Orleans to stem what Gordon Russell of the *Times-Picayune* calls "the steadily rising tide of bloodshed in the city, a wave of violence that culminated Saturday with the shocking murder of five youths in Central City." ["Guard, state troopers to patrol New Orleans," June 20, 2006, front page]

A friend wonders if this effort to have a smidgen of law and order will turn New Orleans into the domestic equivalent of Baghdad. I don't think that can happen in America. Death in America, in New Orleans, is colder than it is in Iraq. Death here is twice as cold as Ice-9. It often looks in a mirror of time and is amazed by its own audacity.

Sam Greenleee wrote a novel entitled *Baghdad Blues*. No one has discussed whether it is at all relevant to what the politically incorrect may one day call the discourse of Mesopotamia. We should use novels to assist us in thinking the histories we can not write?

I wonder if any musician from New Orleans is prepared to write and record "The Rising Bloodshed Blues." New Orleans is killing its music. Someone must pen the dirge and play it like blazing jazz.

June 20, 2006: JUBILATION

I am happy that the Miami Heat beat the Dallas Mavericks tonight and won the NBA Championship. I am especially happy that Dwayne Wade won the MVP award. He plays brilliantly. The man has brain, heart, and game.

OK. Happy time is over. Return to normal.

Yes, like normal is an equation:
United States population = 299,021,637– (5 dead males + 400 people who died before midnight) = 299,021,232.

June 21, 2006, 10:15 a.m.: At the Historic New Orleans Collection

The exhibition "Common Routes: St. Domingue, Louisiana" inspires me to think odd thoughts about the history of Haiti from 1492 to 1804, or, to borrow words from the magazine *Le Tintamarre*, "l'art qui représente le monde du passé." There are three large oils from Ulrich Jean-Pierre's "Haitian Historical Series" and the entire Toussaint L'ouverture Series by Jacob Lawrence, all 41 tempera paintings, that engage my eyes. The pictures bring their own past, as well as the past they represent, into today and into the puzzle of time. All that has been glorious and mundane about Haiti within my lifetime descends like a waterfall. I feel wet pain as my aesthetic responses walk up one road and my efforts to grasp histories race along a different path. The Africans who had to deal with the Spanish, the Taino (indigenous people), and then the French may have had a splintering of conscience similar to mine, as year after year they sought the door through which they could step into freedom. When I leave the exhibit, I am a diasporic centipede looking for a door that does not exist.

June 21, 2006, 7:00 p.m.: Cooking

The second Ray Charles Lecture at Dillard is a conversation between Leah Chase, one of the most admired chefs in New Orleans, and Jessica B. Harris, culinary historian and anthropologist. Mrs. Chase has a sharp memory and a flair for presenting details of New Orleans history from the perspectives of cooking, politics, and restaurants. She also has a wonderful sense of how to perform oral autobiography, using her attractive voice, facial gestures, and body language to transport her listeners and viewers through the avenues of her life. She inspires. Witnessing Mrs. Chase's intelligence and charm at work was rewarding. If one can't see her in person, one can get the flavor of her performance from Carol Allen's *Leah Chase: Listen I Say Like This* (Pelican 2002). The best flavor of all, however, is in her cooking.

Thursday, June 22

Alice Lewis confirmed this morning that I will do a workshop at The University of New Orleans on July 10. She asked for a title. "Letting the Water Write" is the one I chose. There is a geographical or geological metaphor in the title. Water writes on the body of earth. It sometimes writes in that body. The dual personification may work as I try to help other writers (and myself) exploit the flow of water to our advantage.

Friday, June 23: Confirmation by Paper

Yes, I have received mail in various places and in various amounts since August 2005. Julius E. Thompson, my friend and fraternity brother, has been the most active of the people with whom I correspond. He has sent more spirit-lifting letters and cards than I have been able to respond to. The mail today was very special. There were three short letters from Julius. From the University of Georgia came two boxes containing 32 books, this years nominees for the Lillian Smith Awards. I will need to read approximately ten books each week for three weeks to stay on schedule for deliberations with other jurors. Farella E. Robinson of the Central Regional Office, U.S. Commission on Civil Rights sent a letter along with CCR Forms 16-A and B and the Commission's State Advisory Handbook. Ms. Robinson is encouraging me to enter as a candidate for service on the Louisiana Advisory Committee. She knows a great deal about my service for ten years on the Mississippi State Advisory Committee. It is very crucial that a few members of these advisory committees not be partisan pawns. I am a nominal Democrat, but I bear no unfounded ill-will toward Independents and Republicans. Party affliations cut across "race, color, religion, sex, national origin, age, or handicap" lines; they should have a minimal role "in the administration of justice." To some strange degree, civil rights often seems to be a dead issue in twenty-first century America. I am a sucker for championing the underdog. I shall submit my candidacy. Joseph Urgo, chair of the Department of English at the University of Mississippi, sent a Fed-Ex box of materials pertaining to Adam Gussow's bid for tenure. I have agreed to write a letter of evaluation before October. What I have read previously of Gussow's work is solid. I plan to have a pleasant experience as I make notes for the letter this summer. From Joshua Guild came two CDs, the interview he conducted with me on June 2. I must send a thank-you note. Joshua did keep his promise. The Department of English at Grinnell College sent student evaluations of the short-course on Richard Wright's travel narratives that I conducted back in October. The evaluations were more positive than negative.

Today's mail stirred up belief that the joy I took in academic and non-academic work prior to Katrina is not exactly dead. While I was at Tulane University this afternoon, I decided to visit the Amistad Research Center. Under the influence of thoughts about the Richard Wright Centennial 2008, I inquired about manuscript materials the archive might contain. There are two letters: one is a brief letter from Wright to Countee Cullen [CULLEN PAPERS, Box 6, folder 11] dated September 9, 1938; the other is a letter from Wright to Charles S. Johnson, dated May 18, 1947 [CHARLES S. JOHNSON PAPERS (microfilmed),

Box 42, folder 11]. The originals in the Johnson Papers are at Fisk University. These letters attest to the importance of correspondence, of doing things with words. Responding to Cullen's letter of August 18, 1938, Wright wrote to "My dear Mr. Cullen" that "[t]he mistake in the review, which appeared in 'The African,' is of no moment. I am quite certain that the readers understood how such a slip occurred." The slip was apparently the substitution of *Uncle Tom's Cabin*, Mrs. Stowe's title, for *Uncle Tom's Children*, the title of Wright's first collection of short fiction. Wright assured Cullen that, "in speech and in writing," many people used the titles "interchangeably." Nine years later, Wright suggsts to Charles S. Johnson, the President of Fisk University, that not only can one Dr. Langnas, a Jewish man, "fill the bill at Fisk, but more than that, he will make a name for himself in sociology." Wright said he was enclosing a manuscript by Langnas and letters supporting his application for a job at Fisk. At the bottom of the letter, either in Johnson's hand or someone else's is scrawled "no letters enclosed." Wright's failing to enclose the letters might have been unfortunate for Dr. Langnas. What is more important from hindsight is Wright's knowing Johnson well enough to recommend a man who would fit into that generation of Jewish refugee scholars who made careers at historically black institutions. It is unlikely in 2006 that a university president would value such a recommendation from a lionized novelist. It is odd indeed what paper can confirm.

Saturday, June 24, 2006: On Friendship

John S. Page, Jr. and I have been friends since 1960. It amuses us to think that one of our major preoccupations is the will to live past our 50th anniversary as graduates of Tougaloo College. Although I did see him in February, when I gave a presentation at Howard University, I am especially delighted that he has come to New Orleans for the American Library Association convention. John is a very smart librarian at the University of the District of Columbia, far more acquainted with the latest advances in information technology and the electronics of American thought than I am.

With the exception of some of my cousins, John is one of my oldest friends. Some old friends are like old shoes: comfortable, companions for many miles, easy to take for granted. John is different. Perhaps because we see one another infrequently, believe in some values that are now considered antiquated, and have a fierce respect for privacy, our friendship retains its freshness. We do not bore one another with the familiar. We do not probe without invitation.

Having dinner with him on Friday at Cafe Adelaide and today at Ralph's on the Park provided time for us to reflect on the more humorous events in our lives, on the tragic events that demand the insertion of humor to keep human beings from capitulating to unadulterated insanity. The gravity of weaving moments of memory and moments of becoming new persons is especially obvious to us. John is slightly shocked by what he sees and senses in New Orleans. The profundity of destruction smacks him hard. In words and non-verbal expression, he communicates a genuine understanding and sympathy for what has happened to my mind since the advent of Katrina. I appreciate his perceptiveness.

John has brought me gifts: three LPs by Aretha Franklin and a pass for the ALA book exhibits. I am grateful. I am most grateful, however, for the fraternal bonding. As an only child, I always needed brothers like John. When he reads the manuscript of *The Katrina Papers*, he will detect the invisible meanings that breathe under the lines.

Today's poem:

When green leaves / score
the air / people grow
vexed
perplexed
hexed
and scorn unjust desserts.

Sunday, June 25, 2006: The Sacred and the Secular

If Mass at St. Leo the Great was obligatory but not fulfilling, having the Sunday Jazz Brunch at Kabby's stuffed all the gaps.

June 26, 2006

Another busy day. Between the American and British literature classes, I went to the ALA book exhibit at the Morial Convention Center. I had the good fortune of meeting Ms. Diane Burrowes of Harper Collins. She will be my contact person as I work on planning events for the Richard Wright Centennial. I also spoke briefly with C-SPAN2 staff people about the Centennial and how desirable it would be to have them come to Natchez in February 2008. The exhibit is dazzling– more technology than books, but more books than anyone can use in a lifetime. John Page laughs at my reaction, reminding me that this is only a minor exhibit. If I ever attended a world-class book festival, I suppose... well, I suppose the magnitude would swamp my ability to make sense of information overkill. After the late afternoon Shakespeare class, I went to the ALA Black Caucus book awards session at Lowes New Orleans Hotel. It was quite a treat to see Michael Gomez, the historian who conducted the UNCF/Mellon Faculty Seminar in Senegal in 2004. I had met Michael at the October 2003 Association for the Study of the Worldwide African Diaspora (ASWAD) conference at Northwestern. I look forward to using his book *Reversing Sail* in the African World Studies 100 course this fall. Michael is an immensely informed and gifted writer and an admirable human being.

Saturday, July 1, 2006: Commencement

We are graduating 355 students, the largest graduating class ever at Dillard. The ceremony will be very long. The weather will be very hot. This is truly a post-Katrina commencemnt at the new and better Dillard University. It will include the inaugural ceremony for President Hughes, exactly one year after she assumed the office, and ten months after Hurricane Katrina and flooding gave her the formidable task of rebuilding a university.

I get up at 5:00 a.m., shower, put on the lightest clothing I can find. Sitting in cap, gown, and hood in the early morning heat for this academic exercise will be a trial. Bettye Parker Smith calls me at 5:20 to be sure that I am up. I, in turn, call Daniell Taylor, with whom I will get a ride to campus. She isn't up yet but is grateful that I called. We were to leave at 6:00. It is 6:10 when we grab cups of Starbucks coffee and zip over to Dillard in the mounting heat. While we are enroute, I think Tony King's not being able to get his Jeep started this morning is a bad omen. He had called to explain his plight at 5:30. I promise to get help for him from AAA after the ceremony, if no one at the hotel can jump-start his vehicle.

I had to find Mona Jones to get the "Call to Order" script I am to deliver at 7:40. I succeed in finding her and in delivering the call from the podium on time. But before I went to the podium, I had to find Lachandra Pye to give her a letter of recommendation she needs for a law school scholarship. She was in Lawless Chapel with the rest of the happy graduates. I rush from the Chapel to the stage in front of Kearny Hall. Rush, everything is a rush. Cameras, sound equipment, logistics volunteers rushing to and fro. Are the flowers arranged properly? Are the diploma covers in place on the stage? Are the name tags on the right seats for all the people who will be on stage– the Class of 1956, President Ruth Simmons of Brown, Mary Frances Berry, Bill Cosby (the commencement speaker), our President Marvalene Hughes, the academic deans, the Dillard University Choir.

Dillard's Alley of the Oaks is full of anxious parents, assorted relatives, and friends of the graduates, all seated in the sun, happily fanning and chatting as they await the procession of faculty and graduates. I face them. Now I am in a bind. I have announced that the graduates are coming. As I look through the oaks, I see that no one is coming. There is a delay. I feel that I have somehow lied to these people, and I shall never really know why time forced such untruth from my mouth.

The graduates do not begin to march to their seats until 8:20. The audience has waited four years for this occasion, so they do not seem overly annoyed that they had to wait a paltry forty minutes for it to begin. Post-Katrina life has taught us to have maximum patience.

Sunday, July 2, 2006: Floating in Rainlight

You went to 11:00 a.m. Mass at St. Patrick (724 Camp) and felt blessed because the Mass was in Latin and English. You have long felt that a vernacular Mass is an impoverishment of spirituality. Yours is a cultivated misconception, a quirk. God responds to all languages. Your dusty soul responds to Latin.

Your Catholicism was not predicated on the familiar rise and fall of American English. And your childhood faith was hooked on Latin. You dismissed the uses of that tongue in ancient or modern secular life, connecting it exclusively with the worship of God. Your soul was empowered to float by the language of the Church before the liturgical reforms of Vatican I and II. The reforms were too Protestant for your liking; your soul was afflicted by doubt and drought.

There was just enough Latin in today's Mass to induce a high. You had not felt that power since your mother's funeral, had not been touched by such beauty and mystery and transcendental qualities. An arid region of your soul was once again made fertile.

After Mass, you did not walk back to the hotel. You floated in rainlight. You floated as the thunder roared over New Orleans. Small drops of water dampened your skin, hair, summer clothing. As you toweled your hair in your hotel room, for a brief moment the eyes in the mirror assumed a youthfulness they had not seen for many years.

Monday, July 3

My Family/Dual Membership at the New Orleans Museum of Art expires 7/31/06. NOMA asks that I consider a higher level of membership, as if the institution is oblivious to the adverse, post-Katrina circumstances of my life. Institutions, of course, do not have the capacity to care about that or anything else. I do care about cultural institutions, especially if they are designed to increase visual and other kinds of literacy. I shall mail my check to renew membership at the current level in the morning.

It isn't altruism that drives me to write a check. The motive is buying the right to criticize the institution. I am old-fashioned. I believe, in some degree, that the forum for one's mouth is to be secured by the backing of one's money, either taxes or donations. Yes, I know. I am buying into an ideology that may contradict the principles of freedom. So be it.

Mix one-half cranberry juice with one-half Cruzan Pineapple Rum. Although it is distributed from Florida, the rum is distilled in St. Croix, U. S. V. I. Its frosted bottle with a reflective aura label is appealing. The claim that since 1760 Cruzan has defined ne plus ultra of rum is amusing. Obviously, Cruzan has not tasted the quality of rum from other parts of the Caribbean. Nevertheless, Cruzan rum can have the effect of transforming an ordinary person into a "truth" policeman.

Freedom is not an absolute given but a state attained by negotiation, and business matters are dyed with contradiction and ambiguity. Just last week, someone thrust into my hand a badge that reads "I Lie For A Living." Some writers lie for a living and are quite successful. Other writers lie in wait for a living, like Godot. Duration is their cheap substitute for living. I wish I knew where this high-minded, dismissive platitude came from. It is just such crap that gets quoted and requoted and enshrined like other idols of the marketplace. In the aftermath of Katrina, the idols are multiplying.

Invisible water is dripping in your hotel room. You see no visible signs, but you trust your ear. The sound entering your ear is sufficient evidence. Pay no attention to this swerve of imagination. Have another cranberry and pineapple rum cocktail.

As a juror for the 2006 Lillian Smith Book Awards, I have an obligation to avoid all the idols– tribe, cave, marketplace, and theater– that Francis Bacon described so accurately. There are thirty-two books in this year's competition. Each must be given a fair reading. In the process of judging, subjectivity is dominant. Jurors do use standards and criteria which are loosely based on interpretation of what Lillian Smith's life and writing might represent. Invoking some illusion of "objective" reading, judgment, and interpretation only cheapens the mystery about how awards come to be given.

July 4, 2006

Today's obligation is to read "The Meaning of July Fourth for the Negro," the speech Frederick Douglass gave at Corinthian Hall (Rochester, NY) on July 5, 1852.

I remember that on July 4, 2005 my friend Lorenzo Thomas died. In their historically different ways, Douglass and Thomas were masters of language, and they used that mastery to lay bare the more threatening features of American democracy. In a note to myself, I jot down that Douglass used the phrase "fellow-citizens" in addressing the audience in Rochester. And of what were they– Douglass and his auditors– all citizens? Like a bell, Douglass's irony rings and resonates in the contemporary ear. The social contract of 1852 did not include Douglass as a citizen. He spoke as a citizen by virtue of Nature's laws, from a perspective ordained by his membership in the human family. One of the more threatening aspects of American democracy in the twenty-first century is the possibility that one's voice might only be heard as that of the United States citizen. One is threatened by the possibility of one's exclusion within the democracy and must give sound to fear. The larger world may not hear one's humanity outside the cage of specific citizenship. Perhaps natural laws and Nature's laws are not identical. Perhaps fireworks on the Fourth of July are supposed to remind us of American explosiveness, of our violent relations with our fellow-citizens, the people of Tibet, Sri Lanka, North Korea, Mexico, Trinidad and other worldspaces.

July 7, 2006

I purchased a new car today, a sliver Toyota Corolla. Here we buy vehicles to flee the forthcoming disasters. In New Orleans, we enjoy celebrations with friends by thinking about how we must help them and ourselves survive an unguaranteed future. In a normal world one blithely assumes one will step up to the plate in a time of need. Not here. In the new New Orleans— assume nothing and plan everything. Buying a car is a part of preventive planning. So too will be moving from the Hilton New Orleans Riverside Hotel to my house at 1928 Gentilly Blvd. tomorrow.

July 8, 2006: Terminal Beginnings

Hoyt Fuller had been fired as editor of *Black World* and had moved from Chicago to Atlanta. He championed the efforts of Alice Lovelace and others to forge a writers' group that would link some of us who were committed to writing as community action as well as to writing as art. That was one of Hoyt's primal roles in America, encouraging young writers to take responsibility for cultural problems. He had done an admirable job with OBAC in Chicago, pushing Don L. Lee (Haki Madhubuti), Sterling D. Plumpp, Angela Jackson, Carolyn Rodgers, and others into visibility and providing a forum for their voices in *Negro Digest/Black World*. We looked to Hoyt to do something similar in Atlanta. We thought his new magazine, *First World*, would be a forum for Southern voices. We did not know how Atlanta would kill him just as someone or some group was killing young people; we did not know (and still do not) if there was some ungodly and accidental relationship between the Atlanta Child Murders and Hoyt's mysterious death. And why do we not speak of Wayne Williams as a political prisoner? Williams was blamed for the death of 27 children. Is he the scapegoat for our forgetting? Why am I thinking of Williams and Hoyt Fuller this morning? Am I predicting my own death?

It had to be the very late 1970s or the very early 1980s when we had a meeting in Atlanta, at which Alice spoke very boldly of the work required to achieve our as yet unarticulated goals. She spoke again last year, December 2005, at the 21st annual meeting of the National Performance Network in Miami. I copied a few sentences from that speech ("From Chaos to Clarity: The Price to be Paid") this morning:

We must not let truth and beauty slip away. We must become the recorders, those who contextualize; like jazz, we must stretch the human imagination. In addition, we are called on to use the lens of Katrina, to force people to look, to peel away the layers of someone else's dream, help them to see their true destiny.

Must, must, must... the imperatives. I want to use those words at the writing workshop I will conduct at the invitation of another Alice (Alice Lewis) at the University of New Orleans on July 10. The workshop is entitled "LETTING THE WATER WRITE." I want to discover how participants will react to Alice Lovelace's imperatives. I want to know how I might react to them on Monday in a way that is different from my reaction at this moment. I resent the imperatives. Things slip away despite my best efforts. I record and contextualize and wonder whether I am engaged in exercises of futility. Life after Hurricane Katrina allows me to consume pound after pound of doubt. I have become a glutton for doubts. They taste good. They come in 57 flavors.

I have spent many years trying to stretch my human imagination. It still seems to occupy the same small space, the prisonhouse of languages, a blind spot in the eye of the universe.

Limited jazz. A jazz that goes nowhere. I doubt that people ever see any true destiny. They speculate about destiny without seeing it. What Alice Lovelace said is inspiring and positive, yet I recognize the negative, depressing underbelly in her words. Behind every silver cloud is a brass lining. That one must be doing what one did twenty, thirty-three, fifty-one years ago is very depressing. Progress does not last. It appears, shines brightly, vanishes. Old nationalist imperatives bid me to create disappearing. By Monday, I may embrace the imperatives.

Sunday, July 9, 2006: Camp 1928

You count time like coins. Vicksburg, Mississippi: Two weeks in a shelter and three and a half months in an apartment. New Orleans: Six months in the Hilton New Orleans Riverside Hotel. Now Camp 1928. *Counting time is a prelude to assessing displacement.* You are restless this morning. You go to Borders and buy the latest issue of *Foreign Affairs* and a newspaper. You check the shelves for the new edition of Ishmael Reed's poems, but the book is not in stock. You go to Wal-Mart and buy a coffee pot, coffee, and Great Value calorie-free, sodium-free sweetener made with aspartame. You hate Wal-Mart because it looks so trashy, but the prices are reasonable. You stop at Office Depot to photocopy two pages of a document. The clerk does not charge you for the copies. *Instant recall: you hate clerks not because they are clerks but because they are symbols of how big business exploits human labor. Need and greed force you to like this clerk. How petty you have become. How American you have become. It just goes to show that after Katrina your emotions are not reliable.*

Disaster has reduced you once again, but you return to camp from your Sunday morning shopping feeling a little less defeated. You have gone from house to ruined house to a partially restored house that is a camp. The water runs. The toilet will flush. The electricity hums silently. Weeds have established residence on the lawn. The ceiling in the den is naked. It exposes its ribs. One room, where you sleep on an air mattress, has a new hardwood floor. You can still wash and dry your clothes. You can not have a hot shower. Entergy has not restored gas service in your neighborhood. The uninstalled hot water heater stands like a sentry in the laundry room. Your clothes deal better with cold water than your body. They are Spartan.

Your body reminds you that even in a shelter it had the pleasure of a hot shower. You remind your body that it had endured cold showers during the summer after its freshman year in college and in Vietnam. Your body gives you back talk: "Yes, but I was young, young, you hear?" You'd think your body would appreciate the fact that it slept on an air mattress rather than in a sleeping bag. It sulks as you take another sip of coffee. Community Club dark roast freshly brewed in a *cafetera electrica* forces your body to relent. However stubborn it might be, your body does have respect for the ritual of coffee.

Your parents were fond of coffee, especially coffee and chickory. You sit in the well-lit breakfast nook. Nada. Our father who art in nada. Ernest Hemingway. He blew his brains out. Did he like coffee? It does not matter. He has been officially dead for a long time. You are alive and enjoy the coffee.

Rain spoils things. It helps the grass and weeds to grow. It creates more work for you, stealing time you could well use to read the newspaper. Poison oak vines are as persistent as kudzu. You have to clear them away from the palm trees and azaleas and the purple-leafed plant whose name escapes you. Even if the house is not finished it need not be surrounded by a lawn and plants that look abandoned. You want the lawn to announce that you have returned. A neatly trimmed lawn is an announcement.

The lady who lives next door has returned to conduct some urgent business. That is what her daughter tells you as you sweat from pulling weeds and cutting back large palm branches. The daughter, who seems to be in her late fifties, is very friendly, very chatty. She tells you many interesting things about your neighborhood, the place where she grew up. She gives you her mother's telephone number and her own number on a business card. She lives in New Jersey, and you notice that she is a psychologist. She has been caring for her legally-blind mother, but now she is urging her mother to return to New Orleans. "I can't live with my mother forever," she confesses. That is what she reports she said to her therapist. You are sympathetic and yet amused. Here is a psychologist who specializes in gerontology who admits a certain inability to apply what she theorizes in a classroom. Her mother is eighty-five, possesses a very clear mind and good health, and demands the right to be independent, even if she must have two caretakers. You suspect that mother and daughter have a rocky relationship. Rain clouds darken the sky. The daughter's tall friend pipes up, "I should write about mothers and their daughters." Then he laughs. All three of you laugh. The friend is apparently deeply involved with the lives of daughter and mother, for he explains how expensive it will be to repair the slate roof, how they have been cheated by a contractor who was repairing the mother's rental property, and how, should another hurricane beat up on New Orleans, he would urge that they sell everything from long distance. He speaks of affairs as if he is more a brother than a friend. The conversation is developing like a good suspense story. You want to hear more, much more, but the rain has other ideas. It spoils things by bringing the possibility of discovery to a halt.

After having dinner at Lola's, I write an outline for tomorrow's workshop.

"LETTING THE WATER WRITE"

Begin with the following quotation from Carlos Fuentes:

U.S. foreign policy is Manichaean. It's like a Hollywood movie. You have to know who has the white hat and who has the black hat and then go against the black hat. It's *Moby-Dick*. The genius of Melville is that he saw that this is a country that needs a monster. The delusion of one madman, Captain Ahab, meant that the white whale had to go. But as Katrina showed, there are great, great problems within the U.S. without it constantly having to create crusades against the rest of the world.

[From Deborah Solomon's interview with Fuentes, "Novel Politics," *New York Times Magazine*, April 4, 2006, page 19.]

PHASE I

Short explanation: Imagine flowing is primal. Go against it or go with it or seek to go with and against it simultaneously. In the latter case, you will split like an infinite ribbon of cane. We who write can not always control the ideas, the feelings. Images that march or meander in our minds. Lack of control is the easy road to take in post-Katrina time. Often, the hard road is the better one. Take it. Make choices about how to direct your creativity. Water: the Gulf of Mexico, Lake Pontchartrain, rain, water from the canals. To let the water write we must be still. Still water runs deep. We must be still until our bodies accept the emotion of water. Only then can our minds grant water permission to speak.

Exercise #1: Stillness and Motion

The prompt: Who you thought you were/Who you think you are/Who you think you will be (10 minutes)

All participants will read the writing

PHASE II

Suppose our trauma after THE STORM is our recovery. A grief that shall abate but never vanish. It shall be with us like a birthmark, a relentless reminding.

Suppose the "normal" is an illusion, an illusion we want to embrace or to establish. Suppose "normal" is nothing more than the air we breathe.

Suppose we admit that nothing is ever recovered in its original state, including the human body or stolen property or damaged buildings.

These three suppositions can be starting points for letting the water write and for electing to be a river that tells a tale.

Discussion of suppositions.

Exercise #2: Writing that begins "I am a river speaking..." (20 minutes)

PHASE III

If you came back to New Orleans in October 2005, your first impression involved smell (the stench) and minimal sound (the silence of helplessness) and dry vision, the bone-dry brown grey shroud of the city. The rhythm of the city died. Water smashed music. Water smashed the laughter of children. It mocked the sky with blue tarp. Dead rows of homes. Dead traffic lights. The dead dead. The bodies, missing persons. You cried. Water and the human error (the Army Corps of Errant Engineers/the Army Corps of Executioners). Smile for a stranger. Reserve smiles for friends and relatives too. Smiling was painful like chewing barbed wire.

Participants can extend the list of impressions.

Whether our personal losses were small or great, we are witnesses after Hurricanes Katrina and Rita. We seep and twist through impressions in quest of words. Observe those words that might fix or serve temporarily to denote and connote. Love, compassion, ache, resentment, needs, hunger, faith, outrage, loss of faith, uncertainty, joy.

Another order of words: tsunami, mudslide, fires, tornadoes— things elsewhere.

Contexts: hurricane season, death in the Middle East, War on Terrorism, our own terrors, global warming, poverty in New Orleans, failing schools, successful schools, media criminalizes selected targets in New Orleans, mental problems, the unthinkable, a police state, fraud, a culture of corruption, New Orleans is paler, smaller, wealthier, greener.

Exercise #3: Report— Status of My Unfolding Story (your writing to date)

Question: How much time do you want?
Follow-up— sharing reports

PHASE IV

A. What has water exposed about daily life in NOLA that is either shocking or comforting?

B. Designing short writing projects for students, especially young traumatized students.

1. Remainder of workshop to be devoted to discussion of self and exposing the good, the ugly, the bad, the beautiful.

2. End of workshop— therapy of language.

Monday, July 10, 2006: Peeling Spud Dreams

I embrace the imperatives and suggest to the 11 participants in the Greater New Orleans Writing Project that they must write with great passion.

Exercise #1: Stillness and Motion

To sketch my identity, I must move back and forward and back again, dance, hitting moments of a past, the progressive present, the future lurking behind an opaque window. Prior to August 2005, I was a teacher at Dillard, a member of a rich, rag-tag community of writers, colleagues, artists, scholars; a planner of projects; a happy guy after a week at the Beineke Library at Yale. I was simply another college professor trying to do the right thing, whatever that was.

I am now a depressed black college professor who has struggled through a dual semester at the "Dillard Hilton" (two 13-week terms from January to July. I am the resident on Gentilly Blvd. who did not lose his house but lost many contents— books, cameras, LPs, manuscripts, pictures, and... well, I am struggling like my neighbors with loss and recovery. I am not in a crazy house because I write page after page of *The Katrina Papers: A Journal of Trauma and Recovery*.

This time next year I will be the teacher who has mentored post-Katrina students and finished my book. And I will be very much engaged with my Richard Wright projects and the *Cambridge History of African American Literature*. I will still have the post-Katrina burden, the responsibility of helping neighbors, friends, strangers not to cave in— not to abandon all hope that we can live in a very changed New Orleans.

Words the participants used: teacher, activist, dramatic person, writer, cypress, albatross, safe, proud, ashamed of socioeconomic struggle, survivor, ashamed of Louisiana and the federal government, a first-year teacher, be strong, support and return support, Gemini, dual personality, difficult, a lover, a dreamer, a good writer, a bad writer, a mother and caretaker, part of and separate from, person God wants me to be, tough and strong, intelligent, now a shadow, not the real thing, service industry worker, thinker, a work in progress, a mature human being, reverted to mood swings, blah, blah, sporadic cleaner, frustrated with things, more courageous, closer to enlightenment, novelist, liked teaching, now fiction seems trivial, concentrating on returning, teaching after near return to law school, a future is who I am now.

Response to the question: how do we design writing tasks for young students. Alice Lewis: **Do not use prompts. Do not prompt them to write about Katrina. Read to them. Like water they will find their own level**.

Participants mentioned books that might interest the young– *The Lotus Seed*, *The Penny Box*, and so forth. Our discussion about teaching and children was quite good, because we had to examine what the word COMMUNITY is no longer allowed to mean in the context of law.

Writing exercise #2: I AM A RIVER SPEAKING

I am a river speaking like a nonstop jukebox, ranting odd sounds or mellow seductive ones or sentences and paragraphs that seem to mean what they do not mean. I am a river speaking fluently about the ruins, the names, the storm, the pain caused by too much wind and wetness, caused by the parting of waves that tore wife from husband, child from parents, that made grandparents gargle a fatal breath. There are heroes here– first responders, those who risked everything by choice or mandate to save lives. There are heroes certainly who invented ways out for those needing evacuation. That was love. I am speaking, as I run, of media, the calculated images broadcast internationally, the staging to make people seem to be more victim or looter or helpless than in reality they were– the high selectivity that makes news. I am a river speaking that will have a story in progress without end– telling the tale always untold. I can not pretend for your pleasure that anything is ever resolved, that anything is normal by someone's measure, that peace will again flood the earth. I am a river speaking in the pre-future tense of eternal tension.

One participant alluded to Langston Hughes. One said she was a river that had dams. One alluded to Dylan Thomas. One was a river to whom no one listened. Another was a river cluttered with thoughts; the pain is not loud enough. Channel carved the banks. The ever changing scene.

I thanked the participants in the Greater New Orleans Writing Project 2006 Summer Institute for inviting me. Indeed, the water had begun to write.

Tuesday, July 11, 2006

Before Hurricane Katrina, I did not have great reserves of patience. Now, like the water pressure in New Orleans, my patience is declining. Under the slightest of demands, my blood pressure zooms upward. My hands shake; my heart palpitates rapidly. I try to calm down, relax, chill. It is futile. Nothing helps. Nothing relieves the pain of demands that squeeze like a thumbscrew.

I got up very early this morning and finished more than my daily quota of writing before 10:00 a.m. Then I began my slow progress to Dillard's 12th floor offices at 1555 Poydras, stopping first at the main post office to drop off some letters and then driving in circles to find the cheapest parking. Fortunately, I found a lot where I could park for $4.00.

I have not had access to email since Saturday morning. I find 93 hits on my hotmail.com account, plus 18 pieces of junk mail. One piece of junk is from Jeffrey Sammons at NYU, regarding our panel for the Faculty Resource Network Symposium in November– send title of paper and a brief summary, so that he can write up the panel description. O.K. Then Aileen from *African American Review* sent the page proofs for my article on Tom Dent. There are five questions I must answer about the text and supply page numbers. I no longer have the file for the essay. It was, I think, on the hard drive of the computer that water destroyed; I'm not sure. I think I moved the bound copies of *Maroon Tiger,* which I used in writing the article back in 2004, to the attic. I am in the office. The material I need is across town. Quick decision. Trust my memory and answer the inquiries. Have to reply to the nice Hallmark card Cindy Lynn sent from Kansas to cheer me up. I do not reply to the note Alice Lewis sent about yesterday's workshop; I will answer when I can access the Internet with my laptop and send her the April 4 TKP entry. It is already 12:25 p.m. My mouth is dry and I feel dizzy. I only had some coffee this morning and did not eat dinner last night. I wash my face and hands and go over to the cafeteria in the office building next door for lunch: turkey, corn, potatoes, and coffee. The turkey is real, not some pressed composition that pretends to be turkey. The corn is real. The potatoes, on the other hand, were reconstituted from some instant mix, so I am not sure what I am eating. After Katrina, you sometimes have to eat whatever is edible. You also have to put up with people in adjoining cubicles who talk too much. They do still have First Amendment rights.

Stefan M. Wheelock sent the files for his book proposal, book proposal abstract, and letter of inquiry to Duke University Press. He needs quick feedback. What he wants to explore about slavery and reason in the eighteenth century is quite good, but the wording of the proposal, its tone, needs to be modified. It is too stiff, self-conscious, submissive to the cant that folk who are doing work on the African Atlantic must find charming. I have to struggle with the wording of my criticisms. I finally get that done, about an hour's work. While I was working on the critical comments, a fellow from Computer Services stops at my desk to connect my computer to a printer. Oh, happy day. Now I can print out Stefan's proposal with my comments and the email from Carolyn Vance Smith regarding the July 25 meeting in Natchez. It seems a lot of people are coming to the meeting on my plans for 2007 and 2008 and the Wright Centennial.

Suddenly, I am hungry again. A Chinese guy has a snack shop on the first floor. I take the elevator down and pick up potato chips, M & M's, and a granola bar. I munch on chips as I read and delete, read and delete. I delete more than I read. My lawyer calls. There is legal business that must be attended to tomorrow morning. Blood pressure rises. I chew M & M's, although I suspect the chocolate will not help the pressure to go down. The fact that the claims adjuster from my automobile insurance company has not returned my call today does not help. My nerves are playing complicated games under my skin. I need to go home. I do.

There is a yellow sign on the front door from Entergy. **Service Request** is circled. "As you requested, we tried to turn on your gas, but no one was at the location. To reschedule, please call **1-800-ENTERGY**." The Entergy Representative did not sign his or her name or fill in date and time. How the hell can you be at the location when Entergy can never tell you on what day or time the representatives will arrive. So I go through the motions for the ___time. Dial 1-800-ENTERGY. Punch button after button in response to directions from the obnoxious voice machine. I finally talk to someone named Michel, but the cell phone cuts off. Dial 1-800-ENTERGY. Punch button after button in response to directions from the obnoxious voice machine. I finally talk with Michel. Her records show that the representative found water in the gas line and had to send a work order in; perhaps sometime between tomorrow and Tuesday, the crew that removes water from gas lines will appear. I give Michel my cell phone number. The crew can call me when they are on the way. I know they have as little patience as I. I will not be able to come home soon enough to please them and they will leave and tell me to reschedule. And I will cuss a black streak. "Can I help you with anything else," Michel asks. I am tempted to say bring over a tub of hot water, some salad, and Virginia ham. "No. Have a nice day." I did not mean what I said, but I said it because Michel was very courteous. I called Mike Reynolds, my contractor. He doesn't have patience either. So I go directly to the point. I inform him about the call to ENTERGY and ask if any workmen will be coming to my house this week. Yes, the flooring guy will come tomorrow. He has been sick. The plumber might come tomorrow to work on the bathrooms. So, we can put in the hot water heater before the gas is connected, right, Mike? And Mike, I should have telephone service on July 31. Can you put up the sheetrock where you have left two telephone jacks hanging? I guess if I have some Pan-Asian food for dinner, enlightenment and patience will descend and remain until tomorrow morning. After dinner, I can speedily read 344 pages of *The Southern Past: A Clash of Race and Memory* by W. Fitzhugh Brundage. Such penance imposes patience.

Thursday, July 13

A few days ago, a young New Orleans lawyer asked what I thought of W. E. B. DuBois's poetry. People have asked me many questions about DuBois, but for the first time I was asked about his poetry. I had to be honest. I have read some of DuBois's poems. I have never made any systematic study of them, assuming that much of his poetic genius was incorporated in his prose, in those passages where robust words escape from the purple waters of Victorian sentiment. Should DuBois be linked with Frances Ellen Watkins Harper and Paul Laurence Dunbar? Yes, if we are considering his use of poetic devices to express the dreams and the nightmares of his people. But I reserve my highest regard for DuBois the intellectual, not DuBois the poet. His most authentic poetry is in his prose. I tell the young man that DuBois was a competent poet, as competent as any stanza-maker writing in the late nineteenth century. Such an answer can bear the weight of cultural scrutiny.

A few hours later, I recalled a remark Nikki Giovanni once made about how unthinkingly we consumed the talent of Aretha Franklin. We figuratively ate her up. No regard for the hard work of producing beautiful music. No regard for her humanity, for her needs. Giovanni's comment comes up again like a red flag. Are we often more interested in DuBois as one half of the "Bill and Booker Show" than we are in what his lifetime of work tells us about staying the course? I need to give more thought to all of DuBois's works. The odd question the lawyer raised helps me to get back on track. I did not ask why he raised the question. I just responded as honestly as I could. If you are a writer and literary critic in the post-postmodern bog, you are supposed to have an opinion about everything from the Alhambra to the Zulu Social Aid and Pleasure Club.

TKP, Friday, July 14

I resist writing about my arrest and imprisonment in the famous holding cells at Tulane and Broad. When I was a scholar-in-residence at Talladega College, I spent several hours in a federal correctional institution, reading my poetry to some of the inmates and discussing *Native Son* with them. They were an intelligent group. In a different time and place, some of them might have been my friends, my colleagues. Until June 28, those brief visits, and a fact-finding inspection of a juvenile detention center, had been my only contact with the inner workings of a jail.

The experiences I had from the early morning of June 28 to the late afternoon of June 30 were so dehumanizing that I refused to acknowledge that they happened.

They did happen. They were complex. They were signs that within the criminal justice system the guards and the guarded abandon civilization. One guard who weighs 350 pounds walks the halls like a bull rhino.

The experiences were adorned with fears, the shock of verbal abuse, disgust, shame, sympathy for prisoners who suffered greater agony than I. The experiences resonated the Arab slave caravans over the hot sand and the European slave ships cutting the cold water of the Atlantic. Body odors, shit, piss, vomit. Privileged information about the thought patterns of the temporarily criminal men who are being initiated into permanent criminality and the permanently psychotic officers of the law who will never be mentally well until they die of natural or unnatural causes.

I can not lie and say the policemen arrested me under false pretenses. They did not. I broke a law. I can not lie and say that I still have respect for policemen and policewomen. I don't. I don't because they embody corruption of the worst kind. I respect the bravery of people who put their lives on the line 24/7 as they try to keep a semblance of order in this world. I do not expect them to behave normally, especially while they are having post-Katrina stress problems. When they become corrupt official agents of repression, when they cross that line, I have no respect for them. I have come to understand, much to my sorrow, why some people are very anxious to kill policemen, as if killing a policeman would solve a systemic problem. I can not lie and say the poisons that growing up segregated spread in my person, the matters I have long repressed about my Army service in Vietnam, and this new claustrophobia of jail have not enlarged my anger and hate. They have done a wonderful job of expanding my capacity to coil like a huge immortal serpent who is waiting for the right moment to strike any number of life problems.

In jail, language breaks into little pieces; it ignores syntax and grammatical standards; it transgresses for the sake of transgression. Speech imitates the retarded correlative of the environment. Speech imitates the erasure of human rights, the compromising of civil rights...imitates the current postures of our government. Civil rights are dead. The New Orleans lockup is the site for enactments of America's racial contract, and it is a laboratory for observing the dynamics of benign genocide. Abandon hope, charity, and faith all ye who enter Broad and Tulane.

Defecation and urine stuff non-working toilets. They complement the invisible filth that covers every inch of the lockup, the filth that wants to invade the bodies and the minds of the inhabitants. The smaller cells have benches along two walls. The larger cells have benches along three walls and a steel toilet behind a four-foot privacy barrier.

One very large cell has two rooms and a shower that has non-working showerheads.

If more than two prisoners try to negotiate a cigarette behind the barrier, a guard may threaten to do something unpleasant to everyone in the cell. If the prisoners are negotiating marijuana deals behind or in front of the barrier, the guards say nothing. I am sure the guards can not sniff marijuana. *The police academy modifies the brains of men and women so that they can no longer discriminate smells or segregate terror from discipline.* In the best case scenario, the guards supply the marijuana to carefully chosen dealers to minimize the number of prisoners who will act out. Those of us

who do not smoke the reefers can have free-contact highs to keep us calm. This
primitive containment plan works poorly. Too many of the inmates opt not to be
smoked into zombiehood.

Fifty or sixty men are shoved into cells designed to hold thirty. I think of
the slave cells on the Isle of Goree. One cell in particular crawls and claws to the
top of memory, the cell where the bravest African males were murdered. The
biologically-altered Africans in the cells at Tulane and Broad in New Orleans
are shadows of their ancestors; they are brave but they lack pristine bravery.
Those who managed to retain pristine bravery are dead, or perhaps they are alive
somewhere south of Key West, Florida.

Fifty or sixty men are in cells designed to hold thirty. When you are arrested,
you do not expect luxury housing. Nevertheless, you do not expect housing that
is fit only for animals, that ASPCA might condemn. You do not anticipate that,
for more than two days, your identity as a human being will be contested and
mocked. You are unprepared for vile intimacy. You do not anticipate that the
most frequently used word at Tulane and Broad will be "bitch."

In the lockup, "bitch" does not refer to a female dog. It refers to males whom
other males scorn. The plain gender violation is not sufficient in the lockup. The
word must be modified, and those most hated must be called "pussy-bitches."
Such language of outrage is addressed to the guards. It angers them, makes them
less receptive to hearing any legitimate pleas from prisoners who are diabetic
or who have other medical conditions that require monitoring. Let the men
who unthinkingly call one another "dawg" suffer. In the minds of the guards,
the "bitches" inside the cells can suffer. The guards gaze upon suffering with
inhuman glee, their eyes glimmering like those of a predator. Their behavior is
amoral. They are corrupt.

The Latinos huddle together and speak Spanish. Some of them do not
understand the language around them. It has to be translated for them. The whites
who have previous prison records conduct business smoothly with blacks who
have prior knowledge of how to behave in prison. The blacks, whites, and Latinos
who have never been in prison are forced to take a short-course in survival, to
learn the business. I learn real fast.

Prisoners in the lockup are fed two sandwiches per day, once in the morning
and once in the evening. Troubled with a drastic loss of revenue, the city of New
Orleans and the parish of Orleans can not afford to feed prisoners more than that.
The city must husband its borrowed dollars so it can afford to evacuate people
when the next hurricane blows through the city.

If it were not an utter violation of human rights, I think the criminal justice
system would not give prisoners any food and would force them to live on water.
I eat nothing for two and a half days. I give my sandwiches to my comrades, my
fellow prisoners who hunger for something more than white bread sandwiches. I

can afford to lose a pound or two. Those who eat the sandwiches do not die, but
I suspect that the bread and meat (or imitation meat) contains something which
might induce behavior modification. I live on water alone for two and a half days.

One prisoner tells me he was beaten by the police before they brought him
in. He is in pain. He begs me to help him get up from the floor. I help him to rise.
The suffering must help the suffering to rise.

And I sleep in short stretches of no more than five minutes, either sitting on a
bench, or sitting with trepidation on the floor, or standing up. My legs and back
ache. The air bag slammed into my ribs when I totaled my car. Air bag. The air
bag.... Air bags are vicious lifesavers. The police who arrested me did take me to a
hospital to have an examination before they brought me in handcuffs to Tulane and
Broad. The law requires that they exercise minimal human decency. The doctors
or interns— I am too dazed to know to whom I am speaking— determine that my
ribs are bruised not broken; they put a band on my right wrist and send me on my
happy way. Or unhappy way. It depends on who is controlling the perception.

My ribs hurt. I will not lie down on the filth-ridden concrete and use my
shoes and shirt as a pillow. Will not. Will the levees hold when the next hurricane
comes? Will not.

I do not know what time it is. The time I need to know about is not at Tulane
and Broad. It is in the classroom where I am not. It is on Poydras Street, inside
the Hilton New Orleans Riverside, sleeping on a comfortable bed in Room 2843.
It is back at the hotel where I should be preparing to administer final exams and to
attend Dillard's baccalaureate and commencement. I do not know what time it is.
Time knows what it is. It is flowing past the hotel on the surface of the Mississippi
River. I have lost count of how many times I have asked to be allowed to make the
one free phone call I am entitled to make. The NOPD gives as much attention to
civil rights as it gives attention to grammatical issues in Sanskrit.

My t-shirt is uncomfortable, sticky. It is beginning to smell. I should wash it,
put it in the washing machine at home. I am beginning to smell. I no longer smell
Catholic. I smell Sunni or Shiite. I should wash me. I want to take my shoes off.
My shoes tell me they want to stay on my feet. I taste blood in my mouth. I scratch
my face. My beard is growing. White hair is growing on my brown face. I need a
shave. My face says it is June 29.

The walls are grey or green or some ugly color only a convict could love.
The lighting is bad. My eyes are not giving very accurate reports on what they are
looking at. My hearing is good, though, too good.

My ears are weary of sounds of discomfort of the bitches shouting wolf
tickets at the guards who are bitches the nonstop cursing the bitches bitching the
awkward success of the young guys to create rap rhythms why don't they hip-hop
jazz complaints about the lockup blues if they so fucking bad as they claim they
ought to rap criminal injustice I say loud enough to be heard. The guy next to me

looks surprised. You are a professor, he says. You are not supposed to talk like that. I guess he be knowing what he talking 'bout. But I don't give a shit. The rappers stop trying to rap. They go back to burning their lips with "roaches."

The marijuana trade thrives in the lockup. The police officers have blind noses. They can neither smell nor see the inmates who openly suck on joints.

And how does the marijuana get inside the panopticon of the lockup?

I need to be outside the lockup. Claustrophobia– confinement and I have never been friends. The articulate young man from Atlanta sitting next to me is sleeping. His head keeps falling on my shoulder. I nudge it off. He jerks upright without awakening. His head falls again, and again I nudge it off. It falls a third time. Let him sleep. I may need a stranger's shoulder one day.

Meanwhile, one inmate, a skinny little guy, is performing a one-man play on why one should not do drugs. He complains loudly that fleas are biting him. He scratches and slaps his arms, his legs, his head, his thighs. He punctuates his performance with apologies. He calls for his mother. He repeats his scratching and slapping with precision. He says it is heroine. He mumbles. "I'm sorry. I shouldn't be this way. I'm sorry." Some of the brothers who are trying to sleep tell him to shut up. He ignores them. "I'm sorry." The brothers forget him and go back to sleep.

I grab my chest frequently. Several of the inmates ask if my heart is OK. Yes. I'm still breathing. Can't you motherfuckers see that I am still breathing? Goddamn.

The wearier I become, the more I slip into the role of the jailbird, become a member of the clan. It is good to see things from inside the circle. You can witness the mutual destruction of humanity, how quickly people devolve into the state of nature. You can feel the moral ground being swept from under your feet. You can have microscopic views of vulgar madness and racially motivated random violence.

Despite having experience in Vietnam that now serves me well, I am not prepared for the fresh reminders of why soldiers abuse the enemy and feel no guilt. I do not want to contemplate why torture is so delicious, but I do think about torture. I feel tortured. I think of people who were tortured in Mississippi, Rome, France, Uganda, Cuba and Japan, tortured during the period of the Inquisition, tortured in Latin America, in Nazi concentration camps. I think of those suffering the continual rape of their humanity in Guantanamo Bay, in Iraq, in the hidden, top-secret interrogation centers in the hidden geographies of the world, centers that our President and our CIA do not know exist. My flesh screams. This is not New Orleans. We are in Baghdad. We are not in Tulane and Broad. We are in Abu Ghraib. Or Haditha. Or Guantanamo. When I tell one inmate that we are in Abu Ghraib, he smiles and tells me that in New Orleans every African-American male gets arrested or is threatened with being arrested. He says we are not in a foreign land. We are at home. I am glad he pulled my coat and pulled me out of fantasy.

I have been in jail for more than fifty hours before the authorities decide that I can make one free phone call. My friends Thomas (Tony) King and Lolis Edward Elie engineer my getting out of the lockup. I am allowed to make a phone call at 5:15 a.m., and I call Tony, instructing him to notify the Security Chief at Dillard about my whereabouts and to call Lolis later in the morning, because Lolis is not an early riser. Lolis called the jail when he got the news and arranged for me to be released on my own recognizance. Despite the noble efforts my friends make on my behalf, NOPD takes its own sweet time to process me out. I have to be moved to three different cells as they process the paperwork. My legs have to shackled when I am taken upstairs to Traffic Court. After I have admitted my guilt in traffic court, I have to be retained several more hours. When I finally reach the area for out-processing, I have to suffer more humiliation. The young women who have the job of giving us papers to sign and the envelopes that contain personal belongings that were confiscated when we entered are obviously more interested in their plans for the weekend than they are in gettting the job done promptly. They laugh and chatter. They behave like Millennials, like contemporary heifers. A few of us are anxious and restless. Two guys move toward the opening near the counter to see what is the holdup. One of the women looks into the mirror that is angled so that she can see us in the hallway. She yells, "If you don't sit your asses down, you will not get processed out today." My ass sits down on the hard bench. When she calls my name, I think of Walter "Wolfman" Washington singing "Ballgame on a Rainy Day." I feel soaked. It is slightly after 3:00 p.m. when I walk out into the sunlight.

In every country, including our highly civilized society, women and men who have chosen to preserve law and order or sacred traditions transform their jobs into legalized excuses to shed civilization the way a snake sheds skin; they can not resist the temptations of barbarian power. They love to see people cringe. They have orgasms as people suffer. You have to be there to know it. If you have never been in jail in New Orleans, I strongly recommend that you get yourself arrested on a minor charge and spend more than a day in the lockup. You will have an awakening. You will be enlightened. In jail, God speaks more plainly than He does at a Quaker meeting or in a Greek Orthodox church. Your new neighbors will speak plainly also, as they spew yellow elixirs of vomit and unwashed language. You will not have to read Dante's *Inferno*. You will not have to read Amiri Baraka's *The System of Dante's Hell*. It will incorporate you. You will think that Sartre's *Huis Clos* (*No Exit*) describes a suburb of Heaven.

July 15, 2006: On His Birthday

Congratulations. My friend Julius E. Thompson deserves congratulations for having reached a milestone, for having survived the contradictory world for sixty years, for having written histories and books of poetry that document his commitment to remembering. He remembers to write letters to his friends.

His life has been extraordinarily ordinary. That is to say, he has lived without the pretensions which too many people in the academic world embrace. He has been, and still is, a teacher of history with a hunger for scholarship. Rescuing fact from oblivion, he has created a significant body of work from which future generations, the unborn adams and eves, might profit. It they opt not to profit, that is their right in a free world. People have the right, under peculiar circumstances, to fail. And Julius will bear no onus of guilt for their failures.

July 17, 2006: The Coming Surplus of Water

"The minds of human beings prove repeatedly to be fragile instruments for remembering events precisely, especially when we have a point to make."

[Grif Stockley, *Daisy Bates: Civil Rights Crusader from Arkansas*, p. 8.]

Listening today to a brief discussion of *An Inconvenient Truth*, I am remembering no events but words that were once part of an event.

Friends urge me to see the film that is based on Al Gore's lectures regarding global warming. If I happen to see the film, cool. If I don't ever see the film, cool. In either case, the weather in New Orleans can inform me about the progress of global warming. The film I really want to see pertains to the origins of World War Three. It has not yet been produced and edited to protect the guilty.

"If they keep sending stuff up in the air, something bad is gonna happen." I can't remember exactly who uttered those words. Perhaps my mother said them. Or it might have been the neighbor across the street. I can't remember whether they were said in fall or summer. They must have been said at some time when the weather was not behaving as it should have.

"Stuff" didn't refer to airplanes. It referred to objects spinning in outer space that were not there when God designed the universe. How odd. The people who talked about "stuff" may have understood a few principles of chaos theory.

I am fascinated by chaos theory and believe airplanes must be a part of the discourse. They do, I affirm without benefit of truth serum, contribute to the ruptures in the ozone layer. There is necessary and sufficient evidence that planes do more than transport people and things and occasionally crash. In theory, airplanes and butterflies contribute to the greenhouse effect that will hasten the advent of mankind's first genuine global war.

Tuesday, July 18, 2006

I will not check the calendar to confirm that today is Tuesday. In New Orleans, it is not necessary to check the calendar. The day of the week is always a day after Hurricane Katrina. The details window inside the UDISK 25X (F) window informs me that the rich text document was modified today, July 18, 2006, 9:11 p.m., and I know Tuesday was scheduled to occur on that date. It is Tuesday because ENTERGY promised to send a crew to blow the water out of the gas line in my neighborhood. As I expected, the crew did not call to say they were on the way. So, I will have to call ENTERGY again tonight and ask again when the crew's arrival has been rescheduled. When I call ENTERGY, the recorded voice will tell me to please call during regular office hours. I will call ENTERGY on Wednesday. It is scheduled to follow Tuesday.

Kalamu called just after 1:00 p.m. and read his new essay "I'm Weary," because our dinner last week inspired it. I like the essay, how accurately he captured the drift of my emotions and his own. I remind him that he needs to add the phrase "perpetual weariness" somewhere in the piece. That was one of the better phrases I uttered during last week's dinner. This week we agree to have dinner an hour later than we usually do on Thursdays.

In New Orleans, my mind is making good progress as it descends deeper and deeper into insanity. Around 6:00 p.m., I went to Sav-A-Center to buy a salad and Arizona green tea for supper. After eating my salad and a ham sandwich, I brewed a pot of coffee. I need the coffee to help me overcome perpetual weariness, to stay awake long enough tonight to read and write. I want to call Julius about the conference he is planning for November, but when I reach into my pocket for the cell phone I touch emptiness. Did I put the phone on the counter in the bathroom? Was it lying on the air mattress? Did it slip out of my pocket while I was driving to or from Sav-A-Center? Did I unthinkingly lay it down in the garage when I was searching for scissors to cut the top off of the package of RT Dark Roast Coffee and Chicory?

I search my car thoroughly. It is not there. It is not in the garage, not in the bathroom, not on the air mattress, not anywhere in the house. I grow frantic, move to the edge of another anxiety attack. My mind swirls. Did a space alien steal it? Should I call BellSouth to report that the cell phone is missing? Making that call would require my driving to a friend's house. I do not want to drive to a friend's house and bug my friend with my problems. I did not hear the cell phone hit the floor or the ground anytime between now and my returning from the supermarket. Why did the phone go AWOL? Did the space alien hide it somewhere in the house just to cause anxiety? I have not watched television since I moved back to my house, my camp. Space aliens transport themselves into our lives by way of television. So how did this thieving alien get into my house?

My mind thrashes around in the waters of insanity, just as I thrashed seven or eight years ago when a riptide in Daytona Beach tried to drown me. The riptide failed.

Why do I have to endure such minor tragicomedy in my life when magnificent tragedies are playing on every stage on the planet? Why am I so blessed with negatives?

I calm down enough to think that I should return to Sav-A-Center and ask if anyone turned in a cell phone. Perhaps it slipped out of my pocket in the store. I drive back to the store, doubting that the phone is there. If I did lose it there, surely someone walked off with it. When I drive into the parking lot, I try to park near the spot where I had parked earlier in the evening. What did I expect? To find the phone smashed and useless? I go to the Customer Service counter and ask the clerk if someone turned in a cell phone. What kind, she asked. *Cingular.* She reaches into a drawer and pulls out a cell phone. What kind, Sprint, Nextel, T-Mobile... what kind she asked. *Cingular. BellSouth.* I can't tell her what kind, what model, what serial number. Kind? I can not recall. Samsung. The phone is a Samsung. All I know is the provider of wireless service. The phone in her hand looks like mine, but then phones, like pieces of luggage at the airport, often look alike. I tell her to check the saved numbers. *You should see KyS, Chakula, Mike, Glett, Tony.* She checks several numbers. The other clerk behind the counter says "Yes, KyS." He had obviously checked the phone when it was turned in. She hands me my phone. *Thanks very much.* I am very grateful, very grateful. I will be able to call ENTERGY in the morning. I am still wondering, however, why insanity requires so much work. Was this episode another preview of how the space aliens will almost succeed in enslaving humans? I need another cup of coffee.

I should not wonder. Work is a constant in New Orleans. We try to be brave, optimistic about a future in the city, and work to make a future possible. The work is endless. It is one of the causes of perpetual weariness. Each time you move one foot forward, a Claymore mine named "delay" or "barrier" blasts you backward. Static. I hear static. Gentilly Junior is wrapping up his show on WWOZ, so it must be near 10:00 p.m. on Tuesday. As I was saying before the radio interrupted, the invisibles and unaccountables in the city retard real progress. You get up, dust yourself off, surprised that all your body parts are intact. You keep moving forward, anticipating the next invisible setback. You grow wearier. You keep moving. Your arm keeps moving the broom, the mop, the paint brush, the rag damp with some kind of cleaning fluid. You are like Sisyphus. Perpetual weariness, like water, has found its level in your life. You move debris to the sidewalk. The more debris you move, the more debris appears to be removed. You are caught forever now in a nightmare named Mission Impossible. There is some mistake. You auditioned years ago to be in a dream known as Mission Accomplished. The cosmic network cancelled that show.

A midsummer mosquito sings in your ear. A spider is dangling from the ceiling. A big cockroach saunters across the floor. You have to get up and spray it with a generous dose of Raid. *Raid kills bugs dead.* That slogan deserves a prize. Nothing has ever killed anything alive! I take that back. Hurricane Katrina did kill someone alive. Me. I arise from my grave each morning and preach my own funeral.

Thursday, July 20, 2006: Poetry and the Laureates

That the United States has a Poet Laureate is a saddening reminder that public esteem for poetry is very low. This is not to say that poetry, especially in the sense of the creative faculty of imagination, is moribund in our country. It is not. On the other hand, the majority of American citizens deem poetry to be an entity that must be carefully ignored, for they tend to be quite Platonic despite themselves. Within my lifetime, the only national Poet Laureate to win my admiration is Robert Pinsky. During his tenure he had the wisdom to create a Poetry Project. Although the impact of the project was not nurtured after he left office, for a brief time a significant number of Americans declared their allegiance to works that were above the level of greeting card verse. They confessed that work by Whitman, Gwendolyn Brooks, Dickinson, Hughes, Margaret Walker Alexander, John Ashbury, Frost, James Weldon Johnson, Ginsburg, Robert Hayden and others was an essential item in American life. That was good. But like Catholics, after confession they went back to sinning. What so proudly we hailed in the twilight has now disappeared with the last Fourth of July fireworks. Hallmark and product advertising have resumed the managment of tastes in verse.

In the nineteenth century, America received a great and lasting gift. Walt Whitman wrote *Leaves of Grass*. He imposed his book upon people and brought some of the ideals of Ralph Waldo Emerson to fruition. Like the very grass to which it tipped its hat, Whitman's book withered in the American mind, slept for a season, and was born again in the poetry of Langston Hughes and Carl Sandburg. Kalamu forced me to remember today that my first poem "The City" (now lost forever in the realm of the unpublished) was written in imitation of Sandburg. The sound of a national poetry, a poetry of the people, had fragmented into thousands of splinters of individual talent by the mid-twentieth century. The work of Allen Ginsberg made us say that we could still see something in the twilight, but his work was not national enough. Like good post-moderns, we contented ourselves with the baby food of verse. The majority of the American people were determined to prove that verse, not alien poetry, was an authentic element of their character.

A few states and cities have appointed poet laureates, mainly to give credibility to the sugary sentiments wrapped in rhyme that verse usually is. God help the poet laureate who writes an official poem which is not pop cult, bleeding heart streety, or def jammy, or smeared with patriotic gore. Yes, poet laureates may write excellent, thought-altering poetry on their own time, but in public time they must pretend to be incapable of doing so. They must produce little works that trivialize Whitman's ideas about the primacy of crafted utterances. Poet laureates are expected to be goats not lambs or tigers as imagined by William

Blake. When real poetry confronts most Americans, they behave just like Hurricane Katrina.

Friday, July 21, 2006

A month ago, I was asked to become a candidate for selection to the Louisiana State Advisory Committee, United States Commission on Civil Rights. This morning, I decided to complete the paperwork, to increase the likelihood of my entering a battle for civil rights that is decidedly partisan. Among other things, the Commission wants me to describe my "interest and background in issues of color, race, religion, sex, age, disability, national origin, or in the areas of voting rights, or the administration of justice." I attempt to make a concise statement:

> The Commission might evaluate my demonstrated interest and experience in civil rights by reviewing the record of my service on the Mississippi State Advisory Committee to the U.S. Commission on Civil Rights from 1987 to 1997 and giving special attention to the three years I served as chair of the Committee. Most recently I have served as an Election Commissioner in the New Orleans mayoral elections and worked with the New Orleans chapter of All Congregations Together.

> Having lived for a significant portion of my early life in the South where violations of civil and human rights were blatant, I have experiential knowledge of how the uses of color and race in law and public policy can have a devastating impact upon citizens. As a category which is predicated on a sense of difference, race and racial justice must be understood in relation to issues of religion, age, physical and mental challenges, gender roles, national origin, and sexual preferences. As a citizen I have a duty to monitor how successful equal protection under our laws promotes tolerance for difference and minimizes de facto discrimination. My life history and my ideas about the historical dimensions of justice ensure that I have a sustained interest in civil rights. For me, interest in the administration of justice in the United States is not merely a choice; it is an obligation.

I wanted to add:

> I am interested in how constitutional guarantees are modified both in overt and subtle ways by what sociologists describe as the practice of everyday life.

But that admission might frighten members of the Commission.

July 21, 2006 09:46:59 p.m.: New New Orleans

New Orleans, New New Orleans,
your contradictions are so enthralling...
your truth has got to be appalling

Weariness and uncertainty have taxed New Orleanians just short of the point where human spirit implodes and people backpedal into the pre-history of their ancestors. When the human spirit is destroyed or when it begins to recognize the limits of its options, people make risky choices, which lead to terminal points for themselves and others. Such disintegration seems to be occurring rapidly in parts of the Islamic world, in Europe, in Africa, and it can occur in New Orleans. Death becomes attractive, even glamorous. The state of combined weariness and uncertainty is neither unique nor is it without historical precedent. Indeed, from the moment that awareness of the state blossomed in the human mind to the present, it has ravished mankind.

Mankind, of course, has a survival instinct, comparable to that manifested by all animals and some plants. Such a premise may help to explain why New Orleanians refuse to give up, why they insist that getting on with less than desirable forms of living does matter. Living in FEMA trailers or in gutted houses that may not be restored until summer 2007 is better than "missing" New Orleans in Houston or Salt Lake City. They will not render unto the swamp what belongs to the swamp. They recognize that those who went before them struggled under worse conditions. There is an eleventh secular commandment in this city: **Thou shalt honor the faith of the ancestors**. The rule of thumb is to leave that commandment unexamined. Don't question. Obediently observe. Those who have grabbed hope and hang on to possibilities by slender threads, however, ought not congratulate themselves and bad mouth those who have not decided to return or those who have decided never to return. They may live to regret such hubris, for we have no certainty that water shall not again inundate New Orleans. The rainbow sign is as arbitrary, as self-deconstrutive as other signs. Nor do we have undebatable proof that extended psychiatric care will save us from the destiny we have chosen.

New Orleanians must come to grips both with exile as it is conventionally defined and with exile as a condition of being alienated or outcast at home. In the classic sense, exile should contain the possibility of coming home again, however long the period of displacement might be. The conditions of now may prevent the return of those who lived in public housing, who are elderly and living on severely fixed-incomes and requiring specialized health care, who can not manage to pay newly exorbitant rents on what they might eke from a diminished job market, who can not obtain funds to rebuild their destroyed homes. Migration may be the better solution for them, for without support networks they will find that "home" does not exist. They will be forced to integrate themselves into the economies of other places. *Make home where your heart finds itself.* Other places, even as close as St. Tammany Parish, will not host "guests" forever, especially if the guests are irrationally but predictably branded "undesirable."

Among some of those who have vowed to live in New Orleans at any cost, weariness and uncertainty have induced a new awareness of being "exiled" from the wonderful illusion that New Orleans has been since 1718. Given that the gloves are off and more of the physical and political structures of the city have been exposed, the diehard citizens find themselves bludgeoned by issues of race and class that can no longer be "touristed" into oblivion. "Tourist" became a verb after Katrina arrived. They will survive the blows, but the new mindsets that match the new New Orleans will irreversibly change the charcter of "home." Home will never again be organic, because cultural cross-fertilization will no longer happen by accident. It will be the artificial product of civic improvements and business propositions. Perhaps those who were born after 1999 will find "home" in New Orleans to be absolutely normal. Those of us who find ourselves "exiled" by what is drastically new will either adapt or elect to become the living dead. I do hope most of us will reject the latter option, but weariness and uncertainty have positioned me to reject even that hope. Obviously, my instincts need vitamins or legal narcotics.

July 23, 2006: On Teaching at a Black College

Borinski, Ernst. "The Social Science Laboratory at Tougaloo College." *Journal of Educational Sociology* 22.4 (1948): 276-286.

I was five when he published the article and seventeen when I met the author.

Ernst Borinski belonged to that cadre of German Jewish refugees who came to America and made careers for themselves as teachers at black colleges. When I was no longer his student but his colleague, I could look back on how meaningful had been my trying to learn something about sociology, humor born in suffering, German or Russian from him. The backward glace. Ernst avoided the contemplation of the personal past. It was too painful. Tougaloo students learned to avoid asking him about his past, his family. He came from the German Jewish middle class. He had been a judge in Germany. He had been born in an area that was neither Germany nor Poland but both at once. He came to Tougaloo because.... We always came up blank when we tried to explain to ourselves why he was at Tougaloo and not at a white college. When there is no answer, improvise. As Ernst would say from time to time, turn the disadvantage to your advantage. And that is just what we did, those of us who learned from him. Ernst would be alarmed to hear me say that he taught us to forge the weapons to kill our enemies. I would have to explain that I meant "kill" in the sense of minimizing the germ that made white Mississippians hate students at Tougaloo. It is impossible to kill racism and terrorism. You can only momentarily contain them. Ernst understood and was relieved that I shared his dream of a pre-future.

When I read his 1948 article this afternoon, it was pleasant to recall what Ernst had accomplished in a 45 by 15 foot area of the basement of Beard Hall. It was a site for underground education. What he wrote about his lab and its experiments is an important document in the history of Tougaloo College. For me, it is a valuable lesson about how I should design my post-Katrina teaching. The distance between where Ernst was after the end of World War II and where I am after Hurricane Katrina is not very great. To be sure, there is a thin line between the sociology of education and educational sociology. Ernst was very clear about from which side of the line he operated, even if he was blind (as some of his private writing gives evidence) to the flaws he shared with nineteenth-century abolitionists. And those of us who teach the so-called millennial student need such clarity about the underground education we seek to provide, about our alternatives to the orthodox. We too have blind spots. The forward gaze. Often we do need eyeglasses from the past to see what is in the road to a future.

July 24, 2006

Poem Note:

They should be sisters
these women wrapped in Middle Eastern cloth
They could be sisters
these women with raving hair and lucid minds
They would be sisters
these women who chew pita and pray for the dead
They can be sisters
these women wailing grief by the wall
They are sisters
these weeping women
exchanging faces
in mirrors of blood.

Benign Genocide Note: Literature as Improvised Explosive Devices

Gangsta lit is the newest device to invade the public sphere. Whether it shall become a more powerful weapon than the *pimp lit* that Holloway House made very popular in the underground is an open question. And whether like rap it can cross over and become a new genre of *trailer trash lit* or *sexabilly lit* invites speculation. One authority, the author of *On Our Way to Beautiful*, informs us that writers who sell actually find and seduce their audiences. I doubt we shall be more successful in wiping out weapons of massive seduction in the United States than we have been in finding weapons of massive destruction in Iraq. Whatever! As the guy said at the bargaining table in *The Godfather*, it is OK to push drugs in the ghetto. "They're animals anyway." War is the mother of invention. The current level of engagement required that gangsta lit be created to increase pacification efforts.

July 25, 2006, 04:08:08 a.m.: In Hell with Language

Language possesses people. People possess language. Possession does not presuppose reciprocity. Ownership is a black hole of a question.

Language Exhibit A: What you learn about Gustavo Esteva, a writer and founder of the Universidad de la Tierra in Oaxaca, Mexico must be tagged. Your small learning must be shared, for the benefit of the earth, with one of your former students who is developing environmental consciousness.

In an interview conducted by Nic Paget-Clarke (www.inmotionmagazine. com/global/ gest_int_1.html#Anchor-23522), Señor Esteva speaks of the dialogue between corn and man. The dialogue may cast a new light on Esteva's being an advisor with the Zapatista Army for National Liberation (EZLN) in Chiapas, a light that José Torres Tama would understand far better than you. *Corn, man, and a dry toilet.* The implied metaphor crosses a border. It is unequally at home in Spanish and English. The metaphor is not subject to immigration laws. It is neither illegal nor legal. The metaphor is splendidly alegal, free to fly above specific social contracts, above Mexican or United States constraints on behavior. Therein is the horror of languages. They liberate as they imprison. Someone suffers like the little bug that is a spider's lunch. The spider's web imprisons the little bug. The spider liberates the little bug from life. This is the beginning of a story Señor Esteva might tell someone who asked him to solve a problem. Señor Esteva will not give you a fish. He will give you a fishing rod. Esteva is a class-crossed man. *Corn, a fish, a man, a spider, and a wet toilet.* He has ascended, according to his own testimony, from elite status to grassroots respectability. Contraflow. He has entered the double discourse maintained by Martin Luther King, Jr. and Mahatmas Gandhi. The establishment, the people who are most Darwinian in the management of survival, have a peculiar disdain for those who ride the double discourses of Nature. People who share Señor Esteva's

192

sentiments are very daring, very brave. They dwell in the hell of languages.
Language Exhibit B: Lunch. You are learning about your *alma mater* at lunch. The school is a site of mismanagement. This is ghost language, the retribution of what you sought to bury. You are in agony as you listen to one of your former students deliver keen insights about the nature of African American higher education. She rapidly interchanges the rhetorics of commonsense analysis with the language of pain. There is a four-handed tennis match at the table. The rules that apply at Wimbledon have no viability, no authority in this situation. Your head swims. Your heart races. Your eyes swivle down, over, up and back. The table has become a court littered with balls of evidence.

After almost forty years of teaching, you comprehend silently and too readily. You anticipate the backhand strokes. Your face is writing an essay over the fried chicken and potatoes. One book that is dormant in your brain is having future shock. People and activity at your alma mater have descended to dangerously low levels. Shameful levels. Recriminations and counter-recriminations zoom over the net like stealth bombers on terminal missions.

You have *deja vu*. This has happened before in a different life. Your former student's words are factual echoes of words you said thirty years ago. It is July and your former student has not yet been issued a contract for the coming school year. Your essay, like a poor example of academic writing, is marred by Germanic sentences, Latinate avoidance, deceptive logic, and footnotes that spiral to deadends. It pulses with judgments about the agonies of an institution.

Why must your thinking about black schools always, in one sense or another, end up as a personal narrative of bygone happiness mixed with contemporary despair? You can talk about Illinois Institute of Technology, the State University of New York at Albany, or the University of Virginia without overmuch passion. Sometimes you rap about them with no passion. You can not speak of Dillard University or Tougaloo College, especially after Hurricane Katrina, with emotional distance and objectivity. The horror of language stabs you in the mouth. You did not speak without passion before Katrina.

The answers are plain and bloody. HBCU narratives are always autobiographical, stories of collective individuality. It's both a blessing and a bane that the HBCU so entertwines lives that you see your words walking out of your fellow alumni's mouths. This just does not happen at most PWIs. There is no outside the HBCU because there is no inside the HBCU to define it. The HBCU is a historical fact in low cotton. Your lunch with your former student refuses to have an ending.

Thursday, July 27, 2006

AFTERNOON: For the last decade, I have written anniversary of birth poems for myself. I may have published some. These poems are arrogant. They reject condemnation or praise. They hold themselves above the cheapness of such learned reflexes. They sing hymns to the death of artifice. They demand that you get permission from the Source before you address them. They will only listen to what you say if you speak through their linguists.

The Source is more arrogant than the birth poems. It vanishes once the verbal skin of the poem is affixed to paper or entered on cyperspace. It has little use for the surface of the poem. It prefers the arcane underworld. That, the Source pontificates, is where the real poetry resides. That is where one can barter in crucial ways with spaced-out truth. The Source is being mean and nasty this year. It bluntly told the poet to go steal stem cells for his "precious" poem elsewhere.

It is obvious that just like a no-count BABYDADDY, the Source will vanish this year before the poem is born.

EVENING: We dine at Cafe Roma, which has recently reopened. Kalamu and I suspect it is under new management. Four men who seem to have various degrees of authority in the restaurant sit near us, eating pizza, laughing, speaking a language I do not recognize. The waitresses are Caucasian. One is reading *Me Talk Pretty One Day* by David Sedaris and laughing. The kitchen crew is African American. We call them Black Italians when they prepare pizzas. This is an Italian restaurant, but the four men are speaking a brand of Italian that is beyond recognition. Is it a dialect from Sardinia? I am curious. My ear says it is not hearing anything close to Italian.

Despite having driven past the scene of a fresh murder on Broad Street, Kalamu and I are in a good mood. We are smiling and laughing freely for the first time in many post-Katrina months, momentarily forgetting that the police had not yet removed the body when we passed by. I really don't give a damn that a body is on the sidewalk. I don't give a damn about the progress of murder in New Orleans. It has become such a cliché, a cliché that cuts deeply into the myth of recovery, slicing it as one would a watermelon to expose the blood-red pulp. What bothers me is that people are being murdered, and God will not give me the power to stop people from murdering people. Such power does exist. It should not be gathering stardust in Heaven. It should be put to use.

I am telling Kalamu about the wonderful meeting I had in Natchez on Tuesday and how enthusiastic I am about the Richard Wright Centennial. I am telling him, without saying it directly, that my involvement with the Centennial will lessen the pain of perpetual frustration. It will not remove the frustration that is now endemic. I just will not have to smell the stinking albatross minute by minute. His frustration with the fact that education in New Orleans is going to be a mess for a long time is relieved a little by the good news he and others who work with Students at the Center got this week. A Catholic order headquartered in St.Louis made a generous, strings-free gift to the group. Unlike gifts that wind up in strange pockets, the money will be used for the real needs his students have. I deeply admire Kalamu's dedication to teaching troubled students who scorn ineffective, orthodox, and insulting forms of education. His dedication inspires me to rededicate myself to the best ends of higher education.

Neither of us has had a proper summer, a few weeks of vacation. We are working and thinking about writing projects. He sketches out some ideas for a piece on the situation in the Middle East. He has thought about the formation of Israel, about the European motives for creating Israel by stealing land from people in the Middle East after World War II. I make a cynical remark. The land was not stolen. It was God's gift to the Jews. Get your biblical history straight. "O.K. So Yahweh gave Israel to the Jews," Kalamu retorts. "We still have to deal with why Europeans renewed the gift as a reward for thousands of years of Jewish suffering." He has in mind that the gift was a kind of Trojan Horse. He very carefully explains why he understands the will of the Israelies to be vengeful, their super-desperate attempt to annihilate Hezbollah. "That," I say, " is like annihilating terrorism. Impossible." He agrees, but I read some reservations in his eyes. I suggest that if we measure things on a moral plane, we find that the Israelies, especially the Zionists among them, come dangerously close to the line that separates them from the Nazis, from the warlords in the Sudan, from Idi Amin. Kalamu brings our discussion back to the grounding of Realpolitik. He reminds me that the Arabs have a stake in this, that they must allow Israel to exist as a means of preventing the Europeans and the United States from colonizing them in order to extract their most precious resource: oil. This is one of the features I most enjoy about our weekly dinners. Our conversations allow us to work through the messiness of thinking about world problems and to sort out the unanswerable that we must account for in our writing about local or global issues.

As we are leaving the restaurant, I ask two of the men who were talking in a language I could not recognize what region of Italy it was from. They laugh. One said in perfect English, "We were speaking Turkish." As we walked toward his car, Kalamu said the Turks may own the place now, but they had the good sense to keep the Italian name and the Italian food. This is the new New Orleans.

NIGHT: Mayor Ray Nagin is smarter than some people think. At the press conference on July 26, at which he broke his silence about progress in New Orleans, he was surrounded by many of his Republican advisors. The mayor is convinced that the city is making "steady, definitive progress toward recovery." ["Mayor finally breaks post-election silence," *The Times-Picayune*, July 27, 2006, page A- 1.] I was almost about to buy the hype, but a comment Reverend Frank Davis allegedly made at the conference sounded the alarm about the progress being defined by fantasy. Speaking of New Orleanians living in Texas, David said: "We want to get them on the yellow brick road, which everyone knows will take you to the Emerald City, which is New Orleans."[page A-5.] Ray Nagin is smart, but I must request that my city councilperson remind him and Rev. Davis that New Orleans is not in the Land of Oz and that the Wizard does not exist. I will not buy Nagin's republicated deceptions.

SCREED: NEW ORLEANS

a corpse on Broad Street–
transubstantiation in
the late summer sun

Friday, July 28, 2006, 12:54:32 a.m.

POEM 63

The lady you know what I mean you don't understand,
our lady waking herself homeless
on the corner of Canal and Claiborne
you know what I'm saying you don't understand
our lady sanctified in heavy armor summer and winter
the same armor you know what I'm saying
protecting her shopping cart and two neat parcels of belongings
that you don't understand how who is in possession of herself
her mislocated dispossession
our lady is a name immune you don't understand
you know what I'm saying I'm saying our lady is a name
standing still still standing in the flood of misfortune
the same armor standing fall and spring
know what I mean is standing still as peace in New Orleans
on the altar of Claiborne and Canal
our lady her face chubby seriously cheerful
is wrapped in Afro-blue revelations
homesteading homeless security
impervious to pity, to the teflon piety of welfare,
is wrapped in purpose you know what I'm saying

you don't understand how dispossession
translated our lady you know what I mean
under the expressway you don't understand
you know I mean the lady translated
into a mahagony lady will not be moved
you know what I'm saying
will not be moved by waters
homeland liberation
you don't understand
our lady, the lady supreme
possessing your life you know what I mean

Saturday, July 29, 2006

Whenever public education happened to be the topic, I would remark that the public school system in Orleans Parish served its students poorly. A few students succeeded despite the expectation that they would fail. Their peers in the magnet, parochial, or private schools had advantages; if they failed, no one blamed the system. The blame was placed on lack of initiative. In cities where the majority of public school students are African American, it is most convenient to blame the faceless system.

In general, students in New Orleans were left very far behind, as many of them struggled to learn something in buildings that should have been condemned and from teachers who had been driven to the edge of not caring by hostile parents. The parents who were not hostile but far-sighted made common cause to ensure that admission to some schools would be selective. They did not want too many "drug-rats" and other non-traditionals retarding the progress they hoped their children would make, these far-sighted parents who could afford to send their children to private schools and academies.

The meetings of the Parish School Board, at least the ones televised on the public access channel, were embarrassing. Irate parents and community activists shouted at school board members. School board members responded with platitudes, non-statements, and dishwater promises that even a second-grader would not find credible, because they were not prepared to explain fiscal mismanagement and low performance. I often wondered why the departments of education at the various universities in New Orleans did not host a conference on the crumbling public school system and issue recommendations. I guess those, who had more hard evidence and a better sense of the history of education in New Orleans than I, deemed such an undertaking a waste of everyone's time. Hurricane Katrina and the state lawmakers were co-partners in planning a new school system for the new New Orleans. In November 2005, "the state took over operational control of 112 out of 128 schools from the Orleans Parish School Board" and "transferred all public schools in New Orleans that were performing below the state average to a newly created 'Recovery School District' under the aegis of the state Board of Elementary and Secondary Education (BESE)." [Sam Winston,"The New Paradigm," *Gambit Weekly*, July 18, 2006: 19.] Charter schools began to blossom in New Orleans.

When public education in New Orleans happens to be the topic, I am compelled to be silent until I have more information about whether a three-tiered system— private, public, and semi-private (charter)— can be effective in a city that has traditionally put many of its challenging students in a box marked "CONSUMER WASTE." When public education is the topic, I am a cave under the Mississippi River, flooded with light from 1,943 ENTERGY candles. Caves don't talk. They read.

In the opening of "Fate," Ralph Waldo Emerson prepares to dwell on some scheme of events that determines how men live at a given time. He does not start with events. He begins with the visual. A line of his poetry ("Delicate omens traced in air") directs our eyes to the necessity of learning from nature because scribes can tell us little about matters of "vaster character." Emerson is careful to deflect our attention from his role as "scribe," because he is not writing in a conventional sense. He is channeling the pre-Civil War *Zeitgeist*. It is crucial that he genuflects before the hegemony of the visual. The gesture is classical and American.

We would like to believe the nature toward which Emerson directs us is raw and virgin. We know, however, it is processed and violated by drawings, paintings, poetic imaging, photographs, scientific descriptions. Emerson positions himself as a conduit, and we must take him as such in our search for what remains of a nature that can tell us anything about what is of "vaster character."

Among our many American thinkers, Emerson burns brilliantly in post-Katrina discourses, because he has the habit of casting oil on the waters of his philsophy. He guides our motor boats and make-shift rafts through flooded streets of memory to the gates of philosophy, leaving us there to negotiate admission, and if we are lucky, a return Eden. Emerson urges us to think as the physicist Stephen Hawking does; like Hawking, we might find the face of God in the material world. The least intellectual New Orleanian can be drawn into Emerson's widely cast nets, taking untranslatable swipes at Truth and sputtering witty transcendentalisms. Huey Long would have made every man a king. Hurricane Katrina has made every woman and every man a philosopher, a transcending believer in something.

Emerson is on target in suggesting that any question about the nature of Time presupposes a special interest in life. "To me," Emerson confesses, "however,

198

the question of the times resolved itself into a practical question of the conduct of life." He expects us to catch his shifting from Time to the times is consonant with his shifting from the abstract to what is historically embodied in dealing with Fate. We must see Emerson for the trickster that he is.

In New Orleans, we ground our questions about Fate as punishment in such options as we can rip from the process of recovery. Emerson precludes our falling into the fallacy of great expectations. He admits that we are "incompetent to solve the times." Any philosophical response will be instructive but lacking in real force to change behaviors and the course of life. He likens the task of dealing with the *Zeitgeist* to a mathematical operation.

"If we must accept an irresistable dictation" (the words of scribes, authorities) we must accept limits and rely on theory and choices. Such phrasing betrays the lack of rigor in speculative enterprises that mix knowledge and faith. From hindsight we detect more than a little of charm in Emerson's reasoning. We are charmed by his rhetoric. As we speculate about Fate in New Orleans, we may find ourselves charmed by the moves of mass media like naive mice charmed by snakes, by the charms and dictations of our politicians and business leaders. Charm can prove to be deadly.

Emerson is aware of the cognitive whirlpools in his enterprise. He tries to avoid dictation by subjecting "leading topics which belong to our scheme of human life" to balanced argument. Thus, Emerson turns the failure of philosophy into its triumph by bringing individual choice to the foreground. We New Orleanians can gain much if we use Emerson's paradoxical strategies in thinking about the unfolding scheme of events in our city.

Sunday, July 30, 2006 09:36:18 a.m.

we drink syrup, we chew salt
if sorrow sings, it ain't our fault

"Is there anything positive in the uncertainty and frustration that is killing New Orleans? Why bother to ask? The value of dead bodies can be measured by how well they fertilize mud."
From *The Mad Farmer Notebook*

Monday, July 31, 2006: My Birthday

The proximity of death justifies my right to sing the blues.

Should you fail to tell your own story, time will have no mercy. It will leave you hanging without a history. You accept your birthday for what it is: another day in your life.

Tuesday, August 1, 2006

In the Waiting Room

Your cousin, so I hear tell, is dying.
His heart is looking for a place that has gravity,
where his kidneys can retire in comfort.
Is it true a machine is extending his grief?
Yes? Damn. Has your family ever known
what peace is? How to lay a body down?

Thursday, August 3, 2006

In the old days, you could buy a loaf of bread for 14 cents.

Moment #1: When It Rains: Morton Salt Poem for Quo Vadis Gex Breaux

When it rains, we pour
wry libations. We are salt.
When summoned, we testify.
We sprinkle our selves with water
that has holes in it. The spaces left
when it rains. We pour
silence, healing wounds,
work-wrecked backs,
smashed hearts,
trauma-burdened dreams,
paper-split finger skin,
the too-much that comes
when it pours. We are salt.
Post-Katrina, when it pours,
we sprint around the sun,
morph to rock,
gleam like love.

Moment #2: Prelude for a Last Supper

Conversation with Kalamu this evening is marked by the fact that both of us are old enough to remember Fidel Castro's emerging from the Sierra Maestra and his dramatic rise to power. We remember to be concerned that the United

States, having failed in various efforts to kill the man (or the symbol of resistance to U.S. bullying), now wishes to assassinate his brother Raul, create enough chaos in Cuba to initiate a civil war, and assist Cuban Americans to establish a new democratic dictatorship of the elite. We remember that in 1959 Venus, Mack the Knife, Charlie Brown, and Stagger Lee all blew out sixteen candles as they slept-walked to Kansas City. But what has rock and roll or Castro's inevitable dying and canonization to do with Senator Clinton's bold dressing down of Secretary of Defense Rumsfeld and call for his resignation? Everything.

One of the odd legacies of Katrina is excessive interest in everything and in thinking that all events in the world (including the antics of the rich and vulgar) are interrelated. It is a curse. In contrast, memory is the blessing. Memory pertains to the already accomplished, to the future that has a past tense. One does not have to search for yet another folder in the mind in which to store new information and trivia.

I have not exploited this "interest" as fully as I might have under different conditions, because problems with disappearing identity, feelings of isolation, anger, depression and unpredictable moments of deep anxiety, panic and weird physical sensations have priority. One feels condemned to motion on a Moebius strip where progress is ultimately a return to a starting point. Contradiction assumes more significance in one's daily life, and curiosity— well, curiosity kills cats and prompts writers to pay attention. *Give attention to details that people less hooked on languages are free to ignore.*

Even as I grapple with the dense morality of dragging American soldiers to court martial for doing what they have been trained very well to do (to kill people), Kalamu redirects my attention to the political and social justice for which people are demonstrating in Mexico City. The Mexican presidential election of 2006 will not be a replay of the George Bush/Al Gore tragedy of 2000. And we do need some assurance that not every member of the massive 666 Clan shall taste victory and lead their subjects deeper and deeper into the bowels of secular damnation. That Mexican assurance is poetic. Such truth as it might possess is eclipsed by realpolitik actions in Lebanon, Palestine and Yugoslavia, South Africa, North Korea and Japan, the Soviet Union, Iraq, Liberia, the Congo, Israel, Sri Lanka, the Sudan, Siam, Iran, India and China, the pseudo-imperial yearnings of the United States of America. It is legitimate to include the names "Siam" and "Soviet Union" and "Yugoslavia." A change of names is not coterminous with a change of population and landbase. It is unlikely that people in the Gold Coast suddenly felt themselves to be inhabitants of an ancient empire when the land was renamed Ghana!

The impossibility of avoiding everything leads Kalamu to remark that boundary-naming is very arbitrary. *Israel is a wonderful example. So too is Persia. Knock on wood. We are headed toward Babylonian and Byzantinian discourses.*

We are obligated to consider whether there can be any civil discussion of Israel as a nation-state, or of Israel as an enactment of historical repetition. Kalamu proposes to discuss the Jewish question and the question of boundaries with two Jews. I have reservations about how fruitful or enlightening these proposed conversations might be, because Kalamu takes a fairly hard line on what Israel is. He is the brave one; I am less daring, less willing to engage in talks where words may become bloodshed. *I did not ask to be a Palestinian, but I am.*

Kalamu is trying to excavate causes as we have dinner. He finds them in European history or in the history of Western imperialism. He theorizes that the formation of Israel was Europe's solution to *its* Jewish problem and that Zionist terrorism can not be excused or erased any more than one can ignore the geopolitical tricks pulled by the newly constituted United Nations in 1948. They can and have been ignored, but they have returned to haunt us as we recognize how powerless the United Nations of 2006 is in bringing any peace to the Middle East, to any portion of the world. When you note what kind of bed the world powers would have us sleep or die in, you may decide to sleep on the floor.

In the eleven months since Hurricane Katrina, we have shifted our conversations far beyond such topics as African American community; the cultural and literary tugs-of-war between people who self-identify as African Americans and people who make a fetish of their questionable post-x identities. In the Old World, the latter were "been-tos" or "wannabes" or something so-called white people called "tragic mulattos" (the kindest label they could put on the blood kin that frightened them). We have moved beyond shared agony about the destructivenes of permanent poverty and the psychology of self-hatred. Those topics still interest us deeply, but we have moved to issues that define our positions in a world rather than in a community. We are interested in issues that can lead to THE END.

The role of policy in America's *Don Quixote* war on terrorism gives us nightmares. Terrorism, like AIDS, spreads and mutates endlessly. It questions rationales for hope that human beings will stop retreating into pre-histories. Those unsettling questions, whether they be vague or clear, force Kalamu and me to talk about the messy business of World War III, the only war in the history of the planet that shall indeed include all of the world. Put your finger on any inhabited portion of the world and you shall feel the heat of destruction. The fires of a primitive will for power burn everywhere. The world picture is as pretty as photographs of New Orleans and the Gulf Coast taken on September 2, 2005. CNN is our truth-machine. As we look at Senator Clinton's rapidly aging face and read her lips, we sprinkle our fears over *nayo*, spinach, and plantain, and drink our *wanjo* straight or mixed with ginger. Can we have our last supper and disappear into the whatever before World War III arrives?

202

Friday, August 4, 2006

"You Americans buy so many products "Made in China" that I am surprised bamboo underwear is not the latest fashion fad."

—Mr. Lawrence Seagull

"Tell the angels to be careful when they flush the lake."

—Anonymous

In the late afternoon, the day begins to improve. The mail contains two welcomed items: the certificate of title for my new car and an insurance check for about half the 2001 value of the Toyota I cracked up in June. The check will be enough to pay next year's insurance premiums.

Brenda Greene, Executive Director of the Center for Black Literature at Medgar Evers College, CUNY, sent me an invitation to "participate on either a panel or roundtable discussion for our Ninth National Black Writers Conference which opens on Friday, March 28, 2008." The theme for the conference will be **Black Writers: Reading and Writing to Transform Their Lives and the World**. I anxiously accept the invitation. The theme is ideal, because I am writing *The Katrina Papers: A Journal of Trauma and Recovery*.

Writing the journal has been surprisingly transformative. It has forced me to think about how attached we become to where we live. We become attached to our homes, the neighbors and the neighborhood. We take our daily routines for granted. We save our highest regard for one church, one bar, one school, one supermarket. They define what is normal for us. Foods also define us. Where we shop and what we buy is symbolic of our thrift or our waste, of our tastes, our income levels. Do we read the local newspaper? Do we prefer to read the national newspapers? Do we religiously read both local and national newspapers? Unless we have friends in remote areas of the city, it is easy to be inattentive and to think that those areas don't count. How the self chooses to breathe counts. How the city sponsors routines counts. We depend on landmarks to navigate. Street names. Are we at the mercy of streetcar and bus schedules? Do we use our cars to obtain a certain freedom in scheduling how we move through the city? We are disoriented when our landmarks or our cars are destroyed. Walls are metaphors of constraint. We need parks to escape. If we are expelled from the security of our homes, as so many of us were in the months following Hurricane Katrina, we take comfort in alien places. We realize we can find comfort in a relatively small space. However unhappy displacement makes us, we adapt and decorate our adaptation with complaints. And we may envy those who are fortunate, who suffered less property damage than we did. The journal has forced me to adjust my perspectives on the world of New Orleans.

You are fooling yourself about bright moments. All moments from now until the time of your dying shall be dull and prickly. You shall laugh, and laughter will bring you no joy. Sadness shall season all your waking minutes. Peace will exist when your are asleep. You will never be conscious of it. Stop wishing and dreaming. Wake up.

I have to mention dark hours as a part of the writing process. Dark hours have to do with alienation, doubts, extremes of uncertainty. I have had to overcome dark hours and evil thoughts. Overcoming the darkness that has affected my regard for the art of teaching will not be easy. Last August, I had completed the syllabi for my courses and had great expectations for 2005-2006. This year, I am sad and loaded with limited expectations. I have not written any syllabi. The inactivity frightens me. I feel disconnected from course objectives or goals. I fill my mind with trivia that has nothing to do with my helping any student to think well. *I am on a road in 1959. I am walking with Mack the Knife, Venus, Charlie Brown, and Stagger Lee. We have blown out 16 candles and are going to Kansas City.*

Saturday, August 5, 2006

Alpha Phi Alpha: One Hundred Years Cold

You did not attend your fraternity's centennial convention last month, but you did get some photocopied pages from the souvenir journal. A few sessions seem to have been focused on contemporary conditions. Did any of your brothers propose an Alpha KEEP THE MALES OUT OF JAILS *initiative? You hope at least a single brother was interested in the practices of the criminal justice system in the United States.*

Sunday, August 6, 2006: Letter to a Fraternity Brother

Dear J_____,

Thanks very much for sending the Alpha Phi Alpha shirt ("100 Years Cold") and copy of the 100 year convention program. The sessions seem to have been appropriately focused on the condition of black males, and I hope some brothers proposed an Alpha **KEEP THE MALES OUT OF JAILS** initiative. If the initiative were faith-based, I think our fraternity could get a handsome sum from the Bush Administration. I'm sure the matter of incarceration will be one of the more haunting chapters in your next book. The topic will obviously appear in my Reading Race Reading America, and in the essay I am struggling to write about benign genocide.

I continue to deal with the cards life has laid out, although it is tough to tell whether I'm playing solitaire or bid whist with three ghosts. Whatever the game, it is played under the clouds of expecting another hurricane to test the levees and floodgates and the people of the city.

Admittedly, some aspects of life in New Orleans are improving. The postman does bring the mail to my door. I now have gas, water, and electricity and a regular telephone number. On the down side, crime and murders associated with drug traffic have increased. A growing number of New Orleanians have mental health problems. Some to these things will be reflected in the closing pages of The Katrina Papers. I only have 23 more days of writing— short-time as we figured it on our turtle countdown sheets in Vietnam. August 29 will mark a turning point, a segue from Katrina to writing about other literary and social problems.

I'll keep you informed about my fall adventures.

Fraternally,

August 7, 2006

Damnation in New Orleans is living in a world you can not make or remake as Jelly Roll Justice brings you the WWOZ blues. It don't mean a doggone thing.

College libraries are reluctant to shelve paperbacks that have not been specially bound. If they are used frequently, they tend to fall apart. I think the head librarian at Dillard drew my attention to something I knew but had forgotten. She was willing to let me take a number of paperbacks that might be useful for the courses I teach. I chose those that pertained to scholarship, textual criticism, bibliography, documentation and literary terminology. I welcomed these books with a fondness I usually reserve for friends I have not seen for many years. Many of the titles were ones that I lost to the Storm, and I embraced them as if they were prodigal children. They gave me much needed courage to construct an outline for the Introduction to Scholarship course I intend to teach.

In the English profession, which has successfully deconstructed its pre-1950 definition and justified itself as a swamp, books by unreconstructed, recidivist scholars are treated as if they were oldies but goodies, objects designed to gather dust until someone rescues them from oblivion and uses nostalgia to place them on unflooded higher ground. Although Hershel Parker's *Flawed Texts and Verbal Icons: Literary Authority in American Fiction* was published as recently as 1984, it is already an old book if not a forgotten book or a condemned book. Like many members of his generation, Parker did not fall heels over head in love with theory. Instead, he used his hard-won but discredited authority to taunt the young Turks for dissing empirical work. Parker is neither Polyphemus nor Oedipus, a blind man cursing. I am not the man Kabnis spoke with in Jean Toomer's basement or the one who preached in Ralph Ellison's Alabama chapel. As I read his critique of theory, I am amazed by similarities between his position and mine. Despite the fact that Parker and I have operated in parallel sectors of the English profession, it is almost impossible for those with whom we have done combat to see that the twain of our intentions shall never meet, that we may be essentialists in radically different ways. This failure is the shock of recognition itself. It is also a sufficient reason for not abandoning the old scholarship for the newest criticism and for encouraging my skeptical students to be a little tolerant of my antiquity.

Tuesday, August 8, 2006: A Note on Ambiguity

How much Arab blood is required to paint the Grand Canyon?

"We live in tragic times— in an age of disaster, disbelief, and resentment." These are the closing words in Floyd W. Hayes's powerful essay "The Cultural Politics of Paul Robeson and Richard Wright: Theorizing the African Diaspora" in *ChickenBones: A Journal* (<www.nathanielturner.com/culturalpoliticsofpaulrobeson%20andrichardwright.htm, 8/7/2006>). Cyperspace does not allow me to decide whether the essay is in or on the magazine. Such indecision is trivial. It is the pervasiveness of ambiguity, Hayes hints, that counts. Hayes also casts a strong light on the perversity of ambiguity. When cultural politics endows chaos with philosophical terms of engagement, we are likely to experience disbelief and resentment. The intellectual legacies of Robeson and Wright may still describe, explain, and clarify, but they are incapable of effecting solutions. In troubled times, most people want solutions. And Professor Hayes performs a most valuable service in showing us why solutions are not forthcoming.

Hayes selects his words carefully, because he is obligated to distinguish, as clearly as possible, theorizing diaspora from the uncertainties of its lived experience. Thus, he elects to use the rhetoric of war to historicize the activism of Robeson and Wright before and during the Cold War. Hayes would have us understand how Robeson and Wright conducted battles as they addressed what he calls "the ambiguities that are inherent in theorizing the African Diaspora— ambiguities that constitute the discourse of the African Diaspora." Ambiguities are inherent in theorizing the European and Asian Diasporas, as well, and ambiguity as a cognitive category may be central in the making of discourses. Extreme forms of ambiguity reify what the philosopher Charles W. Mills calls the epistemology of ignorance, and it was against sponsored ignorance that Wright and Robeson took their stands. Exploring their lives and works, as Hayes outlines that process may prevent our falling into traps of romantic or idealized expectations.

In short, Hayes illuminates how the referential power of languages is provisional and weak. We are more likely to disbelieve what we hear than to have faith in its sounded value. We know that both reality and actuality teem with disasters and a few events we can legitimately call fortunate. We are becoming aware that biocultural evolution is more tragic than comic, that battles with external nature eventually are transmuted into battles with ourselves. Hayes does not come to an original conclusion about the early years of the twenty-first century by way of his meditating on Robeson and Wright. He comes to a judicious conclusion about ambiguity in theory and practice. In the theater constituted by African and other diasporas, we should only expect to find the clashing of ignorant armies. You are on target, Professor Hayes, when you sing the blues about our tragic sense of life.

Wednesday, August 9, 2006: Lillian Smith Book Awards

Thanks to WWOZ, Billy Dell, and "Records from the Crypt," when I hear music from the 1950s and 1960s, joy courses through my veins.

I got up early this morning to participate in a conference call with other Lillian Smith Book Awards jurors. Although four of us have neared consensus on the winners for 2006, a fifth juror had not yet completed his reading. I had hoped we might have finished our work today. Now we must have a third conference call next Wednesday. Hell, since Katrina, too many things occur in a backassward frame. I would be more tolerant and understanding if the errant juror was from the Mississippi Gulf Coast or the wetlands of Louisiana. The dude is from Central Mississippi. He was not drenched or displaced by a hurricane. What is his excuse? I tamed my anger with a breakfast sandwich and coffee at the Catty Corner Cafe.

This afternoon Lolis Edward Elie and I drove across the Crescent City Connection to visit our friend Raymond Breaux, who had back surgery last week. It was so reassuring to see Raymond standing very erect and smiling on the sidewalk outside his house when we arrived. We had worried about the outcome of his operation. Now we have more evidence that some procedures in modern medicine are effective, that certain kinds of healthcare are still available in New Orleans.

I have driven to Raymond's house several times since I moved to New Orleans, and each time I have had some difficulty in finding it. As Lolis reminded me, I do not have the best sense of direction. We finally resorted to Lolis's talking on my cell phone with Raymond and giving me street by street guidance. The West Bank confuses me easily, and I am more receptive than ever to confusion as we approach the anniversary of Hurricane Katrina. Driving across the Crescent

City Connection reminds me of the wild, wild west. Streets that look familiar are not. They are paths that I have never traversed. Perhaps this disorientation is a normal part of recovering. The paradox of becoming well so that one is in better shape for becoming sick. I can worry about that later. I am just happy that Billie Dell played old recordings by Irma Thomas and Johnny Adams, the Tan Canary. Their voices brought back the New Orleans I can truly love. The music purged bad feelings about this morning's conference call.

August 10, 2006

8:01:05 a.m.: National Public Radio stirs anxiety this morning. Red alerts. British and American airports on alert. Blame someone. Blame people who do not fall on hands and knees and bow five times in the direction of democracy.

Passengers register degrees of fear. Airplanes train their eyes on terrorists. To blink is an insecure movement.

I can see why this would definitely be a problem.

A bottle of water can be an IED. Or a cup of coffee. Perfume, sunscreen, mouthwash, shaving cream, deodorant, toothpaste, wine, cane syrup, and hot sauce are suspect. They may not be carried on the plane. They may be placed in checked baggage. Is this logical? They may be carried from airport A to airport B in the plane's baggage belly, but they may not be carried in the passenger spaces. Is this logical? A well-designed device can be placed in checked baggage, pass inspections, and be detonated by a watch, an earring, or hearing aid that is inside the passenger space. Indeed, a suicidal passenger could drink the explosive liquid.

Accidents may happen inside of precautions. This is not a canard. It is a statement about airports. About New Orleans.

August 11, 2006: WEED ATTACK/HYPERBOLIC MOMENTS

Epiphany #11: Safe gods add a sense of security in a city coping with police trauma and insane newspaper photographers. The poor man who asked the police to kill him was a frugivorous person.

My house sits approximately two hundred feet from the Gentilly Boulevard sidewalk (Mississippi River side) and twelve feet from a second sidewalk that angles eastward into St. Bernard Avenue. My driveway borders the west of this greenspace, or as I like to think of it, mini-park. The city's Parks and Parkways Department maintenance crew has cut the grass once since August 2005. They trimmed it neatly in early April, before the Jazz and Heritage Festival at the Fairgrounds. The Festival was the only reason Gentilly Boulevard got emergency cosmetic surgery. The city officials did not want the tourists attending the Festival to have their holiday mood disturbed by unmitigated proof of urban blight, Katrina's legacy. After the Festival, the city let the mini-park return to a state of nature. What does it matter that my neighbors and I do not like blight, an unkempt green giving the impression that we are slum dwellers? Moreover, the park crew is overworked and the city is broke! Necessity is the mother of initiative.

A park in a state of nature is a wonder to behold. It grows like cancer even during a dry spell. After our daily thunderstorms began, the weeds got religion. Newly sanctified by the drenching, the weeds tried to outdo one another with praise hymns to the god of growth. One weed, which my contractor said was morel, was particularly fruitful and multiplied with passion. I am under the impression that morel is a fungus not a weed, but I am not a botanist and do not correct my contractor. He is a native New Orleanian; he must know what natives eat. He informs me that some New Orleanians would cook "morel" with meat. (I have not seen it listed on a menu in any eatery here). If animals ate the plant, they sickened and died. This plant has tiny white flowers and reddish purple berries. I crushed a leaf and sniffed. It smelled just like plain old stinky grass. The aroma had no kinship with mustards, collards, turnips, spinach, or lamb's quarters. It was not worthy of a pot let alone a mouth. The plant might well be transmogrified pokeweed or poke salad. In my mind it is as valuable as kudzu; its promiscuity must be brought to a swift end. It is my civic duty to restore virtue where vice has taken root.

The weeds are too thick and surly. My old lawn mower can not do the job without some strategy that weakens the target population. The offensive weeds needed pre-cutting, thinning. I borrow a swing blade (the kind called a yo-yo in the vernacular) and begin my crusade in the sweltering heat. Thinning would also allow me to pick up branches, rocks, broken whiskey and beer bottles, soda cans, wrappings and other trash that might dull or break the mower blades. The attack with the swing blade is a prelude to full-scale warfare on the weeds' unwelcomed paganism. The honor and glory of the true religion of urban beauty is at stake.

Powerless against the razor edge of the swing blade, the weeds fell. I turned a deaf ear to their pleas about the sanctity of life. Being a dumb instrument, the lawn mower was less merciful than I in combat. It decimated grass,weed, and anything else in its path, including the little black and white worms that seemed fond of the small plants that reminded me of baby's breath. It was just too hot to wipe out the enemy in one day. The sun forced me to retreat.

But I had the last words. "I shall return. From dust y'all came, and I'm sending you back as quickly as possible." Yes, we will have some law and order in this neighborhood.

August 12, 2006

Epiphany #12: Some benighted soul has claimed that Dio Chrysostom (AD 40-120) wrote the New Testament. Right. And some of us know the year, month, day, and exact hour the world will end.

August 13, 2006: Excerpt from a Letter

I shall miss my weekend escapes to Vicksburg after the end of this month. The rent for my apartment is reasonable, but the burden of keeping an apartment and repairing my house in New Orleans is just too great. It is the solitude I shall miss most, the freedom from intrusions— no radio or television, no telephone, no access to email, no...

This weekend I will draft more entries for *The Katrina Papers* and read *Ashbery's Forms of Attention* by Andrew DuBois. The book promises to be instructive. Why do critics write about writers? The answers are not simple. Why might a writer be treated as a cultural item rather than a human being who belongs to various communities of interest? Minimizing biographical information enables, I think, a sense of distance, of pseudo-objectivity in the humanistic enterprise of critical commentary and theory.

August 14, 2006

Fashion statement: Baggy body is IN. Slender is OUT.
Each year more Americans opt to wallow like hippopotami in their fat.
Lobbyists are pushing for a ban on fat-free foods.
The First Amendment guarantees the right to be obese.

I finished cutting the mini-park this afternoon and must send a bill to Mayor Nagin for services rendered to the City of New Orleans. I don't want cash just tax credits.

I am very tired, but I muster enough energy to sit through the eight and ten o'clock sets Betty Shirley played at Snug Harbor. Ms. Shirley is one of the best jazz vocalists in New Orleans. Voice— sometimes a source of soulular healing. I am very mellow from two glasses of champagne by the time I arrive. I requested that she sing "Love for Sale." Ears redeemed by her styling. In fact, the evening was like a jazz revival— standards that echoed Ella Fitzgerald, Dinah Washington, Betty Carter, Bessie Smith, Carmen McRae, and showed Shirley's ability to caress a song to best advantage— like church. She is a jewel in the world of jazz, a diva modest enough to use the excellence of her vocal range in the service of the song. She held nothing back. Communion. Though the Monday night crowd was too small to fill half the room, she held nothing back. When I left the club at midnight, I carried angelic sound home: the CD "Betty Shirley Sings."

Closure commits a smile.

August 15, 2006: A Small Irony

Does water walk when you swim?

The Parks and Parkways Department crew profited greatly from my having mowed the city's mini-park in front of my house. It was much easier for them to cut the grass a bit lower than I had. The also trimmed the St. Bernard Avenue neutral ground surrounding "Spirit House" and a portion of the public space on the Lake Pontchartrain side of Gentilly Boulevard. They did not cut the neutral ground in the middle of Gentilly. It is likely the crew will cut the mini-park and other public lands three times each year, but I will not place any bets on that possibility. My best bet is to keep the swing blade, the lawn mower, and my muscles in good working order.

August 16, 2006: LILLIAN SMITH AND A FUTURE

This morning the 2006 Lillian Smith Book Award jury reached a consensus about the winners. One book examines African American education in slavery and freedom; the other, the clash of race and memory in the South. The books are nicely matched, focusing attention on overlapping public spheres. Together they remind readers and thinkers of why in the South **remembering** continues to consume much of our daily lives. Near the end of the consensus process, Hiewet Senghor, Executive Director of the Southern Regional Council, informed us about the plans SRC has to revitalize itself by returning to the organization's original mission: informing as much of the world as will listen about race as a permanent feature of economics, politics, and social exchanges in the South.

As I sit listening in Katrina-ravaged New Orleans, I think about the purpose of the awards. They honor authors who, through their writing, carry on Lillian Smith's legacy of **elucidating the condition** of racial and social inequity and **proposing a vision** of justice and human understanding. Who will cast the light on the condition of this southern city? Who will propose the most equitable vision of how it will prevail? Beyond these questions, or maybe prior to them, is the matter of physical and intellectual work needed to sustain the vitality of questions. To be sure, a small portion of the intellectual work should be devoted to reawakening interest in Lillian Smith's writing and in the practice of behaviors that made her life exceptionally meaningful. Smith's books are out of print. Even among members of the Society for the Study of Southern Literature her name is uttered infrequently. Scholarly attention to her work should be supplemented with a vigorous promotion of making progressive change in the South, especially change that will offer children and the rest of us a better quality of life. I sit watching the sunlight of an August morning soften the ugliness of gutted rooms in my house. Yes, we need such light as Smith's works might provide to help with reconstructing gutted Southern lives.

August 16, 2006: Note on my mental condition

I do not feel well this afternoon. I am tired and sleepy and cranky. I give my
ticket for the premiere of Spike Lee's "When the Levees Broke: A Requiem in
Four Acts" to Danille Taylor. I do not wish to deal with the mixed emotions of
the thousands of survivors who will attend the film. Truth be told, I do not wish to
deal with myself and the tears the film would jerk from my eyes and the swords that
would pierce my heart.

I came home and ate an early supper. I took a nap. I woke up at 9:00 p.m.
and drove to Borders. I had a cup of coffee as I read *The Nation*. I bought the
most recent issue of the *New York Review of Books* and the CD "Ella and Louis,"
the 1956 collaboration between Fitzgerald and Armstong. The collaboration is
perfect and so is my choice. It is better for two jazz giants to take me to heaven
than to have Lee's film send me to hell for blasphemy.

Thursday, August 17, 2006

12:07:15 a.m.: Only in New Orleans

Last night at Borders, I saw a blouse having a cup of coffee. It suddenly began
to sing: "God is my pilot, Jesus is my navigator, the Holy Ghost is my steward."
I think the blouse had overdosed on caffeine. On my way home I noticed that
several items of clothing had committed suicide on I-610 going toward Slidell.
I think the clothing had overdosed on a Spike Lee documentary. Only in New
Orleans does the impossible actually happen.

9:42:15 p.m.: Mood— Bitter, Comic

*In the last days, your mood grows more bitter, more comic. It is certainly
comic when it is ninety-six degrees and you, without benefit of eyeglasses, put the
thermostat on "HEAT" and wonder why are you sweating so profusely. You can
laugh at yourself. You can laugh at vanity. You can not laugh when you get an
email from Washington, DC, that informs you that Dillard University is suing
its insurance companies. It leaves a sour taste in your mouth. Your friend in the
nation's capital knows something important about your institution while you stew
in ignorance. You call one of the staffpersons in the Office of Academic Affairs
and ask if what has been reported to you is true. Yes, it is. "I'll send you the article
from* The Chronicle." *The confirmation does not please you. More litigation. A
new strand of problems for your embattled institution. Its future is threatened
by the possibility of severe underenrollment next month. Someone who works
with enrollment figures whispered to you this week that fewer than nine hundred
students were likely to return on September 15. Will your smartassed remarks*

about teaching windows and doors turn out to be more than a bad joke? Will there be neither window nor door to teach in September 2008?

The onus of uncertainty crushes your spirit.

This afternoon you had coffee with Ernest Jones at Cafe Envie [corner of Barracks and Decatur], because the two of you needed to discuss the 2nd Annual WORD FESTIVAL, October 7, 2006. Ernest's brainchild, the festival is an effort to promote literacy and appreciation for local writers in New Orleans. As is the case elsewhere, the work of local writers is usually overlooked in favor of books that get good reviews in the New York Times. The reading habits of the super-literate would be formed by the "superior" reviews in The New York Review of Books, The Times Literary Supplement, or Bookforum, the sites for serious discourses. The super-literate do not need WORD FESTIVAL. People, especially students, who wish to expand their cultural literacy or their knowledge of the creativity of which New Orleans can be proud can profit from how the Festival exposes new work or older works that might go unnoticed. You share with Ernest a secret hope that the Festival can empower people and give them reason to take pride in their cultures.

Ernest tells you it will not be possible to use Congo Square as a venue. No electricity and toilet facilities are available. The cost of renting portable toilets and supplying generators would exceed the modest budget. The Old U.S. Mint, which you can see from the cafe, would be an ideal spot. It could not be used earlier this month for Satchmo Fest; it may not be ready for public use until January 2007. You propose using St. Augustine Church. Ernest mentions we might use the New Orleans Metropolitan Convention & Visitors Bureau on St. Charles Avenue. The audience you want to attract would like the Mint or St. Augustine more, but when options are limited you must be practical. Secure a site and then invite participants. There is little time for doing that. You and Ernest decide you should not give up on having a festival this year. It should be a one-day event involving readings and a panel or two. You must notify the city that your interest in promoting literacy is still standing.

Ernest and I had been chatting over our coffee– a downhome brew with grounds at the bottom of the cup– almost an hour before either of us mentioned WORD FESTIVAL. His son plays on the Dillard University basketball team. He is a point guard, a smart, ambitious athlete. The Athletic Director resigned this week. The recently hired men's basketball coach is very young. The sudden departure of the AD has created anxiety. Ernest's son feels less secure about his status. What if the new coach brings in a new hotshot point guard? What if having missed an entire season is a stumbling block as the team seeks to rebuild its spirit? Will that process parallel the clouded rebuilding process of New Orleans itself? We just don't know.

Ernest's parental concern is all of a mix with the concerns I have as a teacher at Dillard. Will returning students still be in the claws of post-Katrina stress? Will this year's crop of freshmen be underprepared for dealing with college in a city where the normal has been down so long that the bottom looks like the pinnacle? Will faculty members be any better prepared to cope with adversity than their students? Will we have as many or even more logistical problems on campus than we had at the Hilton? We just don't know. There is little time now for taking measures to ensure that students have a decent shot at a good education in our weird post-Katrina atmosphere.

I tell Ernest I feel utterly frustrated. Utterly unsure. I am frightened. I lack energy or enthusiasm for creating the online syllabi for my courses. There is so much reason for grief across the entire continent of Africa, that I fear my teaching of African World Studies 100 will be painful. What should I teach students in Introduction to Scholarship about how languages play a role in sponsoring global conflicts? Am I in danger of spilling my political beliefs in a space that demands "objective" attention? And my new course on Richard Wright, Ralph Ellison and James Baldwin? Will I overemphasize how Baldwin and Wright dealt with human imperfection and be snide when I speak of Ellison's optimism? Or will there be an insufficient number of students to take the English courses? Will I have to teach a couple of sections of writing courses or the sections of American and British literature that do have minimal enrollments? I just don't know. *The longer you walk across the tightrope named "return to normal," the more detailed is the clip of your screaming fall onto a flatbed of nails, razors, burning coals, hypodermic needles, and broken glass.* I do not like the vision of an ending.

We now have acess to Version 7 of Blackboard, and that can be a godsend in the case of another emergency evacuation. We would have a higher probability of being able to continue teaching courses over the Internet. The probability is contingent on course packs, i.e., the students having the required texts and the instructors having prepared attention-holding online courses. I need some special training in how to use the new tools that enable me to spice my courses with visuals and sounds. *If you get the training within the next three weeks, there is no assurance your online courses will be better than makeshift. You shall hate what you create.*

This crisis of confidence intensifies my feelings of trauma. I spill beans with alacrity. Like a good priest, Ernest listens intelligently and patiently to my confession. He tries to put me at ease by recounting his experience of watching all four hours of Spike Lee's documentary "When the Levees Broke: A Requiem in Four Acts" at the New Orleans Arena last night. He assures me that Lee has created a brilliant narrative, a confirmation that every person still breathing in New Orleans is touched with more than a little insanity. My laughter is silent and bitter. *It should be. That a little insanity is not enough is truly a funny thing.*

214

August 18-20, 2006: RETURNING TO THE SOURCES

Some days I feel like a helium balloon one second before the string connects it with the earth.

Compromised freedom has become a major issue in my country since the Supreme Court elected George W. Bush, since 9/11 became the debatable icon of the twenty-first century, since Hurricane Katrina became the name of our national tragedy. We who believe that the United States is the most perfect example in history of what a democracy should be have an enormous problem of explaining to outsiders why suddenly certain freedoms are "unavailable"– unavailable for them and us. Nor is it easy to explain to an outsider why power is a glass tiger. The outsider believes that American citizens, whatever their status, can save the world, or whatever portion of the world the outsider lives in. She or he absolutely refuses to believe that we Americans are not omnipotent, that we can shatter.

I shall blame my friend Kalamu ya Salaam for leading me down a straight-crooked New Orleans street and leaving me in explanatory difficulties. I had to explain the fragility of power as I talked this afternoon to a young man from Angola who lives in Zambia.

We– Kalamu, Mahmud Rahman, and I– are supposed to be on our way to an African dinner and pleasant conversation. Instead, Kalamu turns off St. Bernard Avenue onto North Dorgenois and parks near Mama D's house/home/headquarters in the Seventh Ward.

Mama D (Diane Cole French) is a force to be reckoned with. People who know what the offical mass media is not reporting about New Orleans know that. She is an organizer. She has been called a matriarch. "Matriarch" sounds like an anthropological misnomer used by folks who don't know how to talk about Africans and African-descended people. As far as I am concerned, she is just a brave and ordinary woman who is capable of doing extraordinary things. She organizes life in her neighborhood and calls attention to how disorganized the political leadership of New Orleans is. Call her name and elected officials seek shelter in weird platitudes. She is a very active member of Families and Friends of Louisiana's Incarcerated Children (FFLIC), a truth-teller. She did not flee in the face of Hurricane Katrina. She stayed and got harrassed by the military, FEMA, the first and second responders, as she tried and continues to try to make her neighborhood liveable. She did not wait until the Women of the Storm went to Congress to do the right thing; her efforts were prototypes for what the women wanted to do. Media mavens pretend she and genuine grassroots efforts do not exist.

I think Kalamu wants Mahmud and me to be witnesses.

Mama D has known Kalamu for a long time. She smiles as she welcomes the odd people, Mahmud and me. She has been examining a box of photographs of the neighborhood with a friend, pictures that have to be used in a report. A young African man who is wearing fatigue pants, a fatigue cap, and a National Baptist something-or-other t-shirt is sitting on one of the stump-chairs near the sidewalk. He rises and shakes hands with us. I tell Mama D that people in New York were quite impressed with what she said at the Shabazz Conversation last fall. She nods and gives me some intriguing details about that trip, then informs all of us about her current work, the Japanese newspeople who have documented it, the Vietnamese shopkeepers down the block and their fronting for the drug traffic, the volunteer she sent back to Jerusalem and the other volunteer she helped to rescue from Lebanon, how the City Council is playing games with voting districts and people's lives, and.... "Hey, now...." She goes to greet one of her sisters, who has just driven up.

I ask the young man where he is from. "Africa." I already knew. His face, his body build, his accent said that. "No. I mean which part. I would guess East Africa." His expression changes quickly. "I'm from southern Africa. I think of Africa as one country. Originally, I am from Angola but I live in Zambia. I have a lot of property there." I tell him it is important to be specific about nations or countries. Given what I have to teach students, it is very important to prevent their overlooking details and inventing a continent as a single country. He is undaunted. He has dreams of unification despite neo-colonialism. Bursting with idealism and optimism, he lectured me on the crucial role that African Americans have in saving the continent of Africa.

An African man is trying to save my soul, to convert me to his belief that if we pray, God will answer our prayers and allow Africa to become a country rather than a death-friendly continent.

The man is afflicted with the missionary disease. There are some prayers that God refuses to answer, and no doubt God has legitimate godly reasons for remaining silent.

We do agree on one thing. The world should have rushed to help Robert G. Mugabe appropriate all the arable land in Zimbabwe and restore it to the people so they would be able to feed themselves and minimize the domination of the Other, the post-colonial Other. After all, the then superpowers of the world did not hesitate to help Zionists appropriate Israel in the late 1940s. If we can not avoid having injustice, injustice should be equally distributed.

I have to explain to this young man what I am sure he understands better than I. The destruction of the Organization of African Unity and its displacement by African Union has left Africans at the mercy of the International Monetary Fund and other neocolonial powers that know Africa is the wealthiest continent on the earth and that Africans are peoples who allow their freedoms to be compromised by their leaders and by their deep belief in the human. The image is vulgar because what is happening in 2006 on the continent of Africa is vulgar and obscene. And all the blame can not be attributed to the European white man. We can not entertain that fib to absolve ourselves of shared guilt.

Truth is an adult who does not sit in a playpen with stupidity. Some of the blame is carried by the Arabs, the Muslims and devotees of Islam, who live north of the Sahara and who commit vicious acts of genocide. Some of the blame is festering in American foreign policy. Some of the blame is carried, I tell the young man, by the people from the Middle East, who brought Islam and slavery to a wide swath of his beloved continent, who own the best stores in Dakar and the best seats on the OPEC Board. And soon blame will be carried by the Chinese and their Indian comrades. Read the current trade agreements and treaties. Listen to treason.

Is this young African man a dæmonic agent come to test my sanity? He is forcing me to preview the script for the destruction of Africa in the twenty-first century. The bad dream he has given me of reality is much too painful. It has all the colors and tones of the slave gospel. He is making me wish to wipe Man and Woman from the face of the earth. Do he and I have the same impersonal interest in secular salvation? The same personal Savior? Richard Wright shoots words through my mind. "Man, God Ain't Like That." Can I unbrand the scars inside the young African man's head? Can he batter down the prisonhouse time has erected in my own?

I look very deeply into the ancient eyes of the young man. My gaze has to hack its way through a lot of tall missionary grass to reach the clearing. It is night, but the clearing is brightly lit by the splintered stars that were once the teeth of President Juvenal Habyarimana. The clearing is huge. My eyes sweep across the thousands upon thousands of crucified Hutsi [Hutu + Tutsi]. The signs tacked at the top of each cross read: IN GOD WE TRUSTED.

Here be genocide. The Rwanda genocide. 1994. The names have been erased from the stories and buried. Ethnicity has reshuffled history a thousand times and the narratives are not entitled. Not entitled to be entitled. It must be the season of the witch. Smashed heads, amputated legs and arms, a ginger-colored finger, a nailed foot, raped and sodomized bodies that will not rot— all these bits and pieces of humanity hang on the crosses. The blinding bright eyes of the dead children stare accusations at me. My ears consume cruel French-inflected African laughter. All I can smell is the stench of repetitions orchestrated by the World Bank, the IMF, African Union. I am not devastated. I am demolished, shattered.

He tries to read the writing inside my head. I can feel him turning the pages, puzzling to decipher my handwriting. I tell him that African Americans and Africans have yet to resolve their self-hatred and death-desires, their class and ideological divisions. Perhaps in time we shall. Several hundred more years.

We can cooperate and become kinsmen once more. We must first have separate resolutions for local problems. We must remember that the local is knotted with the universal. These are not problems on which either Africans or African Americans have a monopoly. These are the problems of contemporary Man and Woman, world problems. My young African brother and I are glass tigers, conflicted wretches of the Earth, and we can not help the entire continent of Africa any more than the Italians and the Italian Americans can help the entire continent of Europe. I look at the man's face with tough love. He must go home and help with improving Zambia. I must stay in New Orleans and help with improving Louisiana. We can only help one another by embracing the power of fire. "I believe," I tell him, "in the match." He manages to agree with that veiled message. He and I know that the fires burning now do not belong to us.

Our separate worlds must burn time with our own fires before unification occurs.

When shall we succeed in teaching our children that they must love themselves enough not to kill the people in their towns, townships, and ghettoes or "hoods" – the people who are themselves? When shall we African Americans teach them to love the hair God gave them enough not to make the Koreans, who are only too willing to help them ruin the hair, very wealthy? Or, as Mama D told us earlier this afternoon, she recently had to cuss out a young sister who cut off her beautiful African hair and replaced with the tails of inferior Asian horses. Extensions of African retentions.

The young man believes that if a sufficient number of African Americans left the United States and took all their consumer power with them to Africa (and he was not specific about the destinations of the immigrants), then the world economy would change and Africa would profit. Dreams. The young man is full of naïve dreams. His understanding of world politics is a calculated innocence. I do not want him to become a part of our benign genocide. I want him to live. He is helping me to understand much, much better Richard Wright's *Black Power* and its multiple levels of significance; he is helping me to understand the emotional well from which Wright's anger came when he visited the Gold Coast in 1953.

The Africans in various lands that have all the wrong boundaries will have to first heal themselves and their ancient ethnic hatreds and reset boundaries before they can call upon African Americans for help. And the help, I warn my young brother, will be long in arriving. We are too busy with trying to regain our compromised freedoms in the United States, for we laid our matches down and they got wet.

When the young man hops in his van and drives off to yet another mission, I come back to the late afternoon sunlight, to New Orleans and North Dorgenois, to Mama D, Kalamu, and Mahmud. I glue all the shattered pieces of me together, knowing that I have been to the sources. I am starving for dinner at Bennachin.

It was destined that Mahmud Rahman should have heard parts of the African/ African American dialogue. He, Kalamu, and I are all actors in this post-Katrina performance. He grew up in Bangladesh and now lives in Oakland, Ishmael Reed territory. He is a journalist and fiction writer who knows much about the United States and its ethnic problems. According to his webpage, he is very much interested in "the metaphor of water as the agency of escape, life, death, and reflection." He is in New Orleans, I am sure, to see how the metaphor of water plays its music here. He is on his long trip to home, traveling deeper into writing a novel set in contemporary Bangladesh. After dinner, I assure him the critics will love his novel. They are mad for the postcolonial. I hope Mahmud will come to New Orleans again. I would really enjoy having a conversation with him about the sources and compromised freedoms.

Some days I feel like the earth– a space that is being stepped on without permission.

Chakula tells me that anyone can access information about me from www. zabasearch.com. I check the URL. He told the truth. I email info@zabasearch. com and request that my name and personal information be removed.

Felipe Smith asks if Dillard University can help Common Ground with a major fund-raiser for Hurricane Katrina victims, a program featuring Sonia Sanchez, Amiri Baraka, and perhaps Sean Penn. No, Felipe. Dillard University can not help. The ideal space we might provide under usual circumstances has not yet been remediated and restored. Let Common Ground prevail upon the more fortunate Tulane University for help.

MRE: Meals Ready to Eat. Music Ready to Enjoy. Multitudes Refusing to Expire.

Nayo sends me a very sensitive, very supportive message about my writing, and she has inspired me to do more writing. Jonathan Batiste's brilliant piano playing inspires me, infuses me with a tonic to relieve the weariness that comes with the blues of recovery. A brief conversation with John Page this afternoon lightened the load of living. The prospect of reading Kevin Powell's seventh book expands my desire for a future, as does the likelihood of my visiting Reginald Martin in Memphis later this year. Submitting my review of a manuscript to *African American Review* this afternoon was a small achievement. New Orleans after Katrina is trying to transform me and other people into mental cases. It has had noteworthy success according to recently published reports by mental health workers and the evidence provided by *The Katrina Papers: A Journal of Trauma and Recovery*. But I am a rare phoenix. I shall rise and recover from the most water-logged ashes. Please note there are many rare, invisible birds in New Orleans.

Some days I have no words to describe feelings other than a poem to suggest feeling has not evaporated.

Reconciliation and Truth Came Home

America, the roasting hen crowed three times
before the rooster spoke,
redeeming Malcolm, Mohandas and Marx,
joining the working class red beans
who have divorced you,
divorced you for becoming evil rice women
and rump-fallen men who
have colorblind orgasms with whiteness,
with exported democracies and imported ideologies,
joining the underclass you niggered to create,
joining the ghosts of those you shat upon for centuries with puritanic glee,
those you wetbacked, whipped back, enslaved back, backed back, atomic
vaporized black,
unbaptizing their humanites,
joining the maize and the okra and the yams,
the peanut pepper soups and the sushi
who have divorced your kitchen, the rain that has divorced your global warmth,
the green eagle paper that has divorced your toilet;
three times crowed the roasting hen, America,
redeeming Moses, Marcus and Martin,
before the rooster broke his silence, let his fire verbs
condemn your lynching all patriotic parrots.

Saturday, August 19, 2006

"The Katrina story is so serious and so personal and so tragic it has to be told through humor with social commentary at the same time."
McNeal Cayette

August 19, 2006

Governor's Arts Awards
Louisiana Division of the Arts
P. O. Box 44247
Baton Rouge, Louisiana 70804-4247

To whom it may concern:

When a poet, folklorist, and scholar has devoted a significant portion of her life to enlightening the world about the wealth of creativity in Louisiana, she deserves recognition. Dr. Mona Lisa Saloy's doctoral dissertation (Louisiana State University) was entitled "When I Die, I Won't Stay Dead: The Poetry of Bob Kaufman," and the many years of painstaking research on the life and works of the elusive New Orleans poet Bob Kaufman involved much more than meeting the requirements for a terminal degree. Herself a New Orleanian and poet, Dr. Saloy was aware of the literary historical importance of assessing his poetry in the context of his birthright. In this sense, her scholarship was an extension of her creativity. She was aware also of how important it is to nurture young writers when she developed the Creative Writing Program at Dillard University.

There is much more to say about Dr. Saloy's artistry than the limits of this letter of endorsement permit. Her interest in folklore bespeaks a great sensitivity to the languages of New Orleans, to the many ways the lived experiences and foibles of people contribute to the making of history. Over the years, her New Orleans-inflected poems appeared in such journals and anthologies as Southern Review, Louisiana Cultural Vistas, Louisiana English Journal, From a Bend in the River: 100 New Orleans Poets, and Word Up: Black Poetry of the 80s from the Deep South. The work that has earned national acclaim and is testament to her power as a Louisiana artist, however, is the work collected in Red Beans and Ricely Yours (2005), which won the T. S. Eliot Prize in Poetry. In "Words Can't Describe What Some Writers In New Orleans Lost" (Wall Street Journal, November 1, 2005), Daniel Golden recognized what Dr. Saloy and the world lost as Hurricane Katrina murdered her unpublished metaphors and narratives of folk wisdom. Nevertheless, her words refuse to stay dead as they speak in her recent essays "Social Networks in New Orleans" and "Native Daughter: Growing Up Black in New Orleans" and in the new poems she has been reading in Washington,

Missouri, Florida, and other states.

In recognition of her achievement and of her being a fine ambassador for the arts in Louisiana, I very strongly urge that she be honored with a Governor's Arts Award for 2006.

Sincerely,

Jerry W. Ward, Jr.
Professor of English and African World Studies

Mona Lisa will be on leave from Dillard this academic year. We shall miss her bubbly "Hey Now" greetings, her sparkling cheerfulness, her New Orleans humor. Her presence, like that of her fellow poet Brenda Marie Osbey (who now teaches at Louisiana State University), was part of the intellectual and creative wealth of our Department of English. Their absence will remind me of poverty, the kind that is not much bruited in our government documents on the status of the have-nots and the haves in America.

It is beyond quantification. It is a critical factor in human life that precludes our ever knowing "the truth" about poverty in our cities, especially if we talk about it, as the philosopher Martha Nussbaum would have us do, in terms of **functioning, inclusion, capabilities.** "The truth" would complicate the discourse of economics. "The truth" longs for a moral philosophy that New Orleans rejects in toto.

Thanks to our intellectual limits and the desires of certain politicos and business persons, we shall always have an inaccurate picture of what poverty in New Orleans is. The discourse will remain traditional, nuanced with racialized platitudes. As we approach the anniversary of Hurricane Katrina and the broken levees, the state of poverty worsens. We continue to send Trojan Horse invitations to displaced New Orleanians. We continue to talk in meaningless platitudes about the glory of returning. Return to what? To a city where the jobs they once had have now been outsourced to exploitable workers who do not yet speak like us? To a city where affordable rental units, better-than-average education and much needed healthcare can be measured in a demi-tasse? The broadest sense of what poverty is does matter here. * * In less than a year New Orleans has been transformed from "the city that care forgot" into "the city that does not care for the unchosen." Poverty deepens in an urban space that is a model of perverted liberal and conservative Purtanisms.

* *Gaze upon poverty. Its amoeboid body sprawls from Oregon to Florida, from New Hampshire to California. It is insatiable. This ghost eats in a London alley. It walks boldly

in the streets of Rio and Dakar. In winter, it huddles in rags in Washington, D.C. and New York. It streaks with cell phone through the streets of New Haven. It is shameless. Unlike its amoral step-brother Wealth, it seeks neither understanding nor forgiveness. It is! It is stupid for officials and ordinary people to express alarm that this ghost lives in New Orleans. They are not that dense, that ignorant. Just because the ghost did not show its face in Aspen or on the yacht in the Greek Isles is not a good reason for people to pretend they were unaware of its power. Only the brain dead enjoy such innocence.

August 21, 2006: Reflections in Katrina's Eye

I am watching the first two hours of Spike Lee's *When the Levees Broke: A Requiem in Four Acts* and hearing the profanity of frustration and seeing... what am I seeing? Lee's documentary moves through the yesterday of Hurricane Katrina's sound and fury, moves deliberately and slowly above the heart-jolting explosions of breaking levees and canals so faintly echoed in Terence Blanchard's soundtrack. Afflicted voices filter through memories, drip into articulation, mixing like oil and vinegar in my consciousness. I sit dry-eyed and silent. My breathing matches the pace of the film. The light flickering from the screen reminds me I am in the eye of something. But what am I seeing?

I can't give verbal three-dimensionality to the visual essence of the documentary unless I retreat into a past that seems to have nothing to do with natural disaster in New Orleans. That past, however, both in its 1980s manifestation and in the words I wrote in my journal about it earlier this year, has much to do with Southern writers as witnesses, with the unpredictability of burdens they opt to carry or to drop. I go back to those days when Hoyt Fuller had been fired as editor of *Black World* and had moved from Chicago to Atlanta. He championed the efforts of Alice Lovelace and other Southern writers to forge a group that would link those of us who were committed to writing as community action, as well as to writing as art. That was one of Hoyt's primal roles in America, encouraging young writers to take responsibility for cultural problems. He had done an admirable job with OBAC in Chicago, pushing Don L. Lee (Haki Madhubuti), Sterling D. Plumpp, Angela Jackson, Carolyn Rodgers, and others into visibility and providing a forum for their voices in *Negro Digest/Black World*. We looked to Hoyt to do something similar in Atlanta. Looking blindly to a future, we thought his new magazine *First World* would be a powerful forum for Southern black voices. We did not know how Atlanta would "kill" him just as someone or some group was killing young people; we did not know (and still do not) if there was some ungodly relationship between the Atlanta Child Murders and Hoyt's unexplained death. Wayne Williams was blamed for the death of 27 children. Is he now the vague scapegoat for our forgetting? Why am I thinking of Wayne Williams and Hoyt Fuller? Is it that, after Hurricane Katrina, the brutal facts of life and death have become obsessions?

It had to be the very early 1980s when we had a meeting in Atlanta at which Alice spoke boldly of the work required to achieve our as yet unarticulated goals. She spoke again last year, December 2005, at the 21st annual meeting of the National Performance Network in Miami. I copied a few sentences this morning from that speech, "From Chaos to Clarity: The Price to be Paid":

> We must not let truth and beauty slip away. We must become the recorders, those who contextualize; like Jazz, we must stretch the human imagination. In addition, we are called on to use the lens of Katrina, to force people to look, to peel away the layers of someone else's dream, help them to see their true destiny.

Must, must, must... the imperatives. I want to use Alice's words at the workshop entitled "LETTING THE WATER WRITE." I will conduct at the University of New Orleans on July 10. How will participants, all of them devastated by what is happening in the city, react to imperatives? What will the memory of water force them to say? Will they find that their voices have become eyeglasses to assist our reading of the universe?

I am seeing Spike Lee's idea of how the truth inscribed in disasters challenges the beauty of the human spirit. The collage in motion before me turns me into a witness of all the audiovisual evidence stored in my memory; at the same time, it makes me a juror who must find a verdict regarding the reliability of Lee's representation. What I am seeing are reflections in Katrina's eye. They pose disturbing questions about my obligation as a Southern black writer to be at once witness and juror in the face of event and response. As I try to construct answers, I tear off layer after layer of nightmare, exposing that recovery is a walk through the door of no return.

August 22, 2006

One of the most illuminating scenes in Act IV of "When the Levees Broke" shows the Army Corps of Engineers colonel walking and dissolving into a future that is water. It is inviting to interpret the scene crudely. Knowing the Corps will not construct levees capable of withstanding a Category 5 hurricane reinforced by global warming, the colonel takes a man's final option: he joins Nature. The bureauracracy he represents abandons New Orleans.

Such an interpretation is simple-minded and tangential to the "truth" which a documentary far more volatile than Lee's should throw into our faces. Lee cleverly inserts the initial moment of a film that should shock the world in the footage from the Mississippi Gulf Coast. A doctor who is prevented from going to his devastated home because Vice President Cheney is having a photo-opportunity very nearby addresses the Vice President with the words the Vice President had previously addressed to Senator Patrick J. Leahy. "Go fuck yourself." Whereas Lee's documentary is a polite, almost sanitized, exploration of horror and contradictions in New Orleans, the world needs a briefer, funkier confronting of what Hurricane Katrina and government ineptness in responding to disaster did to the entire southeastern region of the United States. Such a film may prove as ineffective as Michael Moore's "Fahrenheit 9/11" in awakening the nation to its chronic malaise, but the effort should be made to do so.

After watching the second two hours of *When the Levees Broke*, my mind is a Teflon cube. God's purposeful troubling of the water, acid resentments, and collapse and resurrection of the human spirit do not stick easily. Were I outside the post-Katrina circle, I might respond with more alacrity. But I am inside. For me, the review of much that happened in New Orleans after August 29, 2005 is a fairly interesting exhibit. It is like "Without Sanctuary," the powerful catalyst for remembering lynching in America. Residual trauma reduces the impact but not the ultimate worth of Lee's film.

Call us hard-headed, crazy or whatever you will. Because we must fight ideological, racial, and political-economic polarities— fundamental tensions in the United States, we shall not be moved. Whether we have watched four hours or no hours of *When the Levees Broke*, we shall not be moved.

August 22: HAIRCUT

You are cutting grass in your backyard. It is hot. Haircut. Do the roots of grass feel relief when you take away the burden of supporting their long blades? It is hot and humid this morning. Do the bricks you had to remove from the ground and stack on the stump of the magnolia feel any gratitude for being taken out of the mud? Haircut. Hot. Are the gnats annoying your ears really.... Haircut! Yes, haircut. You take off your gloves, enter the cool house, call your barber. He can take you at 9:00 a.m. You have ten minutes to put up the tools, rinse the sweat from your hair, put on a dry shirt, drive to the barbershop. The army taught you to be quick. You arrive at 9:02 a.m. It is OK. You are not late. The barber is still working on his 8:30 a.m. customer. After Hurricane Katrina, the cost of a haircut doubled, going from $10 to $20. You can no longer simply walk into a barbershop and wait for the first available barber. You must now call for an appointment. Barbers have become sophisticated. They want to give the impression that you are receiving personal care. The impression justifies the change in prices. Now that your hair grows slowly, you want to minimize the number of trips you make to the barber. You get a low cut, the kind you don't have to comb. If your head were shaped like Michael Jordan's, you would have the barber shave it. When the barber finishes cutting your hair, your head is grateful that it has less weight to support. You are relieved that you no longer look like a person care has abandoned.

A Letter

New Orleans   August 23, 2006, 7:30 a.m.

Dear Julius,

I have enclosed a copy of "Reconciliation and Truth Came Home," the poem which you have my permission to use for your CLA paper. I sent the poem in the text of my reply to your email, but it won't hurt for you to have another copy. Unless you have a reason not to, I suggest that you include Richard Wright's "Between the World and Me" among the poems that you analyze. It is probably the most gripping poem on lynching in the whole body of 20th century black poetry.

After watching all four hours of "When the Levees Broke" this week, I am feeling like a Teflon cube. The tragedy the documentary portrays washed over me and did not stick. It is not that I was not moved emotionally, for I am sure the film stirred every emotion of which my mind and body are capable. For me the response situation is much like what Frederick Douglass mentioned about being in the circle. When you are inside the circle, you neither know nor appreciate fully what distance and the outside can make obvious. The perpetual frustration, the anger and rage and sorrow, the mind in pain and the body assaulted daily by residual pollution, the suffering and resilience to suffering in New Orleans— it is all locked in the cube that I have become post-Katrina. The cube simply will not be moved. I have to work out the strange complexity of my response in the final pages of **The Katrina Papers**, my sense of the unfinished, of what will not admit conclusion.

Life continues to roll forward here, although it has to carry with it our anxieties about hurricanes between now and the end of November. The changes in the world's climate might make it more than theoretically possible to have hurricanes in February or April. The uncertainty is killing. But I move forward into a future despite that uneasy feeling. Despite my having no metaphysical raft, I drift onward. If I have learned anything from the year-long process of keeping a journal of trauma and recovery, it is a valuable lesson about writing and the world. Writing helps us to possess "worlds" that the inhabited world would deny us. Although these worlds vanish with our minds when we die, perhaps someone will find something useful in the traces.

Fraternally,

Revisiting Feelings at 10:52:38 p.m.

Riding in the Ark of Bones at the bottom of the Mississippi River was an option. Then along came Job and some people you love, meddling in your business, convincing your guardian angel that you must be patient. The angel agreed and served you with a patience summons, but he still refuses to give you a date and time for the trial. That's one of the problems with angels. They do not believe in full disclosure.

I spent several hours this morning in my office on campus. As I took books I had not seen for almost a year out of boxes, I felt trepidation and relief.

Almost a year after The Storm it is extremely difficult to have discrete emotions about anything– it does not matter whether it is filling the gas tank in my car, mailing a letter or ordering a book from Amazon.com, making a peanut butter sandwich, copping an attitude when someone makes me angry or talking with friends, watching a film or listening to music on WWOZ, buying a loaf of bread or a bottle of pomegranate juice, paying an exorbitant ENTERGY bill or dealing with email messages; my feelings are extremely disorganized, and I no longer have plain names for them. Trauma has made my feelings or emotions hyperactively complex. I want to deny ownership. I want to lie and say my declining ability to know and name things is a characteristic of a person who is not me. I am still standing at the controls. Still the clichéd captain of my fate. But it is becoming difficult to prepare faces for the faces that I meet, to wear the mask that is cheerful. Acting normal is a heavy burden. The moments of happiness in my life are brief. Execrations I have not willed into being slip from my mouth. Less able than ever to understand the self I have become, I worry too much and not enough about what the world thinks. Choosing to book passage on the Ark of Bones seems attractive, but I am paralyzed each time I try to walk to the ticket office or to make reservations by telephone.

August 24: Katrina and Harold Pinter's Moment of Truth

I did not write about Pinter's Nobel Prize speech, his moment of truth, in December 2005, because I wanted some distance between my initial reaction to his words about words and my growing awareness of how to live with our domestic and international exercises in distorting what is actual. I listed "moment of truth" as a topic and moved on to more pressing concerns. Anxiety about this hurricane season and those to come dragged me back to Pinter and his perspectives on the political uses of language. The words I hear from Mayor Nagin and City Council members, from Louisiana's governor and congresspersons and senators, from the Commander-in-Chief of the United States of America– the words seem as effective as sand bricks on a beach in Biloxi, Mississippi. We New Orleanians have spent an inordinate amount of time walking on the waters of recovery. Now we are asked to swim in quicksand. Enough is enough. I need Pinter's attempt to speak truth to escape, however briefly, from the labor camp of post-Katrina reconstructing.

The Internet version of Pinter's speech I read on December 9, 2005, was prefaced or "framed" by Sarah Lyall's December 8 *New York Times* article, "Playwright Takes a Prize and a Jab at U.S." We need not debate whether U.S. refers to the United States or to "us" (whoever "we" might be). The absence of a definite article settles the issue. I was much interested in Lyall's choice of words in describing Pinter. In her opinion, Pinter turned the speech into "a furious howl of outrage against American foreign policy," and he was "bristling with controlled fury." I have not seen the video of the speech. I haven't heard the audiotape of Pinter's delivery. I have to imagine a fragile old man behaving like King Lear as he descants on how language obscures reality. It is appropriate that Pinter the dramatist should pay such tribute to Shakespeare, his literary ancestor.

A few days ago I reread the speech in *PMLA* 121.3 (2006): 811-818. This version is glossed by a sidebar: "Art, Truth & Politics"/ Harold Pinter/ a head shot of Pinter copyrighted by The Nobel Foundation / a biographical sketch of 21 lines. The sidebar establishes that Pinter is an honored member of the liberal establishment, not a pre-postmodern Lear. Lyall has firmly implanted in my mind that Pinter is Lear. I like him very much in that role.

The opening strategy of the speech is brilliant. Pinter quotes himself as having written in 1958 that "there are no hard distinctions between what is real and what is unreal." He still stands, as a writer, by his words, but he declares he cannot stand by them as a citizen. "As a citizen I must ask: What is true? What is false? "(*PMLA* 811).

Pinter separates the arena where the true and the false can be identical from the realm of cognition where the false and the true remain segregated. I smell a Trojan horse. Whether the person plays the role of writer or that of citizen, she or he possesses an essence or core that is fixed, that remains in a defining relationship to playful deviations. Like it or not, a person has some responsibility for metaphysical absolutes that might nurture civilization. Even if truth does not exist, we are responsible for it. Pinter tried to come to grips with this inconvenient possibility by making a fine distinction between political theater and political satire. At this moment in his speech, Pinter is busting loose because he wants to deal. According to Pinter, the political theater must not sermonize if the ambiguous freedom of language in art is to be preserved. In contrast, political satire does sermonize. In wishing to maintain such distinctions, Pinter reveals himself to be an honest, conservative liberal or liberal conservative— whichever fits for the purposes of drama and criticism. His speech, at least for me, is an example of why "the truth" quite often does not set us free.

228

Friday, August 25, 2006 09:52:40 a.m.

Asili ya Nadhiri, one of the most original poets you know, a poet capable of creating a language in which to be enormously creative, calls this morning. He is concerned that he has not heard from you for months. You have not responded to voice messages he left on your answering machine in Vicksburg nor to his brief emails. It is not unusual in trauma cases for the patient to respond least to those whom he likes most. Is your case a few steps beyond usual?

I explain to Asili, whom I have not talked with since late January at the Zora Neale Hurston Festival, that I am OK in the highly qualified way one can be OK in New Orleans in late 2006. New Orleans is OK too, if increasing crime and inequity, blooming manifestations of anxieties whose taproots run one mile down in the soggy earth, and blatant denials regarding the limits of hope are indices of what is OK. My voice weaves humor into the serious cloth of conversation.

He seems relieved to know that I can still laugh. Of course I can. Blues people are capable of laughter.

Then he launches the serious question: Have we learned anything?

You pause. "We" does not readily reveal its target.

Human beings have learned how vulnerable they are as they deal with Nature. Caution, careful planning and technological achievements fail sooner and later.

We have learned from the Bush Baby that we must doubt the authority of authority. He has one up on Tricky Dicky and is a far better teacher.

"We" embraces only an almost insignificant number of people in the world's population; if 50% of the people now living in New Orleans have learned these or similar lessons, let us count ourselves fortunate.

Asili tells me that he agrees with this view, but he wonders what has happened to the spirit of resistance in the United States, to our capacity for political protest. He thinks we are witnessing a weakening of national character. I suggest that he remember the USA Patriot Act was passed after 9/11. Even those who have not read one page of that document know what it is capable of putting into motion: one's disappearance from the face of this earth. The bulk of our population does not wish to disappear. Being forewarned, they are meek. I contend now, as I contended months ago in Iowa, Pennsylvania and Arizona, that a large part of our national tragedy is the transformation of citizens into sheep. It is unreasonable to hope that the process can be reversed. Terrorism will most likely preclude that possibility.

Asili mentions he is unhappy with the opening of his high school. His students are... I do not allow him to finish. "What you are seeing in your students, Asili, is quintessential self-hatred." He is taken aback. "You're right." It is simply a matter of ESP and of knowing that students across our nation suffer the same malaise. Drawing upon last night's conversation with Kalamu, I recommend that he put his students in a circle and ask them to write their stories. I predict that several of them will claim they have no story. In that case, he should ask them to write about not having a story.

I make some allusion to Marcus Garvey. Asili laughs. He suggests I should be careful about the company I keep. Asili, I know the difference between possibility and reality, between fantasy and meaningful work. If you see me in a whirlwind, I will not be riding in a metaphor.

As we finish our conversation, I promise to send Asili a few excerpts from *The Katrina Papers*.

Friday, August 25, 2006 10:19:15 p.m.

This week my department chair requested that I teach English 321: British Survey I this fall, rather than English 401: Major Author. This change of plans solves one problem and immediately throws up another. The two-fold motion illustrates how unpleasantries manifest themselves in our hurricane-fractured academic community.

I will have to move back to *Beowulf* and its bloody depiction of a culture that is pre-English, *Sir Gawain and the Green Knight*, Chaucer, Edmund Spenser's allegory of allegories, John Donne's poetry and Francis Bacon's essays, Milton's rewriting of Genesis, Dryden's critical utterances, and the studied civility of Addison and Steele. *Move back* is to be stressed, because I taught English 321 between April and July as part of Dillard's Term 2, Spring 2006. In order to simulate an entire academic year, we conflated 2005-2006 into thirteen-week Terms between January and July. The repetition is not attractive, especially in its reminding me of how very slowly things are moving forward in New Orleans. Thus, in agreeing to teach British literature, I help to solve a small part of Dillard University's underenrollment problem. We have a tacit agreement to teach only those courses that are required for a handful of majors and to delay courses that are elective within the English major. Teaching the required course keeps me glued to foundations. I should be thankful that preparation will be less arduous, but I am not. Circumstances (over which we have as much control as we do of hurricanes) cheat me out of the opportunity to help students explore the interrelatedness of Richard Wright, Ralph Ellison, and James Baldwin. I very much wanted to test the idea that interpretation of a major author is enriched by associating her or him with other authors who have legitimate claims to be major. Very early in my graduate studies, I took courses that would have prepared me to become an

English Renaissance scholar. Later I chose to prepare myself to teach American and African American literatures and to work in the high-tech wilderness of literary theory and criticism. The return to British literature is a forced one. I am sidetracked from my current investigation of African American literature to satisfy my department's need to deal with student underenrollment.

Unplanning is one of the lessons I seem to be learning well as the anniversary of trauma arrives. Like the astronomers who have redefined what a planet is, I have to redefine what I mean when I say I teach with a purpose. Pluto is no longer a planet. It is a visual aid for understanding the universe. My purpose as a teacher is to help students understand that the words in *The Faerie Queene* and those in *The Outsider* are invitations to redescribe the roles of virtue, vice, and violence in our *post-K* lives. My post-Katrina burden is a difficult obligation of helping myself not to cave in— not to release my hold on thinking and dreaming in a changing New Orleans.

Saturday, August 26, 2006 12:47:47 p.m.

The African-American Leadership Project (AALP) has organized "Remembering Katrina Observance" for August 25-29, 2006. I didn't attend the national dialogue "Katrina and Its Meaning for Black Americans and the Nation" at McDonough 35 High School Auditorium last night, nor will I attend today's "Hands Around the Dome Ceremony" or the march and rally from the Superdome to the Convention Center. The AALP hopes that remembrance events "will help everyone to learn, critique, be healed and affirm hope for the future" (announcement flyer).

It rained heavily yesterday, and it is raining now. My healing does not involve standing in the rain. I'm not of a mind to bargain with correctness. If there is bright sunshine tomorrow afternoon, I may participate in AALP's "White Buffalo Day and Katrina Observance" in Congo Square. The drumming, sunlight and the Mardi Gras Indians— "My Indian Red"— should be part of my healing.

Saturday, August 26, 2006 08:33:21 p.m.

*Fascism has killed democracy as you knew it.

*Talk about people of color sounds like noise from a mouth in a chastity belt.

*If a poor man goes to India with an empty bowl, Vishnu will give him trouble and Buddha will give him a bromide.

From *A Book of Wisdom* by Mr. Lawrence Seagull

Meditation on a Sentence

O. Mannoni wrote of a conditional situation that is now a real phenomenon:

"If the desire to break every attachment could be realized, it would lead to a sort of savage emancipation of the adult of a kind seen only among certain species of animals." (*Prospero and Caliban: The Psychology of Colonization.* 2nd ed. New York: Praeger, 1964. 207)

   In the suburban, gated enclaves of the United States, children (who are not children) and young adults have emancipated themselves as they do dope, amass weapons of destruction, and listen to the beat of ghetto fantasy. The number of emancipated suburbanites is statistically insignificant, but the fact that they exist at all is not to be ignored. The fact must be dealt with as mitigating evidence against the unwarranted condemnation of their peers in the inner cities. If reporting on behaviors among the wealthier members of American society were more accurate, we would be shocked to know how widespread abjection is across class lines. Incomplete disclosure regarding forms of savage emancipation helps us to ignore the breadth and depth of our national tragedy.

   Neither the infotainment industry nor the government keepers of data wants the American public to panic. Thus, we have no commissioned reports on tattooing in America as tribalization or databases on the number of Prince Albert operations performed each year. Should gluttony be classified as a deadly sin, an inherited disease, or an acceptable lifestyle protected by the U.S. Constitution? Is military training an effective use of attachment-breaking? Are sports and privatized prisons institutions in an economy of stylized savagery? What do savages in three branches of government celebrate?

   The Cold War may be over, but Iron Curtains and Berlin Walls are still being used to promote alienation of humanity and increasing abjection among Americans. Don't panic. Despite the efforts of skinheads, the World Church of the Creator, and militant neo-Nazis who have vowed to become the terrorists within the United States, Americans do not yet have the monopoly on what Mannoni theorized about return to instinct. Millions of people around the world have beat us to the punch as far as breaking human attachments is concerned. Globalization (economic and cultural) and the dissolving of social contracts around the world have hastened mankind's return to instinct. A century or two from now, savage emancipation shall be the world's norm: authentic savagery, civilization.

Sunday, August 27, 2006

   The sky announces rain. I drive down to Congo Square despite the warning. Although his speech is brief, I learn something quite valuable from Chief Arvol Looking Horse, 19th Generation Keeper of the Sacred White Buffalo Pipe of the Lakota, Dakota and Nakota Great Sioux Nation. The sounds of Native American and African drumming and chanting are instructive. August 27th. White Buffalo Day commemorates the peaceful communion of two ancient peoples. We can practice love and respect. We can make efforts to heal ourselves and Mother Earth. We can try.

Chief Looking Horse delivers a simple message that is pregnant with wisdom. Wisdom speaks against my being blind and chained in Satanic mills. I try to extract the wisdom, knowing that I do not yet understand the lore of White Buffalo. Ancient narratives that invite us to live in balance and harmony are not easy to interpret. It is a hard discipline to be remote from the Grand Romance of Reason. The White Buffalo shall bring me visions that I can understand by being attentive to DNA evidence of my African/Choctaw/European ancestry. I do not want the bad dream the Aztecs sent when I "borrowed" a tiny piece of stone from the Pyramid of the Sun.

It does not rain. I do not have to drown to heal. I do, however, have to practice humility.

Monday, August 28, 2006

Today is the anniversary of my leaving New Orleans before Hurricane Katrina arrived. I do not regret having returned.

My voice shall worry
The peoples of the Earth

Tuesday, August 29, 2006

When my father died on December 25, 1957, my heart was hardened forever against the celebration of Christmas. My mother died in April 1992, but I was able to handle the inevitability of death and grief better. By then I had experienced the rising and falling rhythms of life, had become familiar with the conservation of tears and the utility of laughter.

As the sky over New Orleans changes this morning from black to pearly grey, you are calm. At this very minute a year ago, wind and water were demonstrating how easily they might damage and destroy the Gulf Coast. You believe that the altering of a region, of a city and its population, of a nation partial to the stoic will happen again and again; it has happened before. Nature has many surprises in store for humanity.

Your mood is not indigo, saffron, or scarlet, not any color to sing, secondline, or toast. At this very minute the levees broke a year ago. An old person was dying in water. A baby was rescued from death in many countries. Memorabilia soaked into oblivion. A year ago, Hurricane Katrina became infamous as thousands of people were innoculated with chaos. And a year later, chaos is still the trublem of the world. People are still standing as New Orleans pupates. The city is a conundrum.

At this very minute a year ago, our eyes were watching and our ears were hearing and our minds were sundered. At this minute, I have chosen to say a prayer, to throw some mold-infested dirt in the grave, to co-exist with paper-thick hope, granite disillusions, and all that defies explanation.

Post-Katrina contradictions breed in my soul and body and in the contexts my selves inhabit.

I give mystery permission to celebrate me.

STOP & EXIT

The journal stops. Trauma doesn't conclude. No tidy solutions demand summary.

Stop.

Clear the throat.

Exit into a pre-future of unknowns.

Colophon

About the Cover Art by Herbert Kearney

"All mothers are boats": 67 x 106 inches (detail)
Paint, driftwood, lumber, dirt, masonry, glass, etc.
It was begun pre-Katrina on a wooden wall panel of the studio building
named The Ark. The front window wall was sucked out but the boat
survived. Kicking through the rubble afterwards, I used broken window
panes, floor boards, walls & furniture to build it from its own studio.

across the drained river
the mother boat made it home
a snail in a nautilus shell
smiles in passing
the lizard watches from a black
road for body heat as oil barrels
sink back into swampy crudeness
forgotten by water news
the shimmer of a past cocooned
dragonfly reminder of a millenium
hatched in a moment
gnawing thru the sandy ropes of time
a hedge-shadowed mouse
holds the secrets to the centre
of the earth
a ladybug preens her wings
with the empathy of a road some travelled
the skeleton of her sister lies lodged
in dried tide silt as the muddy rudder
of the last water ship curves her way
across the cosmos
               O
cosmic dust born of a stone egg
mammal memory of the first muddy mother
full-circled thru the eternal umbilical
      life thru death
            for all mothers

–Herbert Kearney